# THE DIVIDING MUSE

# The Dividing Muse

*Images of Sacred Disjunction in Milton's Poetry*

SANFORD BUDICK

YALE UNIVERSITY PRESS
New Haven and London

Published with assistance from the Kingsley Trust
Association Publication Fund established by the Scroll
and Key Society of Yale College.

Designed by Margaret E.B. Joyner
and set in Caledonia type by Brevis Press,
Bethany, Connecticut.
Printed in the United States of America by
BookCrafters, Inc., Chelsea, Michigan.

Library of Congress Cataloging in Publication Data

Budick, Sanford, 1942–
    The dividing muse.

    Includes index.
    1. Milton, John, 1608–1674—Style. 2. Figures of
speech. 3. Christian art and symbolism. 4. Theology
in literature. I. Title.
PR3594.B76   1985        821'.4        84–17270
ISBN 0–300–03288–9 (alk. paper)

The paper in this book meets the guidelines for permanence
and durability of the Committee on Production Guidelines
for Book Longevity of the Council on Library Resources.

10 9 8 7 6 5 4 3 2 1

For Emily

and for Rachel, Ayelet, and Yochanan

# Contents

# Acknowledgments

Partly against my will I have followed a version of Horace's advice and kept back this book until the ninth year. From start to finish I have benefited from the aid of many a friendly Maecius, so many in fact that I am now embarrassed by the small return from their large investment. Among those who have read and improved parts or the whole of my manuscript are M. H. Abrams, Lawrence L. Besserman, Morton W. Bloomfield, Arthur Budick, H. M. Daleski, Antoinette Dauber, Scott Elledge, Geoffrey H. Hartman, Frank Kermode, Maynard Mack, Pamela Schwed, Winthrop Wetherbee, and Joshua Wilner. Needless to say, any errors that remain are mine alone. Ellen Graham, Editor of Yale University Press, Margaret Levene of the Press's editorial department, and Tulin Duda helped me at every turn with their extraordinary efficiency and intelligent attention to detail. Eva Vilarrubi greatly facilitated the preparation of the index.

I wish to express my gratitude to David Rogers and David Patterson of Oxford, who extended a warm and courteous welcome during a happy stay at their university, and to Father Ignazio Mancini, O.F.M., Custos of the Holy Land, who made available to me the large store of his knowledge of Bonaventure.

My confrontation with difficult matters in Ante-Nicene theology was made easier by the learned assistance of my father, Harry N. Budick. My wife, Emily, clarified and fashioned everything that has value in these pages. She knows there is no point in attempting to explain here the extent of her contribution to this project. Our children too played their part in the making of this book. All of Milton's great work looks homeward and onward to the generations that come after. In composing these pages I have hoped that, Deo volente, some part of what I was recording might one day be of use to Rachel, Ayelet, and Yochanan.

# 1

❀

# Milton's Imagery and the Force of the Nonvisual

It is no simple matter to speak of the special characteristics of Milton's images. Not only is the subject of any great poet's imagery complex in itself, but, in the case of Milton, many readers are understandably deterred by Eliot's warning that the distinguishing qualities of Milton's image-making actually render his verse alien to the traditions of European literature.[1] Few of us who love Milton's poetry wish to deepen his isolation—and ours. But there is, perhaps, another way to approach the phenomenon of poetic differentness. Indeed, except where Milton is concerned, no one has done more than Eliot himself to create tolerance for the interplay of sameness and difference in poetic tradition. The advent of a unique talent, suggests Eliot, is the crystallization of newly revealed aspects of our collective literary consciousness. If we are willing to learn about the materials and the powers of the individual muse, we inevitably see the points of continuity between the individual and the tradition he enlarges.[2] And in its turn, I may add, the willingness to learn how a poet manifests his tradition is first and foremost expressed by asking appropriate questions in appropriate ways. This too has not always been easy when the subject is Milton.

## G. E. LESSING AND R. M. FRYE

Among those who do manage to put the right questions with particular cogency are a number of eighteenth-century aestheticians who inhabit the marchland between the Enlightenment and proto-Romantic worlds.

Burke, for example, tries to understand how it is that Milton can pre-sent "terrible things . . . in their strongest light by the force of a ju-dicious obscurity." He is persuaded that Milton's texts furnish an opportunity for glimpsing a large, powerful truth: "So little does poetry depend for its effect on the power of raising sensible images," he writes, "that I am convinced that it would lose a very considerable part of its *energy,* if this were the necessary result of all description."[3]

Some may be inclined to dismiss Burke for a sentimental attachment to vagueness, but his views in fact represent part of a finely distin-guished approach to poetic meanings. Following the similar leads of du Bos and Mendelssohn, Lessing, most notably, proceeds rigorously in the same direction by attempting to discriminate the symbolic usages of poetry from those of the visual arts. Lessing too uses the special case of Milton to point to the essence of a poetry qua poetry, as opposed to verbal approximations to pictorialness. Against Count Caylus, who urges that poetry must contain vivid pictures that the imagination can seize upon, and who (like Eliot) castigates Milton for his poetic blind-ness, Lessing counters that Milton's verse offers the supreme instance of a poetic order of symbols that have little to do with images of the visual kind: "Milton cannot fill picture galleries, it is true. But if the range of my physical sight must be the measure of my inner vision, I should value the loss of the former in order to gain freedom from the limitations of the latter."[4]

Milton's avoidance of fully rendered objects, in other words, is not seen as a liability but is used by Lessing to reinforce his conviction that poetic signs do not attempt to convey "the corporeal whole ac-cording to its parts." Lessing's reasoning seemed very attractive to Coleridge when he came to frame his own notion of the special nature of Milton's imagery. Lessing elaborates:

> I do not deny to language altogether the power of depicting the corporeal whole according to its parts. It can do so because its signs, although consecutive, are still arbitrary. But I do deny it to language as the medium of poetry, because the illusion, which is the principal object of poetry, is wanting in such verbal description of bodies. And this illusion, I say, must be wanting because the coexistent nature of a body comes into conflict with the consecutive nature of language, and although dis-solving the former into the latter makes the division of the whole into its parts easier for us, the final reassembling of the parts into the whole is made extremely difficult and often even impossible.[5]

For Lessing "the illusion, which is the principal object of poetry," is achieved by a defining omission, as it is for Burke by a judicious obscurity. In Lessing's view the activity of selective omission establishes poetic "illusion" as an unmediated form of rational knowledge. In his comments on Milton's nonpainterly imagination, he emphasizes that we are here confronted with a kind of sign that can communicate a more purely intellectual knowledge than other aesthetic forms. Milton's signs, he implies, can cross the gap between allegedly subjective and objective kinds of knowledge by virtue of a visual subtraction willed or recognized by the perceiver in the perceived. Lessing believes that this kind of knowing is the effect of a Platonic or Kantian imagination that has more to do with ideas than with images:

> The poet does not want merely to be intelligible, nor is he content—as is the prose writer—with simply presenting his image clearly and concisely. He wants rather to make the ideas he awakens in us so vivid that at that moment *we believe that we feel the real impressions which the objects of these ideas* would produce on us. In this moment of illusion we should cease to be conscious of the means which the poet uses for this purpose, that is, his words.[6]

We need not subscribe to the creed implicit in Lessing's Idealist language to reap the benefits of his insight that the exercise of one kind of poetic imagination is a rational activity in which meaning becomes a function of pictorial deficit. We "see" the object because of what is left out. Description of this kind is continuous with the meanings of differentiation that Milton's images represent. The experience of these differentiations is what Lessing calls "ideas" of objects felt as "real impressions." Reality, in this view, is the experience of differentiation or of rationality itself.

I have thought it worthwhile to disinter Lessing's hypotheses concerning Milton's imagination both because they help explain the nature of Coleridge's invaluable defense of Milton's imagery and because right at the start of modern criticism they put the emphasis squarely where I believe it belongs: on the rational or distinguishing activity of Milton's imagination. Lessing may have erred in not allowing for the existence of other very different kinds of poetry (and of different kinds of painting and sculpture as well). But his remarks greatly illuminate the abstractive habit of mind offered by Milton's verse.

In fact, the tendency of Lessing's criticism is in accord with the views of many contemporary scholars and has even formed one major trend in modern Milton criticism. Striking, even memorable, examples of this criticism abound with regard to countless Miltonic images. Don Cameron Allen, for example, points to the similarities between Milton's description of the amaranth and Clement of Alexandria's denial that the flower had any earthly or physical existence. Amaranth, says Allen, is for Milton "not a real flower at all but an ideality inexpressible in terms of earthly flora. . . . As a consequence, this flower, beyond the things of earth, has neither color nor form."[7] In a similar vein, Douglas Bush counters Leavis's objection that Milton's phrase "vegetable gold" is "incompatible with sharp, concrete realization" by pointing out that Milton's two words "suggest a mysterious growth hardly to be approached in words . . . each word is altered and quickened by the other; the richness of 'gold' glorifies the simple product of nature, and the rich natural life applied in 'vegetable' gives pliant form and vitality to metallic hardness and removes the idea of unhealthy artifice and evil which in *Paradise Lost* is associated with gold."[8]

Most recently, as a more or less direct development of the lines of defense laid down by Allen and Bush, Leland Ryken has paused over what he calls Milton's mystic oxymorons: living sapphire (*Paradise Lost*, II.1049–50), flowing jasper, liquid pearl (III.518–19), and others. Ryken draws attention to the ways in which Milton repeatedly gives us "a picture of contradiction," one that derives its power from the fact that "in earthly experience something cannot be simultaneously fluid and static in its essential nature." The "solution" to the contradictions, Ryken observes, is in "combining two empirical phenomena to suggest a transcendental realm in which the sum is greater than the parts." Ryken proposes a similar explanation for Milton's use of "conceptual terms" to create "poetic texture" (as in IV.288–95: glory, truth, wisdom, sanctitude, severity, purity). By Milton these terms are given being in a transcendent realm in which abstraction is prima facie *real*: "Each of the terms names a quality which is no less real and distinct than a tangible object perceived through the senses."[9]

With so much acute commentary celebrating the nonvisual dimension of Milton's art, it would be easy and comforting to conclude that we are dealing here with a poetry wholly different from all and any verse that depends upon imagery. But, as most readers have realized— indeed, as Eliot will not let them forget—the case cannot be settled in this way; for in spite of their difference from other kinds of figures and metaphors, Miltonic images, for better or for worse, do exist and do function in important capacities in Milton's poems. Before I proceed, therefore, to Coleridge's view of Milton's sublimating imagery, and before I try to apply his insights to an inquiry into the nature and origin of the Miltonic imagination, it is worth considering the most painterly aspects of Milton's images. To do this efficiently I shall turn to Roland Mushat Frye's landmark study, *Milton's Imagery and the Visual Arts*,[10]—a work that, interestingly enough, actually enlarges the significance of Burke's and Lessing's observations by emphasizing precisely what they choose to omit: the visual contours of Milton's imagery.

By more than one standard, the appearance of Frye's book is a significant scholarly event. Three centuries of misgivings about Milton's re-creations of physical reality are here brought to a climax, with the intention of defending Milton against his detractors. All the principal objections are inventoried, classified, and discussed, image by controversial image; and an immense catalogue raisonné of related imagery, in all the relevant European periods of the fine arts, is set before us. Though Frye stops short, I think, of attaining the full results he intends, his investigations are greatly beneficial to any informed reading of Milton. He sums up his working assumptions and his conclusions in the following way:

> We will understand *Paradise Lost* and *Paradise Regained* only partially if we cannot accept the poet's invitation to *see* persons, events, and things. For Milton, imagery was rarely if ever merely decorative, but was developed to express or suggest or support an idea. Time and again, his challenge to us as readers is both visual and intellectual, and we cannot meet such a challenge without some familiarity with traditional systems of visual iconography. It was by carefully wrought and carefully selected poetic references to such iconography, still familiar when he wrote his great epic, that he sought to guide the vision of his audience and to vitalize subjects which might otherwise have seemed forbiddingly remote and abstract.[11]

Note that Frye does not deny the intellectual character of Milton's verse. The main effort of his book, he says, is to make clear the iconographic aids that Milton uses for his own special ends. He hopes to beckon us onward to understand the ways in which Milton transforms iconographic concreteness into poetic consciousness. We should not, therefore, misapply Frye's evidences to suggest that Milton's poetry cultivates a visual way of apprehending reality which is virtually opposed to that which, as Frye recognizes, Milton actually employs.

Two epitomes of Frye's analysis will illustrate its usefulness, as well as the areas of critical understanding that remain to be filled in. In both passages below Frye touches on phenomena with which any serious criticism of Milton's imagination must contend. After adducing rich catalogues of analogous works of fine art, Frye writes,

> When Milton refers to the "mouth of Hell" and to its "ravenous jaws," or when he writes of the falling angels that "Hell at last / Yawning received them whole, and on them closed," he was using a very ancient symbolism, but one which had by no means yet lost its visual force and vitality. In these words, brief though they are, Milton sketched a picture that would have been instantly recognized by his contemporaries. . . .

> When Milton describes the landscape of Heaven, he is in no wise innovative, and an awareness of the artistic representations of the Celestial Paradise is important to a full appreciation of his achievement. It is not that he provides precise and detailed descriptions of scenes represented in any particular art works; on the contrary, his pastoral descriptions are general and evocative, rather than meticulously drawn. But if our minds have been stocked with the traditional images of the visual arts, we will find his descriptive phrases to be extraordinarily rich and visually allusive.[12]

Frye's observations in these and similar passages are significant and indisputable. Careful study of his pages brings to life a highly dramatic element of Milton's imaginative communication and, correspondingly, of the informed reader's appropriate response. Frye has in effect pointed to a pattern of imaginative progress in which visual evocation forms one large, preparatory step. He has shown more fully than any other commentator that such evocation occupies a pivotal place in Milton's verse.

But Frye does not explain how the pivoting is executed and in what direction the poetic imagination is finally propelled. Frye himself hints at the necessity for such a multistage account in a number of instances.[13] He suggests that Milton's descriptive passages—for such they are, even if they do not produce the descriptions expected—are manifestations of an imagination that reached full flower. As he intermittently acknowledges, they are carefully constructed object lessons. Their force of denial, we may say, urges Milton's poetic world toward the pole of the nonvisual and the abstract or rational. Visual countercurrents are certainly allowed significant play in Milton's verse. But the overall flow is never in doubt.

We can turn here to Joseph Mazzeo for a metaphor from the history of ideas that is, I think, closely analogous to Milton's individualized poetic world. Mazzeo has shown that in the Augustinian cosmos there is a dominant movement which is essentially unidirectional even if counter-realities sometimes occupy the center of our field of vision: that movement is "through the words to the realities themselves, from the temporal realities to the eternal realities, from talk to silence, and from discourse to vision."[14] The image life of Milton's poetry, I suggest, is controlled by half-interdicted images that similarly point to his abstractive goals. His poetic meanings are a migration of this kind.

The nature of these goals remains to be discussed in later chapters. Here I will attend to what I am persuaded is the characteristic pivotal moment in Milton's verse, the moment when the poetry is made to resist the pressure of the visual world that Milton himself has evoked. Frye has helped us to appreciate this moment. For all of the images discussed above by Allen, Bush, and Ryken, Frye can provide iconographic parallels which undoubtedly could, and in many instances actually did, endow Milton's descriptions with a visual element that has an important imaginative function.[15] At the same time, these other commentators perform exemplary service by pointing to the nonvisual realm of meaning that strains against this iconographic domain.

In the chapters that follow, I attempt to specify as fully as possible the link between these apparently opposed elements of the Miltonic image. Milton's journeys on the *via negativa* and the *via positiva* are continuous. In fact, the meaning of each way is only realized by combining it with its inverse. Systematically and deliberately, Milton, I believe, sets visual analogies into motion with an eye to their imminent depletion. Visual duration in Milton's verse is not imagistic life but imagistic half-life, interminably regenerated, endlessly disintegrated. His poetic progress is a meaning unto itself. It is a distinctive way of revealing the world, a different symbolic order. As Lessing, and Coleridge too, understood, we must be willing to grant Milton his imaginative individuality, his combination of depleted "physical sight" and enlarged rational "vision."[16]

## ELIOT AND COLERIDGE

To answer Eliot's charges against Milton's "black fire" and "darkness visible"[17] we must go the whole route of Milton's imagination. Eliot appreciated fully that Milton meant every nonvisual effect he worked to create. He recognized that as a wielder of images Milton represented something decisively different from Eliot's own poetic platform (though, ironically enough, perhaps not very different from Eliot's poetic practice). In fact, Eliot's critique of Milton offers insights into the defining differentness of Milton's poetic imagination.

Eliot was convinced that the individuality of Milton's image-making could not be tolerated because it was the effect of a turning away from what Eliot terms *visual imagination*: "The most important fact about Milton, for my purpose," he wrote, "is his blindness. . . . Milton may be said never to have seen anything." In *Paradise Lost* particularly, Eliot argued, "a dislocation takes place, through the hypertrophy of the auditory imagination at the expense of the visual and tactile, so that the inner meaning is separated from the surface, and tends to become something occult, or at least without effect upon the reader until fully understood."[18] Behind Eliot's condemnation of Milton, as is well known, lay a specific theory of poetry and a carefully meditated account of modern literary history. Both are strongly linked to Eliot's concept of "dissociation of sensibility." More than anything else, perhaps, his theory and his history affirmed the necessity of rebridging the gap between feeling and thought by finding "objective correlatives"—"external facts [that] terminate in sensory experience"—for the emotions we wish to express. "Not only all knowledge, but all feeling," Eliot declared, "is in perception."[19] He early identified Milton as one of those chiefly responsible for the dissociated condition of our perceiving consciousness. For Eliot, Milton's failure to provide objective correlatives was a principal determinant of the contemporary condition of our poetry.

Eliot expressed astonishment at the "success in the world" of his phrases *dissociation of sensibility* and *objective correlative*.[20] But historical hindsight shows that his views and his phrases rode the crests of the dominant movements in poetry and criticism of the early twentieth century. The afterglow of the French symbolists taught the world the necessity for reinstituting the luminous dilation of the purely represented object, the wedding of mind and symbol that alone was believed to be capable of assuring an unbroken continuity of consciousness.[21] And the New Criticism, working out its own complicated relationships with Eliot, furnished a broader coherence for his sketchbooks.[22]

A significant ingredient in the success of this object-focused poetics has been the ability of its expounders to argue its historical primacy and to affirm its continued dominance in Western aesthetics from Greek literature to the present. William K. Wimsatt, Jr., has written, for example, that it is through New Critical formalism—

an interest, that is, in poetic order and hence in poetic reality—that recent critics participate in a kind of Aristotelianism and even scholasticism—or let us say, more liberally, in the ideas about order, harmony, and unity which we may read in neo-Platonic sources of late antiquity, Pagan or Christian, in the medieval scholasticism of Aquinas, in early modern aesthetic speculation such as that of Leibniz or Baumgarten, in the theories of later German transcendental philosophers and English romantic poets, and most recently in the neoscholasticism of Maritain, Gilby, and others.[23]

The value of Eliot's historical account and his animadversions on Milton lies in his description and enactment of a kind of circularity in literary evolution—of the kind also suggested by Wimsatt. Eliot's critique had the illuminating effect of describing two closed circles, each antagonistic to the other. To Eliot, Milton was not merely a colossus who failed. Milton's nonvisual poetry, like Joyce's nonvisual prose, represents for Eliot a death threat to a circle of tradition and talent in which Dante and Donne and Eliot point to each other. The circle described by Eliot has since been traced in a multitude of familiar ways. Its locus, we say, is symbolic, imagistic, iconic, Thomistic, emotional-intellectual, meditative, and so on. We may not agree to its best single name, but we acknowledge its self-defining continuity. But what of the wheel to which Milton is tied? What is its name?

To proceed in this other task of description, we should remind ourselves that the dream of an undissociated sensibility and of a poetry constituted by objective correlatives was, as Eliot himself sometimes seemed to acknowledge, a version of Coleridge's doctrines of imagination.[24] In the English tradition that Eliot represented, Coleridge's dazzling *obiter dicta* have formed the basis of the dominant romantic and post-romantic poetics—through to the middle of the twentieth century, and even, retroactively, of the English Renaissance. The famous phrases are second nature to us: "imagination . . . reveals itself in the balance or reconciliation of opposite or discordant qualities: of sameness, with difference; of the general, with the concrete; the idea, with the image." For the purposes of this discussion it should be noted that for Coleridge the "idea" and the "image" are poles apart. The distinction between them is operative in Coleridge's categorization of the imagination's two faculties or phases, which offers, in effect, a receipt for sublimating the imagined object into secondarily imagined idea:

The IMAGINATION then, I consider either as primary, or secondary. The primary IMAGINATION I hold to be the living Power and prime agent of all human Perception, and as a repetition in the finite mind of the eternal act of creation in the infinite I AM. The secondary Imagination I consider as an echo of the former, co-existing with the conscious will, yet still as identical with the primary in the *kind* of its agency, and differing only in *degree,* and in the *mode* of its operation. It dissolves, diffuses, dissipates, in order to re-create; or where this process is rendered impossible, yet still at all events it struggles to idealize and to unify. It is essentially *vital,* even as all objects (*as* objects) are essentially fixed and dead.[25]

Few early critics did more than Coleridge to prepare the way for Eliot's poetics, in both its inclusive and exclusive aspects. Coleridge articulated the relation of visual symbol to the *motus animi continuus,* to the nature of consciousness itself in both its quotidian and artistic manifestations. In effect, Coleridge proclaimed anew that the dead fleshly object must be made to live in the assimilating vitality of the individual *logos* imagination. And yet, strangely enough, it is to Coleridge that we can turn for intimations of the poetic, philosophical, and theological conceptions that justify the ways of Milton's imagination. With Coleridge's help we can begin to see that Milton's imagination is dependent upon a *logos tomeus,* a logos that *divides* and distinguishes rather than resolves.

Coleridge, unlike Eliot, would not reject Milton's imagination, even if he too recognized its departures from a pictorial aesthetic. With Lessing's considerable help, Coleridge tried to confront the fact that although Milton had sojourned in Italy during the apprentice years of his imagination and although his talents were exercised primarily on scenes that were favorite subjects of the Italian masters, "in no part of his writings," as Coleridge puts it, "does Milton take any notice of the great painters of Italy, nor, indeed, of painting as an art."[26] Instead of lamenting or condemning this fact (a "fact" which, in light of Frye's work, must now be reformulated), Coleridge attempted to include Milton's scenes in an alternative theory of poetic meaning.

In his comparison of Milton's and Wordsworth's imaging, Coleridge rejected the "minute accuracy in the painting of local imagery" that he saw in Wordsworth's *Excursion.* Echoing Lessing, he remarks that comprehending Wordsworth's contiguous images in that poem is "like taking pieces of a dissected map out of its box. We first look at one part, and then at another, then join and dove-tail them; and when the successive acts of attention have been completed, there is a retrogressive effort of mind to behold it as a whole." In Milton's poetry, Coleridge believed he had found "*creation* rather than *painting*, or if painting . . . the co-presence of the whole picture flash'd at once upon the eye" by the effects of a subtractive imagination. He chooses his aptest example of this creative co-presence in Milton's description of the fig tree to which Adam and Eve repair in their hour of guilt and shame. He begins to quote as follows:

> The fig-tree; not that kind for fruit renown'd,
> But such as at this day, to Indians known,
> In Malabar or Decan spreads her arms
> Branching so broad and long, that in the ground
> The bended twigs take root.

From this point on, Coleridge gives his quotation special emphasis:

> *and daughters grow*
> *About the mother tree, a pillar'd shade*
> *High over-arch'd, and* ECHOING WALKS BETWEEN:
> *There oft the Indian Herdsman, shunning heat,*
> *Shelters in cool, and tends his pasturing herds*
> *At loop holes cut through thickest shade.*

From Eliot's point of view Milton's description, bound down in "echoing walks between," supported by "pillar'd shade," and shaped from "thickest shade" could only be reckoned as so much reverberating darkness. But for Coleridge these were "*creative words* in the world of imagination."[27] Coleridge was certain he could envision here the co-presence of a whole, rendered integral by the complementary activities of imaginative construction and equally imaginative *rejection*. In Milton's poetry, he says, "the imagination is called forth, not to produce a distinct form, but a strong working of the mind, *still offering what is still repelled*, and *again creating what is again rejected*; the result being what the poet wishes to impress, namely, the substitution of *a sublime feeling of the unimaginable for a mere image.*"[28] The strong working of the mind is the act of a continual substitution, not the sublime feeling itself. This strong working of the rational, discriminating imagination is in Coleridge's view the characteristic activity of Milton's image-making.

The differences between Coleridge's and Eliot's approaches to Milton are determined by the fact that, whereas Eliot is an Aristotelian, unswervingly committed to activities of human perception, Coleridge, a founding father of neo-Aristotelian criticism in England, is also a

Platonist, yearning, as he says, for constitutive ideas.[29] Eliot's position
with regard to Milton is consistent with his general poetic theory.
Coleridge's rationale for Milton's imagination is inconsistent with his
own emphasis on the aesthetic centrality of the concrete image. His
apology for Milton points us to the other pole in his theory of mind,
the pole he described as "pure reason . . . the power by which we
become possessed of principles—the eternal verities of Plato and Des-
cartes, and of ideas, not images."[30]

Many commentators have noted that the discontinuity between secondary imagination and reason is never bridged in Coleridge's thinking.
Yet his comment on Milton's description of the fig tree reflects, I believe, his desire to close this gap. Though Milton's description may
seem, at first glance, to be one of his most painterly passages, Coleridge
senses that it possesses a principle of growth and change that moves it
toward the condition of reason itself. He attempts to use the passage
to illustrate how the imagination can go beyond visualization and become part of the distinction-making activity of human reason.

Coleridge's effort to identify in *Paradise Lost* a process of imagination that departs from conventional imaging is, I suggest, part of his
effort both to acknowledge the qualitative uniqueness of pure reason
and to claim for imagination, contra Kant, a continuously active role in
a process of intellectual disembodiment. The aesthetic that he desires,
but that he cannot achieve on his own terms, would be constituted by
the resolution of subject and object in the activity of perception formation, rather than in the percept. It would be achieved in the continual delimitation of images, rather than in images themselves.

Although Coleridge did not fully describe a metaphysics and poetics
along these lines, he frequently identified their expression in a long
intellectual tradition. Particularly in his accounts of the Neoplatonic
dialectic of the Greek Church Fathers, he associates the distinction-
making activity of the imagination with the logos Divider-Creator. His
writings on these matters in seventeenth-century British theology, especially in the work of Milton's contemporary Richard Baxter, similarly
run parallel to his concern with the special nature of Milton's imagination. These Coleridgian and Baxterian matters are included in
Appendix C. In addition, many of Coleridge's preoccupations will figure prominently in the unfolding discussion.

# 2

❀

# Patterns of Division
# in the Nativity Ode

To a large extent, modern interpretation of *On the Morning of Christ's Nativity*—the first considerable project of Milton's differentiating muse—has turned on the significance of harmony or peace. As many readers have recognized, in spite of the apparent thematic centrality of concord or resolution at certain vivid moments, harmony such as we might expect to find is actually far from the poem's overall imagery and structure. Indeed, dissonance and disruption play major roles throughout the poem. Don Cameron Allen has put it this way:

> The power of this poem does not spring from a true reconciliation of its intellectual and emotional disunities, but rather from the fact that they are not reconciled at all, or, better still, that they are erased in a unity of a higher order. When we observe the conflict in its separateness, it seems like a tug-of-war between teams of gigantic stallions—the thesis and the antithesis pull oppositely, the synonym and the antonym stretch each other, the myth dashes itself into divergent metaphors.[1]

Nonetheless, a significant number of commentators have felt confident that a unity of a higher order such as Allen describes must surely be demonstrable, not merely as a projection to a realm beyond the last line, but as a substantial function of the text itself. However, even learned attempts to locate this higher reconciliation have more or less had to restrict the interpretative field to what the poem tells or proclaims rather than what it shows or does. Indeed, from this point of view it is not too much to say that many critics have been willing to

regard the Ode as a mysterious effusion that on the deepest aesthetic
and conceptual levels defies analytic comprehension of achieved meaning.

Before I leap into the controversy about whether in fact Milton's
poem expresses harmony or discord, and, if harmony, then what kind
of harmony, it will be useful to review the argument of one proponent
of this latter view. Rosemond Tuve believes that "Milton has . . .
formed our understanding of the full import of the mystery he celebrates by a kind of orchestrated weaving of themes carried by great
symbols traditionally used to present such meanings."[2] By her terms
"understanding" of "meanings" Tuve describes the reader's a priori
acceptance of a dialectical agency and a dialectical process that manifest
themselves principally as accomplished facts of resolution or synthesis.
This telescoped activity is, for the poets, divine harmony and concord.
It is, Tuve in effect argues, a well-known quantity, and properly prepared readers will know when the appropriate signal has been given
for summoning it up in its extensive, developing form.

In Tuve's view, then, the Ode states a "vast single theme: God's
reconciling of all things in earth and heaven to Himself, principle of
Light and principle of Concord."[3] This reconciling, like the mystery
with which it is coextensive, is not matter for a progression of analytic
and then synthetic understanding, but for intuitive recognition and
ritual appellation: "Music, Harmonia, Concord (Love, Reconciliation,
Peace, Order, Unity in multiplicity) becomes the greatest and most
conceptually necessary symbol of the poem," says Tuve, "except for
that of Light, and the two interpenetrate each other."[4]

Yet the truth is that we still very much need to ask how Milton
strives to achieve harmony in his poem, what kinds of image structures
he uses, and, most important, what variety of dialectical agency constitutes the harmony he produces. This after all is a poem in which
Peace is said to work by peremptory force of separation (see stanza iii
of the *Hymn*). It should not be surprising to discover that Milton has
found a way to have his harmony and his lack of reconciliation at the
same time, even in the same structure.

Yet by insisting on formal considerations I do not mean to suggest
that the historical depth of Milton's images should be disregarded.
Indeed, to progress in our understanding of the Ode we need to bring
forward a new range of archaeological siftings. What I propose, however, is that we reexamine the clues Milton has given us for the site of
our diggings; and that we be certain that the materials recovered for

display are closely identifiable, most particularly, with the controlling components of Milton's poetry. Some clues are provided outside this text, in a poem that Milton composed less than a year before the Ode.

## ELEGIA QUINTA

Near the beginning of his fifth elegy Milton reproduces a commonplace image and manages to invest it with extraordinary urgency and depth of meaning. The emerging poet, yearning for partnership with the energies of spring, views and then reviews the approach of Apollo, the god who can somehow bestow poetic power:

> Delius ipse venit—video Peneide lauro
> Implicatos crines—Delius ipse venit.       [13–14]

Apollo himself is approaching—I see the locks that are braided with Daphne's laurel—Apollo himself comes.[5]

Separated and set in relief by poetic laurel, the phrases of epiphany are made to represent a complex conception of regenerating creativity. The dynamic shape of the symbolic form is clear enough, even if we do not yet comprehend its significance: Apollo, the god of light and poetry who is anxiously awaited, is always approaching, but he does not arrive. The poet strains and glimpses his glory, already intertwined with the gifts of poetry. And yet—Apollo, the god of light and poetry, is arriving, never to arrive in the way imagined. What can this deferral of his arrival possibly signify? With what other concerns is it associated in the elegy?

Apollo's non-arrival and the pattern that it introduces sharply define other aspects of the poem's imagistic and thematic structure. It is, I would argue, the germ of the elegy's larger meaning. Broadly considered, the fifth elegy can be said to represent simultaneously the supernatural rebirth of nature and the reawakening of vivid human awareness of that nature. The allegorical elements of the poem project aspects of a devoutly wished consummation between Apollo and the mythical personations of nature. But the consummation, as in the frozen scenes of a Grecian urn, is, like Apollo's coming, always in an interdicted future: "Et fugit, et fugiens pervelit ipsa capi"—"She darts away, but, though she runs, she hopes to be overtaken" (130). Continuing desire on both sides, it would seem, depends upon prolonged frustration. If the spring season of human vitality is to be kept fresh and alive, winter must be kept close at hand. Winter, indeed, is somehow part of the essence of spring. Deferral, in other words, implies an acceptance of absence, even of loss. In the highly compressed elegy as a whole, this recognition rises to a condition of poetic creativity.

In the lines quoted above, for example, the beloved desired by Apollo has died and been transformed into a tree, which has in turn yielded its green to shape the poetic braidings of Apollo's locks. Still, and because of the continual incompleteness and loss, Apollo comes. As Milton shapes him in the elegy, the figure of the sun god of poetry represents the essence of both objective and subjective vitality, nature as well as art. This is the case chiefly because he is eternally approaching and yet always departed: it is that doubleness and the absence of a fixed here and now that, in the poet's view, lights up the world for us. It does so by demanding our breathless pursuit of the particularity of apparently available objects. The poet also joins the indeterminate and interminable procession of poetic awareness thus located. His elegy ends not with exultation in perfected spring, but in recognition of ineluctable winter. This seemingly incidental recognition is his best hope for an activating, renewed springtime consciousness:

> Tu saltem lente rapidos age, Phoebe, iugales
> Qua potes, et sensim tempora veris eant;
> Brumaque productas tarde ferat hispida noctes,
> Ingruat et nostro serior umbra polo.          [137–40]

At least, O Phoebus, drive your swift coursers as moderately as you can and let the spring-tide pass slowly. Let the foul winter be long in bringing back its endless nights and let the shadows be later than their wont in attacking our pole.

In the fifth elegy Milton is engaged in a passionate reexamination of conventional vehicles of poetic creativity. His rehearsals, piled swiftly one upon the other, suggest a poetic gift urgently searching for a reliable form of self-expression. As the poet says in the moment just prior to turning to the shaping image of Apollo,

> Concitaque arcano fervent mihi pectora motu,
> Et furor, et sonitus me sacer intus agit.          [11–12]

My breast is aflame with the excitement of its mysterious impulse and I am driven on by the madness and the divine sounds within me.

This grasp of reality is intensely sexual in nature. Not accidentally, the poet's season of youth is mirrored in the pivotal section of the poem, which concerns the Earth's reviving desire for fulfillment of the

Sun's never-fulfilled approach. Earth ends her entreaty with these lines:

> Nec me, (crede mihi) terrent Semeleia fata,
> Nec Phaetonteo fumidus axis equo.
> Cum tu, Phoebe, tuo sapientius uteris igni,
> Huc ades, et gremio lumina pone meo.      [91–94]

I have no fear, believe me, of a fate like that of Semele, nor of the axle that smoked when Phaeton was the driver of the horses. When you shall have put your fire to wiser use, come hither and lay your glories in my lap.

The image of sexual opposites and the attractive force between them dramatizes a scrupulously delimited field of reality. Yet the repeated bracketing of such images in dramatizations of sexual desire within a contemplative, quasi-narrative framework suggests the poet's awareness of limitations in the world view he is provisionally espousing. In any case, this vague sexual view of things does not produce (or is not allowed to produce) any notion of the world's purposefulness beyond the future fulfillment of sexual desire—or the maintenance of high human consciousness in prolonged sexual frustration. Such an attempt to take hold of reality can only be expressed in endless eddies and whirls. It lacks a stable center. And we sense, perhaps, that the poet of *Elegia Quinta* knows that he is only recapitulating a passing phase. A reliable and stable form of self-expression still eludes him.

Yet the images of what may be described as binary opposition, and of incompleteness or interruption at the heart of fulfillment, retained an important place in Milton's development. Indeed, by disposing these two classes of images in new combinations he soon achieved a powerful, highly stable mode of expression that could encompass the representation not only of a world of opponent forces but of the eternally unchanging Judeo-Christian theological realities as well. This was his next order of large-scale business.

## "THE PARTING GENIUS"

By contrast with the fifth elegy, the mood and the orderly, progressive form of *On the Morning of Christ's Nativity* suggest a mind calm and secure in its choice of an appropriate poetic access. This too is a poem about the rebirth of nature and the human spirit, and the interrelations of those renewals. But the necessary acknowledgments of loss crystal-

lized only at the end of the elegy are already included in the carefully
delineated subject of the Ode: this is a poem about winter rebirth. In
the climactic section of the Ode a near relative of the Apollo figure
appears, his features and power so distributed that he becomes subordinate to a still more encompassing image. We do not have to commit
ourselves to any of the tenets of a so-called genetic interpretation to
see that within the Nativity Ode itself the following lines are part of a
complex effort, similar to that of the fifth elegy, to locate the sources
of human creativity:

> From haunted spring and dale
> Edg'd with poplar pale,
>    The parting Genius is with sighing sent;
> With flow'r-inwov'n tresses torn
> The Nymphs in twilight shade of tangled thickets mourn. [184–88]

What the reign or skill of this parting genius might be is left mysterious. He is sent and in that sense he is *de*parting, but the very
redundancy of that meaning forces the word to mean something else
as well. Does the parting have something to do with the inweaving of
flowers in tresses, with the tearing of those tresses, with the inevitable
fate that the nymphs mourn, or perhaps with an unnamed force of
division that rules not only this scene but the larger scene of which it
is only an emblematic and ephemeral part? What kind of parting genius, in other words, might Milton have symbolized in the local deity
and local representation of his larger poetic vision?

Within the universe of Christian patterns generated by the poem,
it is natural to ask such questions; and the Christian answers are quickly
forthcoming within the poem itself. The parting genius mourned by
the nymphs is in part a shadow image of the spirit of God, who at
Christ's baptism

>                     came softly sliding
> Down through the turning sphere,
> His ready Harbinger,
>    With Turtle wing the amorous clouds *dividing*,
> And *waving wide her myrtle wand*,
> She *strikes a universal Peace through Sea and Land*.
>                   [47–52; emphases added]

In some sense the same parting genius is also a figuration of the "sleep-
ing Lord" (242) who has come to be crucified and to divide the warring
elements of good and evil so that

> Th'old Dragon under ground,
> In straiter limits bound,
> Not half so far casts his usurped sway.       [168–70]

But the parallelisms created by the poem are more highly specified and more deeply informative than they may at first appear. The Christ who is endowed with, and simultaneously earns, a special efficacy of parting is characterized from the beginning of the poem as the god who laid aside his godhead in an act of *kenosis* (emptying) or retirement or departure from divinity. Not only, in other words, is his divine mission on behalf of humanity to be accomplished through the crucifixion of his adopted humanness, but his divine personality is characterized by his desire or willingness to suffer the loss of such personality.

Within the fabric of Milton's poem the fact that Christ's relation to loss is primary and essential, and not one of accident or means, is represented by a totally circular configuration of similes. The secession of Christ from "Trinal Unity" (11) brings about the supersession of nature:

> The Sun himself withheld his wonted speed,
> And hid his head for shame,
> As his inferior flame,
> The new-enlight'n'd world no more should need.       [79–82]

The victorious Christ, who controls the "damned crew" (228), is in his turn likened to the sun that he has even now overshadowed. The extended simile that Tillyard called grotesque[6] may only be meaningfully strained and complicated by the need to represent a sun that is both adequate to its remaining tasks and yet partially superannuated and reclining, even if not actually declined:

> So when the Sun in bed,
> Curtain'd with cloudy red,
>    Pillows his chin upon an Orient wave,
> The flocking shadows pale
> Troop to th'infernal jail.       [229–33]

The Christ whose nature is reflected in this simile is, as the next (last) stanza notes, also reclining. This parallelism is appropriate not only because he has come to be sacrificed, so that the repose of the manger prefigures the pietà; but because, like the gracefully recumbent sun, Christ's fitness for his task is associated with the acceptance of loss, of diminution of self.

Perhaps the most obvious implication of this shadowy association is that we are forced to reconsider the function of the series of stanzas (xix–xxv) describing the displacement of the pagan gods. We begin to recognize that these stanzas form an essential part of the theological meaning that the poet affirms, fully as much as they illustrate the idolatry that the poem denies. Milton summons up the pagan gods not merely to damn them, though undoubtedly that too is one of his aims. The striking parallelism between the stories of the pagan gods and the life of Christ are not offered by Milton as ironic elements in a simplistic disqualification procedure. Rather, within the framework of Christ's triumph over paganism, the distantly separated contrasts are made to suggest patterns of recurrence and antecedence. In stanza xxii, for example, Ashtaroth,

> Heav'n's Queen and Mother both,
>     Now sits not girt with Tapers' holy shine,

and in the first stanza of the poem the poet is quick to specify that his subject is the Christ who

> Of wedded Maid, and Virgin Mother born,
>     Our great redemption from above did bring.

The resemblances between the pagan Mother-Queen of heaven, surrounded by tapers, and the maiden mother of God who brings forth the heavenly redemption—and who will, as everyone knows, be perennially adored with multitudes of Roman Catholic tapers—are too close for uncomplicated comfort. The parallelism is swathed in particularly potent ambiguity because the poet does not really say that Ashtaroth has in all senses ceased to exist. We hear only that she "sits not girt with Tapers' holy shine."

Milton's handling of Osiris in stanza xxiv is striking in this same respect:

> Nor is *Osiris* seen
> In *Memphian* Grove or Green,
>     Trampling the unshow'r'd Grass with lowings loud:
> Nor can he be at rest
> Within his sacred chest,
>     Naught but profoundest Hell can be his shroud:
> In vain with Timbrel'd Anthems dark
> The sable-stoled Sorcerers bear his worshipt Ark.

Osiris is surely damned and his cult is surely empty of meaning—now.

But there was indeed a god Osiris and his potency was associated with his having been murdered, as was Christ. His image was worshipped, whereas his tomb was mysteriously empty.

What kind of power did the pagan gods have, in the poet's view? Of course, no fully explicit answer to this question is possible; but it would be grossly inaccurate to say that in the Ode the poet exposes the illusory being of the pagan gods. Just as he carefully avoids any direct specification of Christ's continuing and far greater divinity, he winds the divinity of the pagan gods in shroud within shroud. Yet the special kind of ambiguity that he associates with the existence of the pagan gods is significantly expressive, and not about the pagan gods alone. Stanza xix is full of oblique communications of this sort:

> The Oracles are dumb,
> No voice or hideous hum
>     Runs through the arched roof in words deceiving.
> *Apollo* from his shrine
> Can no more divine,
>     With hollow shriek the steep of *Delphos* leaving.
> No nightly trance, or breathed spell,
> Inspires the pale-ey'd Priest from the prophetic cell.

The clear implication, deeply entrenched in carefully constructed ambiguities, is that there was a god Apollo. It is not clear when and under what conditions his words of divination became deceiving, but in the world of question marks here associated with divine power it is surely possible that Apollo once could indeed divine. And if he could divine, his truth, like the power of the parting genius in the next stanza, had to do with leaving with hollow shriek the shrine of his divinity, as the voice *runs* through the arched roof and as the spell is breathed *from* the cell. The parallels suggest the ways in which Christ's truth became known when he laid aside and emptied his godhead in leaving the heavenly heights—as well as, later, the steep or vertical of crucifixion. The pagan priest could very well have been inspired, the poet implies, by the spectacle of leaving; and his cell might well have been rendered, then, truly prophetic.

The fact that Milton again and again represents the supersession of the pagan gods as a parting from a former state of supernatural efficacy should not be lost on us. Within the structure of the poem these descriptions are given the climactic place of honor because they help make intelligible, almost on the natural level, a pattern of divine abridgment

of divinity. What we have here is not merely a chain reaction of dis-
placements that are brought about by Christ's initial parting from godhead (indeed, in *Paradise Lost* Milton explores the possibilities of a
still earlier departure, or, more precisely, *retiring* of divinity).[7] Rather,
a significant part of Milton's achievement in the Ode is the creation of
a symbolic form that could represent a highly specified theological
reality.

Milton's recurring shorthand for this new or reinvigorated representation of the divine is a music that has not been heard since the
creation and is perhaps not aurally heard even here; music, he calls it,
"as never was by mortal finger struck" (95). Two aspects of this music
are particularly important for the meaning of Milton's poem. First, it
is characterized or even defined by a kind of harmony that is substantially different from the harmonies generally known to us: "such harmony alone," we hear, "could hold all Heav'n and Earth in happier
union" (107–08).

> Such Music (as 'tis said)
> Before was never made,
>   But when of old the sons of morning sung,
> While the Creator Great
> His constellations set.                                    [117–21]

Second, it is a musical harmony that is directly associated with hollow
sound (or hollow reverberation) and with a kind of thrilling or piercing
of conventional sound continuities, which are thereby punctuated by
deep silence and sharp cessation. This implication is first hinted at in
stanza x:

> Nature that heard such sound
> Beneath the hollow round
>   Of *Cynthia's* seat, the Airy region thrilling,
> Now was almost won
> To think her part was done.

By the end of the poem, when the final image of the bringer of the
redeeming Word is thrown into high prominence by a species of perfect
quiet, the reader knows that the poet's notion of divine efficacy has to
do with the re-creation of an analogous kind of framed silence,[8] an
adoring silence befitting the inviolable rest of a divinely human child:

> Time is our tedious Song should here have ending;
>
>  .  .  .  .  .  .  .  .  .  .  .  .  .  .  .  .  .  .  .  .  .  .  .

> . . . all about the Courtly Stable,
> Bright-harness'd Angels sit in order serviceable.    [239–44]

Both as a component and as a product of divine harmony, this silence somehow provides a key element in the "full consort" or "Angelic symphony" (132), the "Harping in loud and solemn choir, / With unexpressive [inexpressible] notes to Heav'n's new-born Heir" (115–16). That this is not silence as we conventionally think of it is somehow the converse of the fact that the poem is not really tedious but rather replete with recovered meanings. The poet's ending becomes an intrinsic part of the divine service: by falling into silence he joins the assembled company of those who only stand and wait in attendance.

It is clear that the silence and silencing of the oracles and the pagan gods play an active part in reproducing the harmony that Milton associated with Christ's new or renewed music. In that sense the dumbness of the oracles (173) is itself a functional element in Christ's "happier union" (108). And it is noteworthy that the same kind of mysterious music is suggestively located within the pre-Christian world of the oracles and pagan gods. That is, it is located within the nebulous syntax which is both the world of pagan myth fragmented and the world of fragmentation enshrined in pagan myth, as well as, perhaps, the pagan myth that foreshadows its own demise. Apollo or his priest leaving, as was their wont, the place of Delphic frenzy, runs with *hollow* shriek (178, emphasis added). The parting genius goes sighing (186). The sorcerers accompany the ark of Isis with a music of synaesthetic silence: "with Timbrel'd Anthems dark" (219). Similarly, when Christ was born the "Trumpet spake not" (58); conversely, when Christ on the judgment day will create his full harmony of apocalypse, he must sound his "trump of doom" (156), the special music that can untune the sky.

## New Music, Logos Division

The special meaning of the Ode's silence-punctuated harmony was not invented by Milton, even if his poem recapitulates the creation of that meaning. Laurence Stapleton, following a suggestion made by Gretchen Finney, has noted that Milton's presentation of the new music in the Ode is strikingly similar to Clement of Alexandria's use of the new music in his *Exhortation to the Greeks*. Not only, Stapleton notes, does Clement associate Christ the logos with a "principle of creation" that, says Clement, "arranged in harmonious order this great world," but Clement, like Milton, lays heavy emphasis on the simultaneity of his coming and the right hearing of this logos music and the silencing of the oracles and the pagan gods. Whether we regard the *Exhortation* as a specific source for the Ode or only as a highly informative analogue, this in itself is an important observation. For it is one more plausible indication that the Greek Church Fathers were of special interest to Milton, even the early Milton.[9] But the potential importance of the parallelism to an understanding of the Ode appears greater still when the actual nature of the "new" music described by Clement is considered.

Clement's brief chapter on the new music, which opens the *Exhortation,* is part of his definitive statement concerning the kind of music that Christ brought to man. He brought it, Clement emphasizes, by having "emptied Himself" to become man.[10] Clement sees the harmony of the Word's truth as a music made by transitions between visualized emptiness and fullness. He cites Isaiah 54:1, "more are the children of the desolate than of her that hath an husband," as prologue and type for his comments on Luke 1. The mysterious dumbness of Zacharias, husband of the barren Elizabeth, father of John, provides divine witness to the new-born Word. Speaking of the new music, Clement writes,

> in some such ways as this John, the herald of the Word, summoned men to prepare for the presence of God, that is, of Christ. And this was the hidden meaning of the dumbness of Zacharias, which lasted until the coming of the fruit which was forerunner of the Christ,—that the light of truth, the Word, should break the mystic silence of the dark prophetic tidings, by becoming good tidings.[11]

It is clear that for Clement the mystic silence has an important role in the composition and propagation of the new harmony. It is also clear that this silence is somehow analogous to the silencing of the oracles, which he describes in a neighboring passage. The context and specification of his musical meaning, however, is left undeclared; Clement is not given to summary statements of his theological intuitions.

Yet in the fifth book of the *Stromateis,* where he presents his most extensive analysis of the structure of divine symbols, Clement leaves no doubt about the kind of harmony that he associated with the divine Word. Here his principal text is the Mosaic blueprint for construction of the mercy seat above the ark of the covenant (Exodus 25:17–22). What concerns him particularly is the kind of cosmic harmony that the text in Exodus 25 expresses with the symmetrical cherubim separated by the axis that is drawn from the "voice" or Word above to the ark below. Here the harmony described may be said to be essentially visual, though the movement of the spheres that Clement invokes implies a harmonics that is implicitly and immensely musical. His interest is in rendering a gnostic harmony as a structure of intelligible objects or terms:

> And those golden figures, each of them with six wings, signify either the two bears, as some will have it, or rather the two hemispheres. And the name cherubim meant "much knowledge." But both together have twelve wings, and by the zodiac and time, which moves on it, point out the world of sense. . . . Whether [the ark] is the eighth region and the world of thought, or God, all-embracing, and without shape, and invisible, that is indicated, we may for the present defer saying. But it signifies the repose which dwells with the adoring spirits, which are meant by the cherubim. . . . The face [of each cherub] is a symbol of the rational soul, and the wings are the lofty ministers and energies of powers right and left; and the voice is delightsome glory in ceaseless contemplation.[12]

Corresponding to and explaining Clement's conceptions of the logos music and divine mercy, which have silence or emptiness somewhere at their heart, is his larger image of the logos-divided cosmos. Musical or structural division, of one kind or another, is by Clement systematically associated with the nature of the divine Word. It is the Word, he says, that "discriminates all things."[13]

As we might expect, Clement's symbols are also derivative and carry with them a burden of inherited meanings that would have been well known to anyone familiar with the traditions of thought that had produced his exegetical world view. Most relevant to the present discussion is the fact that Clement's symbols of the logos discriminator were borrowed in detail from the writings of Philo of Alexandria, which Clement knew "virtually by heart."[14] Philo's discussions amply flesh out Clement's skeletal tracings. In abundant interpretations of the mercy seat blueprint and the Mosaic patterns of animal sacrifice, Philo explains that the cosmos owes its form to the divisions of the logos severer.[15] That immaterial, severing logos stations itself between the "material elements" to keep them "apart . . . so that the universe may send forth a harmony like that of a masterpiece of literature. It mediates between the opponents amid their threatenings, and reconciles them."[16] The forces of cosmic existence represented by the cherubim, whom Philo

glosses as "recognition and full knowledge" (thought to be the direct
source of Clement's own gloss),[17] are separated by the logos "severer
of all things" (the probable source of Clement's logos discriminator).[18]
For Philo and for Clement the harmony created by the logos is a structure of divided, separated parts with immateriality or the Word at its
center.

## THE SERVICEABLE ORDER OF MERCY

The terms of inherited meaning carried by the materials Milton chose
to employ and the development of those materials within the Ode are
closely related. Indeed, the musical metaphors discussed above furnish
an avenue of approach to an inner realm of highly specified meaning
that would otherwise remain inaccessible. The poetic and divine order
represented immediately by the Ode's metaphor and mimesis of an
interrupted music is also presented in a series of controlling symbols
of cosmic separation. That is, the metaphors of music blend into a range
of visual symbols and deliver us virtually unawares into a world of
special topographies that parallels the music that "never was by mortal
finger struck."

   This is the scene that is first intimated when the spirit of God "the
amorous clouds dividing . . . strikes a universal Peace through Sea and
Land" (50–52).[19] What is the nature of this dividing and striking, heavily suggestive of a miraculous parting of the waves, where "Birds of
Calm sit brooding on the charmed wave" (68)? Something like a sat-
isfactory answer to this question can be provided by specifying as carefully as possible the visual elements entwined within the musical and
then identifying the biblical class of these combinatory metaphors or
symbols. Three key stanzas that promote the recurring pattern into a
common denominator of schematized meaning are iii, x, and xv:

iii

But he her fears to cease,
Sent down the meek-ey'd Peace;
   She crown'd with Olive green, came softly sliding
Down through the turning sphere,
His ready Harbinger,
   With Turtle wing the amorous clouds dividing,
And waving wide her myrtle wand,
She strikes a universal Peace through Sea and Land.

X

Nature that heard such sound
Beneath the hollow round
   Of *Cynthia's* seat, the Airy region thrilling,
Now was almost won
To think her part was done,
   And that her reign had here its last fulfilling;
She knew such harmony alone
Could hold all Heav'n and Earth in happier union.

XV

Yea, Truth and Justice then
Will down return to men,
   Orb'd in a Rainbow; and like glories wearing
Mercy will sit between,[20]
Thron'd in Celestial sheen,
   With radiant feet the tissu'd clouds down steering,
And Heav'n as at some festival,
Will open wide the Gates of her high Palace Hall.

In all three stanzas the renewed harmony, which is differentiated by exception and silence, is inwoven with an act of division that in its turn parts or separates major components of the imagined scene: Sea and Land, Heaven and Earth, represented Truth and Justice. The affiliation of images suggests its own logic. The divided elements of the first act are subsumed in one divided element, Earth, of the second act, as the elements of the third are the result of a division of one element of the second group, Heaven, after Earth and Heaven have been separated.

It would be wrong to suppose that the goal pursued here is finally the rarification or etherealization of earthly reality. Instead, the poet's aim is the location and mimetic stationing of the central, all-organizing, all-dividing entity within the totally divided and ordered cosmos. By Milton and the tradition behind him, this enthroned entity is called Mercy.[21] It is represented by inset immateriality or silence. In the 1673 version of the Ode, the lines that made the source text all too obvious—perhaps slavishly so, in Milton's later view—were changed for an image that was more mysteriously allusive, though just as masterfully controlled by the biblical image and its heavy theological burden. The original lines were:

Th'enamel'd *Arras* of the Rainbow wearing,
And Mercy set between.

Here, complete with the holy curtain of the ark of the covenant (described in Exodus 27 as a tapestry woven of blue, purple, and scarlet threads), is a vast allusive projection of the mercy seat or propitiatory scene reflected in Psalm 85 and derived from Exodus 25:20–22. These are the lineaments of the same master image that Clement, following Philo, glossed in his explanation of the divine harmony. The verses in Exodus are these:

> And the cherubims shall stretch forth their wings on high, covering the mercy seat with their wings, and their faces shall look one to another; toward the mercy seat shall the faces of the cherubims be.
> And thou shalt put the mercy seat above the ark; and in the ark thou shalt put the testimony that I shall give thee.
> And there I will meet with thee, and I will commune with thee from above the mercy seat, from between the two cherubims which are upon the ark of the testimony.[22]

In his allusive phrases, Milton has created the image of God's self-manifestation and self-representation by mirroring the Philonic-Clementine allegorical assumption that the heavenly creatures who stretch forth their wings are God's rational potencies, Truth and Justice. In addition, Milton has stipulated that God's reality is more than the knowledge of his truth and more than the effect of his justice; it is also the band of logos division, corresponding to divine musical silence, that is here called Mercy.

For Milton the use of the inherited polar pattern undoubtedly represents a markedly dialectical meaning, but it is, I should emphasize, dialectical meaning of a special kind. What is found repeatedly in the Ode is dialectic with continuous separation or differentiation at its organizing, stabilizing center. This combination of visual and conceptual pattern is the matrix form of the poem's principal images. From it, for example, proceeds Milton's dramatic elaboration of Isaiah's correlative combination of cherubim and seraphim who are the "full consort," which produces the "Angelic symphony" that prepares the way for the "order serviceable" of the bright-harnessed angels in the poem's conclusion:

xi

At last surrounds their sight
A Globe of circular light,
  That with long beams the shame-fac't night array'd,
The helmed Cherubim

> And sworded Seraphim
>   Are seen in glittering ranks with wings display'd,
> Harping in loud and solemn choir,
>   With unexpressive notes to Heav'n's new-born Heir.

And this image of divine symmetries is powerfully associated, within the same set of Philonic and Clementine exegetical axioms, with God's first covenant with his people. This is the covenant of symmetrically divided sacrifice in Genesis 15:8–10, where the logos was understood to have manifested itself as both dividing force and separating, undivided bird:[23]

> And he [Abram] said, Lord God, whereby shall I know that I shall inherit it?
> And he said unto him, Take me an heifer of three years old, and a she goat of three years old, and a ram of three years old, and a turtledove, and a young pigeon.
> And he took unto him all these, and divided them in the midst, and laid each piece one against another: but the birds divided he not.

These undivided, dividing birds at the center of covenant division provided one authoritative prototype and source of power for Milton's dividing dove. In the progression of Milton's Ode, this is the same dove or logos or spirit of God that gradually merges with undivided mercy.

What can be said about a poetic pattern of such large comprehensiveness and such mysterious division at its heart? What does this ordering of reality mean within the Nativity Ode? And how might it be considered "serviceable"? Part of the answer to this multiple question can be sought in Milton's identification of his muse with particular structures of paradox. From the very beginning of the poem his efforts are articulated as an attempt to release his poetic gift into the no-man's land between historical past and historical present. The opening line, "This is the Month, and this the happy morn," refers to two real Christmas mornings and to a nativity in the poet's mind. It is by virtue of the purely imaginative nativity that, following his "sacred vein" (15), he hopes to interpose his muse in and between the sequence of recorded time:

> See how from far upon the Eastern road
> The Star-led Wizards haste with odors sweet:
> O run, prevent [anticipate] them with thy humble ode,
> And lay it lowly at his blessed feet.                    [22–25]

Even at this early point the poem's particular structures of paradox are associated with both the sacrificial altar, surrounded by birdlike presences, and the angelic bird choir that is also a choir producing heavenly music:

> Have thou the honor first, thy Lord to greet,
>     And join thy voice unto the Angel Choir,
> From out his secret Altar toucht with hallow'd fire.          [26–28]

At the end of the poem it is no surprise that the poet takes pains to point out the necessity of falling into silence: "Time is our tedious Song should here have ending" (239), he says, apparently in self-deprecation and resignation to failure:

> Heaven's youngest-teemed Star
> Hath fixt her polisht Car,
>     Her sleeping Lord with Handmaid Lamp attending:
> And all about the Courtly Stable,
> Bright-harness'd Angels sit in order serviceable.          [240–44]

But his phrase "time is" is not really colloquially diffuse—reflecting, as we may have been led to expect, the looseness of a mood of defeat. Rather it is absolutely compact and precise, a perfectly decorous acknowledgment and realization of divine order.[24] The patterning of interruptive silence has created the universe of special time wherein divine reality most clearly manifests itself. The poet's own silence will complete his attempt to reproduce the new, higher harmony. By withdrawing and by presenting his gift he has suggestively joined his voice "unto the Angel Choir." The implicit ordering of his poem has become a "secret Altar." The double preposition "from out" perhaps signifies the simultaneous emergence of a number of representational patterns: in sight, in sound, and in other imagined dimensions of reality as well.

Yet for all the solid gains made by the poetic persona, the poem is not made to reflect an identification of poetic and divine egos. In the final rehearsal of the dove, angel, mercy-seat pattern, the child who furnishes the sacrificial middle merges with the space of divine parting. He alone is the center point. This final image is tremendous in its impact: it is nearly, that is, in the nature of an aesthetic trauma, an overwhelming meaning almost (but not quite) beyond meaning as it is usually conceived. For here theological meaning and cosmic form are focused in a virtual image of human and divine personality that is completely obliterated, yet the frame within which the virtual image might be said to be self-sacrificing or self-canceling remains intact; and we know precisely where it hangs. The poem both regenerates and retains the biblical archetype of the virtual image.

The concluding mood of calm sufficiency is the gift of separation and sacrifice. It comes as the largesse of Christ's efficacy as redeemer. G. Wilson Knight complained that the Ode lacks an "inter-knitting . . . of central action with design."[25] It seems more likely, however, that in the Nativity Ode Milton worked for just such an inter-knitting. If we follow his dividing activity, we understand that he executed an extensive, consonant design.[26] The serviceable order stands firm "all about," with the divine will and the divine presence of separation at the cosmic center.

Having achieved this complex of meaning, Milton stored it up for other uses. Before long, the patterns embodied in the Ode began to appear in his prose as well. With his left hand, he was soon showing that by virtue of the dividing Word, analytic reason and theological imagination were the same.

# 3

❀

# The Shape of Discipline
# in Milton's
# *Reason of Church-Government*

In the Preface to *The Reason of Church-Government* Milton makes clear that the reformation of ecclesiastical polity and the renovation of civil order can only be accomplished by the exercise of human reason. But what kinds of reason are required for precisely which tasks Milton does not immediately reveal. Indeed, his precedents from Plato and Moses declare the transcendent difficulty of finding and maintaining appropriate rational regimens even as they encourage us to believe in their great desirability. For the task of bringing about the reformation of church government or "discipline," Milton considers a number of different kinds of reason. These can be lumped together under the heading: the Christian's rational activity in his search for salvation. Milton, it is true, even describes points of continuity between the kinds he mentions. But in the Preface and in the pamphlet as a whole one kind of reason comes to occupy a position of special importance in his argument. This reason is identical to the true church discipline. It is a form of rational activity that Milton offers as a model for the individual Christian mind. In his view, Christian discipline of this kind is characterized by a continuous process of division and by an emerging divided shape that together constitute the operation and location of God's redeeming Word.

## REASON'S WAYS

The kind of reason that Milton mentions first in order of apparent persuasiveness is not of ultimate significance for the argument of his treatise. In its degenerate form, this is the reason of the prelates. Milton calls it informed understanding of "that government which the Church claimes to have over" its members: that is, claims on their behalf—as distinct from "in Gods behalfe"—as a reason or condition, attested by syllogism, for improving their chances of winning eternal life. Aside from the love and service of God for His own sake, nothing could be more technically important for the Christian life. Yet Milton's specification of other kinds of reason soon makes us aware that in his view we must keep open a substantial part of our rational agenda and that the first-named kind of reason is inadequate by itself even for its own proposed end.

In fact, it is not surprising to find that Milton gradually assigns this calculus of spiritual self-interest to a realm of "carnal support-ment" (I.827) or fleshly establishmentarianism that is starkly opposed to the higher rational efficacy of the gospel Word of Scripture.[1] Quite soon he will tell us that in fact he hopes to cut the knot of this reasoning with the aid of the "quick and pearcing" Word of Hebrews 4:12:

> But let them chaunt while they will of prerogatives, we shall tell them
> of Scripture; of custom, we of Scripture; of Acts and Statutes, stil of
> Scripture; til the quick and pearcing word enter to the dividing of their
> soules, & the mighty weaknes of the Gospel throw down the weak
> mightines of mans reasoning.                                    [I.827]

The operative meaning of this dividing Word in *The Reason of Church-Government* is not specified at the outset, but it gradually acquires great significance.

Because for Milton every kind of reason is to some degree in the immediate cure of the church's power to prescribe and proscribe our ways of thinking, he acknowledges that his second kind of reason has also been substantially obscured by fleshly concerns. But he believes that we may yet restore its original status as a spiritually independent entity. This second faculty or way is (or could be) right reason itself. It is the consummation of "spirituall knowledge" won by "those inner parts and affections of the mind where the seat of reason is" (I.747–48). In Milton's present, when the church prelatical all too directly reflects our fallen condition, this divine capacity is left to languish as the "grosse distorted apprehension of decay'd mankinde" (I.750). Later he will reveal his belief that, afflicted as we are, we may attain to the "sorer burden of mind" that comes of knowing "any thing distinctly of God" (I.801). His emphasis will be on a power of true distinction that has been blurred by the false distinctions of "these sensual mistresses that keep the ports and passages" between the understanding and objective knowledge or truth. Milton thus implies a close connection between one kind of "ecclesial jurisdiction" and the incapacitation of our judging faculty by "those wily Arbitresses" that have come to dominate human thought (I.831). The promotion of the sorer burden of mind is for Milton clearly a vital aspect of the reformation of church government.

To complete his trisected circle of reforming reason Milton describes a quantity that does not seem to be a kind of *ratio* at all, yet that upon closer inspection turns out to be the visible shape of virtue or reasonable action (I.751) and in many ways, as I have suggested, the principal subject of the pamphlet. In Milton's view this is our one remaining access to the true religious life. Our spiritual knowledge, he writes, is both a function of the "manner and order" of church government and an embodiment "in Gods behalfe" of "a service intirely reasonable" (I.748). This operative reason of church government is the reasonable form of church activity that is coextensive with the living form of reforming reason. Milton devotes the first two chapters of his treatise to a circumstantial description of this vital form. He calls it by the name most closely identified with it by Calvin: discipline. This is the disciplinary ideal that, in 1642, was for most Puritans the conceptual nexus of reformation and revolution.[2] In Milton's pamphlet it appears as the living, acting, symbolic form of reason understood as "the quick and pearcing word" that enters swordlike to the dividing of men's souls.

What I wish to recover from the pamphlet is consonant with Stanley Fish's central insight in his stimulating essay, "Reason in *The Reason of Church Government*," although some of his conclusions seem to me in need of revision. Reason, he argues, "is very much the subject of *The Reason of Church Government*, but" he maintains, "it is an antisubject (almost an antichrist)." Milton, he believes, works to "bypass the reasoning *process* and redefine reason to mean self-validating reason." In this view, the treatise "undermines its own pretensions and repeatedly calls attention to what it is *not* doing. It does not express truth, or contain it, or process it. Indeed, its elaborate rational machinery operates only to emphasize how independent truth is of the validation that reason and rational structures can confer. At best, it turns the mind of the reader . . . in the direction of truth." Its "locus of meaning is not the printed page."[3]

If we linger, however, to inquire into the nature of that reason of church government which Milton elaborately describes as the local and cosmic workings of discipline, we realize that only the syllogistic kind of reason, the first kind described above—and that, only when it is abused—is Milton's antisubject. At least one other kind of reason, the meaning of which is very much on Milton's printed page, is a professed and real meaning of his treatise. Milton does not slyly undermine his stated meanings in favor of meanings that he trusts to the reader's articulation. He has set out to "warre a good warfare" by expounding the "heavenly structure of evangelick discipline" (I.758). His treatise both expresses and contains all the truths that interest him, whether or not the reader is interested in, or capable of following, his way.

Fish's emphasis on the word *process* implies a distinction between static and dynamic form. But Fish does not explain the distinction. He tells us only that the dynamic variety is not to be found in Milton's pages. Most seventeenth-century logicians, particularly of Ramistic persuasion, would not have allowed a distinction between static and dynamic forms of reason. Nor would they have granted that there can be such a thing as self-validating rationality. For them, right reason is animated by divine intelligence; it is always both scripture-validated and God-validated. The revelation and reading and copying out of God's Word constantly renew our dependency on its rational structures.

It might be argued that the whole of this process is not after all in the text. But innumerable Ramist tomes of systematized dichotomy (to take just one example) show just how easy it is to conceive of apparently static rational structures as all the process worth caring about. One man's stasis is another man's dynamic cause sufficient. Yet if process means the dramatic renewal of God's rational patterns in our civil and religious conceptualizations, such process is certainly not lacking in Milton's pamphlet. First to last, these renewed conceptualizations are presented by Milton as the structures of a reforming discipline. The reader's task in perusing the text is to make out Milton's rational structures of discipline in all their specificity. Milton could not be clearer about his belief that the structures of discipline embody a decidedly active principle. Almost as if he is anticipating the misconceiving of discipline—and of his treatise—as a mere immobilization of unruly energies, he asserts that "certainly discipline is not only the removall of disorder, but if any visible shape can be given to divine things, the very visible shape and image of vertue." He emphasizes that discipline is the principle of rational organization within all regenerate activity: "all the moments and turnings of humane occasions are mov'd to and fro as upon the axle of discipline. . . . Nor is there any sociable perfection in this life, civill or sacred that can be above discipline, but she is that which with her musicall cords preserves and holds all the parts thereof together" (I.751).

Milton's complex use of the word *moments*—here meaning turning point and torsion as well as motion[4]—is emblematic of a rational discipline that is both a pattern of understanding and a shape of action. It acts as an unmoved mover, an axle that turns everything yet is itself stationary. It functions as a musical harmony that preserves and holds all moving things in "the regular gestures and motions" of its heavenly paces. Discipline has motions and paces yet its place is as unchanged, we learn, as the throne of God at the center of its thronging angels— "as the Apostle that saw them in his rapture describes." Milton's conception of discipline involves a structural principle that appears merely static yet comprises a marked dynamism. Even more important, though it seems to suggest familiar models of dialectical resolution, it is in fact sharply distinguished by continuous formal separation. Precisely as in Plato's memorable exemplification of the distinction-making activity that is dialectic, the turning axle is, in Plato's terms, at "rest" and is not one with its surrounding, moving objects.[5] Milton makes clear that the music which turns the spheres is the impulsion of a separate "she," which is the divine spirit.

Of course, the special attributes of Milton's disciplinary reason were not his own invention. He inherited all their leading features from well-known Christian sources. In particular, the model of a rational discipline centered in continuous formal separation corresponds in ruling conception as well as circumstantial detail to the authority for all Calvinistic disciplinary conceptions, the endlessly quoted twelfth chapter of the fourth book of *The Institutes*. It is difficult to overstate the intellectual richness of Calvin's statements on this subject, most of which had their own depths of inherited meaning. A contemporary Puritan would likely have been offended by a footnote such as most modern readers require to point to Calvin's "The Discipline of the Church: Its Chief Use in Censures and Excommunications."[6] He would have recognized instantly that the first two chapters of Milton's pamphlet, as well as his handling of the central problem of schism, are built directly upon the foundation of Calvin's complex rendering of discipline as a rational symbol. Calvin's meanings inform Milton's.

## CALVIN, AUGUSTINE, AND THE SWORD OF DISCIPLINE

The idea of church discipline occupies the place of honor in Calvin's larger account of the dialectics that order Christian salvation.[7] Indeed the formal embodiments of inspired rationality in ecclesial form bear much the same relationship to his announced subject in "The Discipline of the Church" as they do in Milton's *The Reason of Church-Government*. The key to Calvin's thinking about disciplinary reason is his conviction that its formal activity, like that of the divine separating Word that it expresses, is simultaneously a dividing and a bonding: it separates and unifies at one and the same time. Calvin's aim, he says, is to teach us

> how the spiritual jurisdiction of the church, which punishes according to the Lord's Word, is the best support of health, foundation of order, and bond of unity. . . . Those who trust that without this bond of discipline the church can long stand are, I say, mistaken.          [1231–32]

The true church edifice reflects a structure of disciplinary concepts. Its bond of disciplines maintains the bond of unity even while it punishes by excluding or separating transgressors. Calvin can locate the activities of binding and dividing in the same conceptual space because the bond of unity (or "bond of fellowship" or "bond of peace," as he variously calls it) is an agency that is essentially different from the elements that it both separates and maintains in unity. The force of binding in ecclesiastical censure is itself the force of dividing. The gospel divisor is always identical with the bond of fellowship, unless by a disproportionate separating severity we ruin the ratio and relation of the whole and "slide down from discipline to butchery"—"ne ex disciplina mox delabamur ad carnificinam" (1238).[8]

 Calvin's exposition of the coincidence of binding and dividing in the tolerant handling of separation and schism functions, as it does for Milton, as the conceptual heart of disciplinary reason. His expansions upon this central matter are presented as a series of lengthy attributed quotations from Augustine, principally from *Against the Letter of Parmenianus*. Calvin clearly wanted to be sure that there would be no

doubts about the authority of his difficult conceptualization. Here is
Calvin:

> What Augustine writes is very true: "Whosoever either corrects what
> he can by reproof, or excludes, without breaking the bond of peace,
> what he cannot correct—disapproving with fairness, bearing with firm-
> ness,—this man is free and loosed from the curse." In another passage
> he gives the reason: "All pious method and measure of ecclesiastical
> discipline ought ever to look to 'the unity of the Spirit in the bond of
> peace' [Eph. 4:3], which the apostle orders us to keep by 'forbearing
> one another' [Eph. 4:2], and when it is not kept, the medicine of pun-
> ishment begins to be not only superfluous but also harmful, and so
> ceases to be medicine." "He who diligently ponders these things," Au-
> gustine says, "neither neglects severe discipline in the maintenance of
> unity, nor by intemperate correction breaks the bond of fellowship."
>                                                                [1238–1239][9]

Calvin shows that his own model of rational discipline is no more
and no less than Augustine's elevated representation of the dividing-
binding Word working as church discipline. The power of Augustine's
disciplinary conception stems from its breadth and clarity. A dialectic
of church discipline that includes the dividing-binding Word that both
separates and binds is for him no tentative speculation. Augustine sees
it, rather, as an inevitable corollary of the logos activity that initially
ordered and now maintains the cosmos. In *The City of God* he explains
in detail how God made

> the world's course, like a fair poem, more gracious by antithetic figures.
> *Antitheta,* called in Latin opposites, are the most elegant figures in all
> locution: some, more expressly, call them contra-posites. . . . So is the
> world's beauty composed of contrarieties, not in figure but in nature.
> This is plain in Ecclesiasticus, in this verse: "Against evil is good, and
> against death is life; so is the godly against the sinner; so look for in all
> the works of the highest, two against two, one against one."    [XI.xviii]

We refresh our memory of the symmetry of Augustine's dialectic
without difficulty. It is perhaps harder to remember that he also specifies a particular bond of separation between the contra-posites. Immediately after citing the verse from Ecclesiasticus, for example, he
searches "the meaning of that text 'God separated the light from the
darkness'" and concludes that God "only could make separation" in
creating and keeping apart the clean and unclean angels (xix). From
Ecclesiasticus and the symmetrical arrangement of good and evil, he

thus moves gradually to Hebrews and the discerning Word of God that divides and distinguishes all things, both in the act of creation and in the understanding or knowledge of that creation: "All these the angels discerned in the Word of God, where they had the causes of their production immovable and fixed, otherwise than in themselves" (xxix). [10] In Augustine's dialectic of rational discipline as in Calvin's, the dividing Word stands between, even while it is the turning axle of all heavenly and earthly creation. Indeed, Augustinian and Calvinistic discipline is one immense manifestation of that dynamic divide and its operation. This is its special kind of activity and what might be called its processing of reality.

I could dig further into the history of Milton's and Calvin's ideas and reveal the strata just below Augustine's formulations, but that would not, I think, significantly enhance the reading of *Church-Government*. And as I suggested in chapter two, the tradition that provides those formulations is in any case not conceptually different from the model he presents. [11] By recalling the outlines of Calvin's and Augustine's conceptions we can more easily see that the visible shape and image of Milton's handling of discipline are graphically substantial. Milton could assume that readers would understand these inherited meanings as a part of his own, both when he rehearsed their distinctive conception of discipline and when he applied it in the cases and in the manner stipulated by his august forebears.

### The Schism that Binds

In the management of these inherited materials Milton advances on Calvin by a more systematic equation of the benefits of separating discipline and what he calls "quiet schisme" (I.783). The equation is more than implicit, as we have seen, in Augustine's and Calvin's thinking as well. But in Milton the impassioned identification is raised to the pitch of revolutionary Christian liberty. Quiet schism and church discipline become obverses of the same bond. They are manifestations of the *idem in alio* of the dividing Word.

Quiet schism, Milton argues, is mysteriously healthful to the church body. To try to outlaw it altogether, to fail to tolerate it in some moderate form, is paradoxically to cause a fatal breach in church government. Dynamic renovation is the church's flourishing condition. Milton's expatiation on this point stands out as a particularly rich and complex moment. He may even be momentarily conjuring the spirit of a higher loss from his *Elegia Quinta*. Of the prelates who claim to save us from the catastrophe of unleashed schism he writes as follows:

> Doe they keep away schisme? if to bring a num and chil stupidity of soul, an unactive blindnesse of minde upon the people by their leaden doctrine, or no doctrine at all, if to persecute all knowing and zealous Christians by the violence of their courts, be to keep away schisme, they keep away schisme indeed; and by this kind of discipline all *Italy* and *Spaine* is as purely and politickly kept from schisme as *England* hath beene by them. With as good a plea might the dead palsie boast to a man, tis I that free you from stitches and paines, and the trouble-some feeling of cold & heat, of wounds and strokes; if I were gone, all these would molest you. The Winter might as well vaunt it selfe against the Spring, I destroy all noysome and rank weeds, I keepe downe all pestilent vapours. Yes and all wholesome herbs, and all fresh dews, by your violent & hidebound frost; but when the gentle west winds shall open the fruitfull bosome of the earth thus over-girded by your impris-onment, then the flowers put forth and spring, and then the Sunne shall scatter the mists, and the manuring hand of the Tiller shall root up all that burdens the soile without thank to your bondage.          [I.784–85]

The meaning of this passage is dependent upon Milton's simulta-neous revision of the apparent significations of schism and winter. Both are released as new meanings from the old ones in which they have been buried. By avoiding the excesses of what Calvin calls a butchering discipline, itself aimed at the excesses of a licentious separation, the attributes of a moderate or quiet schism are learned. Quiet schism turns out to be the same as moderated discipline. Indeed, schism of this special kind is by Milton's implication the intelligence of the soul, the active perspicacity of the mind; it expresses the rational acumen of an exercised discipline. England has been kept unpersecuted and whole by such schism and such discipline. A little disease of this strain is, it turns out, a healthful thing. Milton does not choose his climactic metaphor to deny the necessity of rigorous discipline any more than the inevitability of seasonal change. His aim rather is to suggest that the interruptiveness of discipline, as of quiet schism, is a providential part of the cosmic plan. Only when that frost-like interruptiveness becomes violent and hidebound is it a bondage rather than a fruitful bonding.

In the last lines of the *Elegia Quinta*, Milton completed his vision of a renewed springtide of human consciousness by setting at its heart the recognition of inevitable winter.[12] In *Church-Government* as well,

near the core of Milton's conception of continued spiritual life we find
the divinely contained winter—here quiet schism and rational discipline—that performs a secret ministry to inner well-being.

Milton shows us how to regard apparently unwarranted resistance
to our sense of truth as an opportunity for achieving a still higher truth
than that initially contemplated. He implies a divine mediation or me-
diate presence in the processes of human knowing. For him as much
as for Augustine the benefits of a true discipline and of a tolerated
modicum of schism are directly related to the dialectic of perfectibility
and improving knowledge that they organize:

> Other things men do to the glory of God: but sects and errors it seems
> God suffers to be for the glory of good men. . . . For if there were no
> opposition where were the triall of an unfained goodnesse and magna-
> nimity? vertue that wavers is not vertue, but vice revolted from itselfe,
> and after a while returning. . . . . If sects and schismes be turbulent in
> the unsetl'd estate of a Church, while it lies under the amending hand,
> it best beseems our Christian courage to think they are but as the throws
> and pangs that go before the birth of reformation, and that the work it
> selfe is now in doing. For if we look but on the nature of elementall and
> mixt things, we know they cannot suffer any change of one kind, or
> quality into another without the struggl of contrarieties.          [I.795]

The reformation is already occurring. The birth is already in progress.
The throes and the birth are connatural. The sects and schisms suffered
by God and by the amending hand of discipline represent the glory of
good men and the visible emergence of a reformed church. The dialectic of moments and turnings maintained by the intervening axle of
discipline is moved equally by quiet schism and deliberated discipline,
for they are providentially coequal.

One cannot read the above passage without thinking of the similar
passage in the *Areopagitica*, published just two years after *Church-
Government*:

> He that can apprehend and consider vice with all her baits and seeming
> pleasures, and yet abstain, and yet distinguish, and yet prefer that which
> is truly better, he is the true warfaring Christian. I cannot praise a
> fugitive and cloister'd vertue, unexercis'd & unbreath'd, that never sal-
> lies out and sees her adversary, but slinks out of the race, where that
> immortall garland is to be run for, not without dust and heat. Assuredly
> we bring not innocence into the world, we bring impurity much rather:
> that which purifies us is triall, and triall is by what is contrary.[II.514–15]

Milton is here considering the spiritual benefits of allowing possibly erroneous religious opinions to be printed and read. His meanings and usages are extraordinarily close to those of *Church-Government*. Here too his emphasis is on the dialectic of contraries that can perfect man's soul. And here too it is man's ability to keep the contraries intellectually separate—"and yet abstain, and yet distinguish"—which causes the dialectic to work. Later in the *Areopagitica* Milton even shows us how much a divided dialectic has been at the back of his mind when he cites Ephesians 4:2–3 to precisely the same effect as did Augustine in advocating the toleration of a measure of schism in a just discipline. Where Augustine wrote, "All pious method and measure of ecclesiastical discipline ought ever to look to 'the unity of the Spirit in the bond of peace' [Eph. 4:3], which the apostle orders us to keep by 'forbearing one another' [Eph. 4:2]," Milton says, "those neighboring differences, or rather indifferences, are what I speak of, whether in some point of doctrine or of discipline, which though they may be many, yet need not interrupt *the unity of Spirit*, if we could but find among us *the bond of peace*" [II.565].

The bond of peace that is tolerated distance and tolerable interruption is the key to the unity of spirit. Just such, Milton emphasized in the *Areopagitica*, is the function of schism in the larger spiritual architecture of the church temple. The following passage is so much of a piece with passages in *Church-Government* that I only hesitate whether to think of it as gloss or text. What Milton particularly suggests here is that the discontinuity of the temple's symmetry is the divine secret of its strength and purity:

> There must be many schisms and many dissections made in the quarry and in the timber, ere the house of God can be built. And when every stone is laid artfully together, it cannot be united into a continuity, it can but be contiguous in this world; neither can every peece of the building be of one form; nay rather the perfection consists in this, that out of many moderat varieties and brotherly dissimilitudes that are not vastly disproportionall arises the goodly and the gracefull symmetry that commends the whole pile and structure.                    [II.555]

For Milton the idea of a spiritual architecture is a unity that includes division and separation and distance. This is what ultimately creates the structural stability as well as the well-supported space of the whole.

Using this passage as a gloss it is apparent what Milton in *Church-Government* meant by the "heavenly structure of evangelick discipline" that can create "that elegant and artfull symmetry of the promised new temple"—the "inward beauty and splendor of the Christian Church thus govern'd" (I.758). Milton tells us that God "by his owne prescribed discipline" casts "his line and levell upon the soule of man which is his rationall temple" [I.757–58].

In all this, discipline and schism occupy the space of distinction made by God's dividing Word and man's power of rational differentiation. The true church, in other words, stands on the sustained counterforces of freedom. According to a vision of this kind it is clear that the apostle who "in his rapture" (I.752) described even the angels as divided and ranged in order around the throne of God saw nothing less than the heart of the comos. It is perhaps no accident that when later in *Church-Government* Milton digresses on the subject of whát is worthiest for a poet to undertake, his enumeration of projects is in one' instance unusually specific: "to celebrate in glorious and lofty Hymns the throne and equipage of Gods Almightinesse" (I.817). It is hard to imagine that Milton was not thinking here of the special importance he attached in his treatise to the axle on which the universe moves and to the image of the angels divided and ordered by the median throne. John the Apostle had actually seen this heavenly archetype of the disciplinary image. In addition, it seems likely that by mentioning poetic hymns on that same throne and equipage, Milton alludes to the glittering, bright-harnessed angels in the throne and equipage of his own well-divided Nativity *Hymn* (see 110–16 and 240–44).

## THE WRITER'S DISCIPLINE AND THE WORD'S DIVISIONS

I have so far discussed a number of the ways in which Milton conceives of the visible shape and image of that discipline that is a chief reason of ecclesial forms. I should like now to observe Milton in the process of acting out the disciplinary form in the structure of his treatise. His last specific word on the discipline, which "is already come to passe" in contemporary church reformation, is that "through all the periods and changes of the Church it hath beene prov'd that God hath still reserv'd to himselfe the right of *enacting Church-government*" (I.761; emphasis added). Milton is anxious to serve that enactment in this text.

All along, he has associated discipline with measuring. Discipline's "golden survaying reed," he tells us, "marks out and measures every quarter and circuit of new Jerusalem" (I.752). When Christ, he says,

by those visions of S. *John* foreshewes the reformation of his Church,
he bids him take his Reed, and meet it out againe after the first patterne,

for he prescribes him no other. Arise, said the Angell, and measure the Temple of God and the Altar, and them that worship therein. What is there in the world can measure men but discipline? Our word ruling imports no lesse. Doctrine indeed is the measure, or at least the reason of the measure, tis true, but unlesse the measure be apply'd to that which it is to measure, how can it actually doe its proper worke[?]
[I.760–61]

In the first chapter of the second book, after his personal digression, Milton circumstantially details "the first patterne," which is the measure and measuring of Christ's discipline. If we attend closely, the "visible shape" emerges:

Who is ther almost who measures wisdom by simplicity, strength by suffering, dignity by lowlinesse, who is there that counts it first, to be last, somthing to be nothing, and reckons himself of great command in that he is a servant? . . . To doe the work of the Gospel Christ our Lord took upon him the form of a servant. . . . The form of a servant was a mean, laborious and vulgar life aptest to teach; which form Christ thought fittest, that he might bring about his will according to his own principles choosing the meaner things of this world that he might put under the high . . . those meaner things of the world, whereby God in them would manage the mystery of his Gospel.     [I.824–26]

The form of a servant derives its strength from the acceptance of weakness, as the author of Hebrews asserts in "out of weakness [we] were made strong" (11:34). At the center of the servant's form is being nothing and suppressing the principle of self for the great command of service.

Of course, from one point of view the conversion of weakness to strength is simply a divine mystery, ineffable and beyond human comprehension. But Milton works to reveal the components of its recurring symbolic form. In this life the choice must be made between the self-effacing form of a servant and "the Lordly form of Prelaty" (I.826), which is unwilling to allow any such suspension of self-will and subjectively organized identity. The choice is palpable. The disciplinary form of a servant is thus correlative with the extended symmetry of the temple measured out and divided by God's grace. The church discipline that reflects this form is perfectly manifested by the schism it tolerates in the bond of fellowship. The lordly form, by contrast, is totally incapable of accommodating difference and division. Its whole ambition is for absolute conformity and uniformity. For Milton's eyes this shape too is fully visible:

> I say Prelaty thus ascending in a continuall pyramid upon pretence to perfect the Churches unity, if notwithstanding it be found most need-full, yea the utmost help to dearn up the rents of schisme by calling a councell, what does it but teach us that Prelaty is of no force to effect this work which she boasts to be her maister-peice; and that her pyramid aspires and sharpens to ambition, not to perfection, or unity[?] . . . Prelaty if she will seek to close up divisions in the Church, must be forc't to dissolve, and unmake her own pyramidal figure . . . which she hating to do, sends her haughty Prelates from all parts with their forked Miters . . . according to their hierarchies acuminating still higher and higher in a cone of Prelaty.          [I.790]

Instead of the disciplinary rational temple with its eternal sufferance of an infinite parallelism of contraries, prelacy demands the convergence and collapse of free intellection—in pyramids and cones of inevitable and absolute identity. Prelacy abandons the first pattern of Christ the servant. Thus, Milton is not simply joking when he advises the prelates to emulate the action of Marcus Curtius, who saved Rome by riding into the chasm that had opened in the forum: "for the Churches peace & your countries . . . leap into the midst" of the "wide gulph of distraction in this land . . . her dismall gap." The serious core of this advice is that the prelates must commit themselves to the deep symbolic action that will reenact the form of a servant: "for then you wil not delay to prefer that above your own preferment" (I.792).

Milton's vehemence in the final moment of the treatise is directly related to this highly serious joke. His concluding sentences may represent a partial tonal failure, for he is here working so close to his ideal rule of discipline that he seems to drift into an empyreal, nonhuman sphere. But his failure (if it is that) is immensely instructive about the architectonic or symbolic patterns that inform his meanings throughout *Church-Government*. If, Milton says, prelacy "be found to be malignant, hostile, destructive . . . as nothing can be surer,"

> let your severe and impartial doom imitate the divine vengeance; rain down your punishing force upon this godlesse and oppressing government: and bring such a dead Sea of subversion upon her, that she may never in this Land rise more to afflict the holy reformed Church, and the elect people of God.          [I.861]

This concluding image is as much an integral part of Milton's rational vision of the shape of discipline as is his invocation of the form of a servant. His penultimate request to the Lords is that in the "midst of rigor" they might "think of mercy," even such a mercy "as may exceed that which for only ten righteous persons would have sav'd *Sodom*" (I.861). Again, for Milton, tolerant mercy in the midst of rigor is one of the two principle forms of church discipline. It carries with it that reinstatement of separation which maintains life itself.

But when that kind of mercy is no longer applicable, another kind, equally life-giving, becomes necessary. Prelacy has brought about "the greatest schisme of all" (I.790), one that eliminates the possibility of all quiet schism. When one kind of schism, which has free play in the zone of toleration, itself denies the possibility of all other alternatives, a different kind of reformative separation becomes necessary. This is what Milton calls the rigorous incision in the very midst of rigor. As Calvin explained, "Augustine especially commends this one thing: if the contagion of sin invades the multitude, the severe mercy of a vigorous discipline is necessary" (1240).[13] Milton's call for a "severe and impartiall doom" is mercifully austere. The dead sea of subversion is not destruction simple and pitiless. Rather, it is the re-creation of the rift or space of division that makes this land whole again. Only in this way might the discipline of a free church be restored to all its members.

In *Church-Government*, as in Milton's writing generally, patterns of an ascetic or excising kind are not allowed to amount to a withering asceticism. Milton's interest is in a band of division and exclusion within the dynamism of life. In his conception, this band of division prevents the collapse of life into death. This he suggests is the great mystery of God: Christ's high design in fulfilling the form of a servant is to give life by "smothering and extinguishing the spirituall force of his bodily weaknesse in the discipline of his Church" (I.849). This discipline is "a mortifying to life, a kind of saving by undoing" (I.847). As an operation of the rational intellect Milton views it as the *disentailing* or detaching of unwarranted church jurisdiction. Disentailing of this sort sweeps away the "sensual mistresses that keep the ports and passages between" the understanding and its objects (I.831–32). It can do so because such abrogation restores the zone of distinction that is required for knowing anything distinctly of God (I.801).

Milton speaks here of theological knowing, but his conception may invite generalization to a notion that the consciousness of the subject can only know the object distinctly, as a thing with its own definitive existence, when the mind succeeds in creating a space of separation between subject and object. Otherwise, the ambition to know and possess totally results in the loss of knowledge. Very much in accord with such a conception, the dynamics of church discipline express themselves in a rigorous incision. Milton says that they inure us to the habits of what St. Paul calls *"casting down imaginations, and every high thing that exalteth it selfe against the knowledge of God"* (I.848). In this exercise of incision or excision they produce the sorer burden of mind (I.801) that Milton mentioned virtually at the beginning of the pamphlet.

Finally, it is important to see that this proposal for rigorous incision is not offered only at someone else's expense. The author of *Church-Government* has himself not delayed to leap into the dismal gap. In the treatise as a whole there is no more vivid enactment of the form of a servant than the oft-quoted personal digression that stands at the fulcrum of Milton's entire argument. Perhaps more than any other determinant, it was the decorum of the form of a servant that required that the author's self-abnegation stand at the center of the work rather than closer to the end, where classical orations usually located the speaker's digression on his own chararcter. By dividing his argument to show specifically with "what small willingnesse I endure to interrupt the pursuit of no lesse hopes then these" (I.821), Milton gives active symbolic form to the ideas of service and interruption of ego. His rhetorical and psychological posture of confessing to be half in doubt (I.824) and of finding his "thoughts almost in suspense betwixt yea and no" (I.830) further emphasizes his acceptance of the suspensive state of mind that is the form of a servant. He has "come into the dim reflexion of hollow antiquities," where he must "club quotations with men whose learning and beleif lies in marginal stuffings" (I.822). That he himself speaks from the depths of an internalized gulf of distraction strongly suggests that the quick and piercing Word has entered to the dividing of his own soul. This is his personal warrant for expounding the reason of church discipline that is God's dividing Word.[14]

In *The Reason of Church-Government*, as in the Nativity Ode, the logic of Milton's imagination dramatically conforms to the pressure of the Word. These are not idiosyncratic occurrences. In order to recognize the familiar meaning of this conformity in Milton's age and in the fabric of his works, it will be helpful to survey a variety of the forms in which he acquired and cultivated this same discipline.

# 4

❀

# Milton's Image of
# Divine Analysis:
# Provenance and Meaning

The logical structures of seventeenth-century poetic images in general and of Milton's imagery in particular have been the object of considerable though inconsistent attention in modern scholarship. James Whaler and Rosemond Tuve early made us aware that few poets and few ages have more systematically exploited the potentialities of poetic images to embody logical contents. During the past forty years a host of perceptive commentators have discussed, from diverse points of view, the logical components of many of Milton's images. But in most of these discussions it has seemed to be a foregone conclusion that the analytic role played by Milton's imagery cannot be coextensive with the larger meanings of his finished poetic products.[1] His imagistic use of logical analysis, in other words, is in this view necessarily a handmaiden of art, which, at the crucial moment, discreetly defers to the grander business of synthesis and resolution that we necessarily expect of truly poetic completions.

These assumptions, it seems to me, do not finally clarify (and perhaps they even obscure) the unique meanings of Milton's poems. Geoffrey Hartman has begun persuasively to counter the formulas of synthesis and resolution that have pervaded Milton scholarship. By analyzing a series of images of "the observer ab extra" in *Paradise Lost*, he has argued that the "poet constantly suggests, destroys and recreates the idea of an imperturbably transcendent discrimination."[2] Analytic reason of a higher order is thus assigned by Hartman a special figural centrality in Milton's verse. The abiding significance of such figuration is greater even and more deeply founded, I believe, than Hartman's insightful remarks indicate. As I have suggested, Milton's poetic meanings depend upon theological structures that are themselves organized by continuous division and distinction. At this point, however, a mild caveat is in order. Even if the well-accustomed view that Milton's images everywhere create harmony out of discord, synthesis from analysis, is rejected, it does not necessarily follow that, where Milton is concerned, the concept of poetic unity must altogether be abandoned. Varieties of reader-oriented poetics have undoubtedly proved to be very fruitful in interpreting Milton's poems.[3] But even those works that are accessible to such interpretations may establish criteria of independent wholeness that are of a different order from those shown to be absent by affective readings. We must, that is, consider the general possibility that Milton's images of divine analysis have a denotative meaning that has so far been grasped incompletely. And we should consider the further, specific possibility that Milton's compositions regularly accord analytic structures a theological value that is primary rather than secondary, ultimate rather than penultimate.

My aim here is to describe in more or less systematic fashion the intellectual origins and poetic meanings of one particular image of deific division that recurs frequently in Milton's writing. The image, which stands as divine rationality itself, is markedly analytic in its own form and is associated with a significant theme or activity of dialectical discrimination. This dialectic, like the analytic shape of its characteristic image, is highly individual. So too is the context of intellectual and religious history in which Milton found it and deployed it for his own purposes. I shall survey briefly some additional representations of this divine analysis in Milton's poetry, and then attempt to identify its roots and efflorescence in his theological milieu. For an awareness of the depth of these affiliations can, I believe, enlarge our ultimate understanding of the kinds of meaning and poetic unity achieved in Milton's works.

### THE MUSE THAT DIVIDES

It is quite possible that Milton himself announced the link between poetic analysis and divine division in the Nativity Ode. In the opening

lines of *The Passion*, composed within a year of the Ode, he had this
to say about the genre or method of the earlier poem:

> Erewhile of Music and Ethereal mirth,
> Wherewith the stage of Air and Earth did ring,
> And joyous news of heav'nly Infant's birth,
> My muse with Angels did divide to sing.

Of course, divide can mean only to "execute 'division', or rapid melodic
passages," as Carey puts it, though as he adds, "elsewhere in Milton's
poetry 'divide' means either 'share' or 'separate'."[4] But given what we
have seen of the thematic significance of division or "parting" in the
Ode, it seems likely that Milton's direct reference to the dividing muse
of the Nativity Ode is to the specialized muse that (among other things)
proceeds by acts of systematic separation. The musical meaning is not
thereby cancelled. Quite the contrary. In the Ode, divine division and
the angelic new music occur in integral relation.[5]

Two other examples, which will come in for fuller discussion later,
will help illustrate the number and variety of Milton's poems that recur
to mercy-seat division. The predicament of his sonnet *When I Consider* . . . (ca. 1652) can be formulated in many ways, but in all of them
a central element must be the contradictory claims of passive acceptance of God's will and the obligation to act in order to fulfill other
expressions of that same will. The apparent resolution of these coun-
terclaims comes as a realization of an underlying theological verity. In
the much-glossed closing lines, patience speaks from a transcendent
realm. She states the one unchanging truth that stands behind our life
of shadow objects:

> Thousands at his bidding speed
> And post o'er Land and Ocean without rest:
> They also serve who only stand and wait.

The scholarly quest for the exact order and neighborhood of the angelic
thousands and the standing attendants is well worth pursuing, for it is
plausible to assume that the precise quality of Milton's acceptance of
his fate is minutely reflected in these heavenly specifications.[6] But the
goals of the present restricted inquiry can be served even by focusing
on a point made by Grierson seventy years ago and reiterated recently
by Harry Robins: in the last line of the poem Milton re-creates an
image of the divine throne that was given special emphasis in a long
tradition exemplified by Pseudo-Dionysius and Aquinas.[7] For Milton's

more immediate exegetical milieu, the same point may be made more simply by noting Calvin's frequently quoted gloss on the extended wings of the propitiatory cherubim in Exodus 25:18: "to mark the readiness of their obedience, for the extension of their wings is equivalent to their being prepared for the performance of whatever God might command. Thus they are said to turn their faces towards the mercy-seat, because they are attentive to the will of God."[8]

In Milton's description as in Calvin's, divine being intervenes between its emanated potencies. The contradiction of fulfilling active being in perfect stasis is resolved in a discrimination of incoincident potentialities. Placed at the very end of the sonnet, the described structure itself suggests a terminal stasis. It is an immovable band of division that subsists beyond and within the emanations of motion that constitute the created world. Milton elevates and redeems the shattering disruption of life and creativity by suggestively incorporating it within God's own pattern of immobility within deputed motion. That framed image—part visual and part nonvisual—of intervening, unmoved, moving godhead is revealed as the source image of divine power, divine presence, and divine grace. Thus the unstated, invisible, dividing component of the last line—God's medial throne—has the effect of raising the image and the sonnet towards the condition of a sublime idea.

My second example is from the very end of Milton's career, from *Paradise Regained*. The thematic significance of the mercy-seat division in this instance is extensive and complex. I shall scrutinize it in chapter seven. The appearance and function of the image are sufficiently schematized, however, for even a brief sketch to produce a working acquaintance.

In the Nativity Ode the fulfillment of God's meaning is somehow prophesied in the extension of the symmetry of the propitiatory to the opening wide of heaven's gates. In *Paradise Regained* the same image life is compassed in an elongated series of very similar image movements. Here Milton begins slowly, almost in a retarded movement, with a triple iteration of the opening of heaven's doors (I.29–32, 79–85, 280–88). In spite of the repetitions, the significance of the opening doors is left unexplained and mysterious, just as the image counterparts of the opened doors are for the time being left unmentioned.

In the third of these passages, for example, Christ recounts,

> as I rose out of the laving stream,
> Heaven open'd her eternal doors, from whence

> The Spirit descended on me like a Dove;
> And last the sum of all, my Father's voice,
> Audibly heard from Heav'n, pronounc'd me his,
> Mee his beloved Son, in whom alone
> He was well pleas'd; by which I knew the time
> Now full, that I no more should live obscure,
> But openly begin.

Somewhat reductively stated, the drama of *Paradise Regained* concerns the fact that in spite of the declared centrality of the baptism revelation and in spite of Christ's unequivocally spoken understanding of its meaning, he does not at all openly begin. Instead he is immediately moved to retire into the wilderness. He does just so, once more, in the final moment of the poem. Directly after the angels have sung, "on thy glorious work / Now enter, and begin to save mankind" (IV.634–35), Christ emphatically returns, unobserved and private, home "to his Mother's house" (IV.638–39). The time may well be full (I.287) for Christ's fulfillment of his mission, but fullness clearly has a special meaning in this poem.

The initial image pattern of the heavenly temple, with its symmetrical portals from which issue the divine spirit and voice, is itself fulfilled by the image of the godlike man as "Holiest of Holies" (IV.348–49). It is summed or gathered up, that is, in Christ the "true Image of the Father . . . enshrin'd / In fleshly Tabernacle . . .ʹ Wand'ring the Wilderness" (IV.596–600). Milton thus borrows Paul's theme of "edification" or of transposition of the pre-Christian, material temple to the immaterial, inward, and heavenly temple, a favorite topos in Puritan writing.[9] The cherubim of glory that the author of Hebrews (revising Exodus 25) similarly envisions around the transposed propitiatory are also not forgotten by Milton. At the moment of symbolic triumph over Satan, before Christ again retires rather than enter on his glorious work, the fixed Old Testament mercy seat is reconstituted as a propitiatory "couch" without specified location:

> straight a fiery Globe
> Of Angels on full sail of wing flew nigh,
> Who on their plumy Vans receiv'd him soft
> From his uneasy station, and upbore
> As on a floating couch through the blithe Air.    [IV. 581–85]

The most striking aspect of Milton's use of the mercy-seat pattern must for the time being be stated even more skeletally than the above points, for it is the most intricate and requires the most ample commentary. In the final temptation Satan imagines that by bringing Christ to the highest pinnacle of his father's house (IV.549–52) he will either heighten his humiliation or ensnare him in hubris. Instead, he only aids Christ in fulfilling triumphantly his subordinate elevation as Word or voice of God. How this fulfillment relates to the holiest of holies, the mercy seat, and the cherubic wings that surround him is not yet clear. But here too a particular image of divinely centered symmetry is intimately associated with Christ's office.

## IMAGES OF DIVINE DICHOTOMY

In the cases briefly reviewed above I have suggested that Milton pays special attention to the images of divine division that for him constitute a particularly vital species of analytic image, and that these images are generally found in a derivative or familial relationship with the biblical pattern of the propitiatory throne of God. Let us next consider the parent images of that family and, following that, some of the characteristic ways in which Milton's age regarded them. Few other periods have been as systematic in their attempts to discover and delineate the shapes and functions of rational images, especially those of sacred origin. Perhaps it was a perfectly natural gesture for the last pre-Enlightenment age.

The two largest biblical images of propitiatory pattern have become so commonplace in Christian thought that they are in a sense always beyond, or rather nearer than, the reach of ordinary allusion. They recur in a multitude of ways throughout the prophetic literature and they are so frequently dissolved, in high concentration, in Christian writing, that they may be precipitated or redissolved at any moment. God's instructions to Moses in Exodus 25:20–22 are the starting text:

> And the cherubims shall stretch forth their wings on high, covering the mercy seat with their wings, and their faces shall look one to another. . . .
> And thou shalt put the mercy seat above upon the ark; and in the ark thou shalt put the testimony that I shall give thee.
> And there I will meet with thee, and I will commune with thee from above the mercy seat, from between the two cherubims.[10]

No other Old Testament text specifies so precisely the habitation of divine presence; and no other text is more central, architecturally as well as thematically, to the delineation of the holy temple. It was, of course, just this geographical location of centralized meaning that was transposed in the New Testament into a divine process without place. In Hebrews the process of incarnation and atonement is represented as an internalized and universally available structure of intercessory holiness. Here again is the movement from Old to New Covenant that is expressed by the Pauline idea of edification. In Milton's terms it is the preference of God for the redeemed heart, upright and pure, before all material temples.

The most direct New Testament commentary on these matters and on the above verses in Exodus is the following passage of Hebrews 9:

1   Then verily the first covenant had also ordinances of divine service, and a worldly sanctuary.

2   For there was a tabernacle made; the first, wherein was the candlestick, and the table, and the shewbread; which is called the sanctuary.

3   And after the second veil, the tabernacle which is called the Holiest of all;

4   Which had the golden censer, and the ark of the covenant overlaid round about with gold, wherein was the golden pot that had manna, and Aaron's rod that budded, and the tables of the covenant;

5   And over it the cherubims of glory shadowing the mercyseat; of which we cannot now speak particularly.

6   Now when these things were thus ordained, the priests went always into the first tabernacle, accomplishing the service of God.

7   But into the second went the high priest alone once every year, not without blood, which he offered for himself, and for the errors of the people:

8   The Holy Ghost this signifying, that the way into the holiest of all was not yet made manifest, while as the first tabernacle was yet standing;

9   Which was a figure for the time then present, in which were offered both gifts and sacrifices, that could not make him that did the service perfect, as pertaining to the conscience. . . .

11   But Christ being come an high priest of things to come, by a greater and more perfect tabernacle, not made with hands, that is to say, not of this building;

12   Neither by the blood of goats and calves, but by his own blood he entered in once into the holy place, having obtained eternal redemption for us. . . .

15   And for this cause he is the mediator of the new testament, that by means of death, for the redemption of the transgressions that were

under the first testament, they which are called might receive the promise of eternal inheritance.

The *occupatio* or *occultatio* of the fifth verse, concerning the mercy
seat itself, was traditionally understood to be the key to the entire
description. The mystery shadowed forth by the mercy seat is too great
to be spoken of directly; but the meanings elaborated in all the verses
relating to the tabernacle as a figure of Christ's redemption are extensions of the central structure of propitiation and interposition. And in
the fifteenth verse, the Old Testament placement of the propitiatory
above the tables of the law and below the point of God's communion
is reflected in the structure of mediation.

Milton's learned acquaintance John Diodati nicely sums up this
complex of relationships in his *Annotations* (a work that at least one
contemporary believed Milton himself had translated into English, or
had at least seen through the press).[11] On the word *kapporeth* in
Exodus 25:17 Diodati writes:

> the Hebr. word signifieth also a mercy-seat; and so the Apostle calls it,
> *Heb. 9.5. viz.* a means of purging and expiating sin; because that this
> cover signified Christ, who with his righteousness covereth all our sins,
> and containeth within himself all the Churches righteousness, as the
> tables of the Law were inclosed under the cover; and interposeth himself
> as Mediator, between the Law which accuseth us, and God our Judge,
> as the cover was between the said Tables, and the majestie of God,
> which shewed it self present over the Cherubims of this Cover, as sitting
> upon his throne.[12]

Diodati emphasizes that for the author of Hebrews the mystery shaded
between the two ends of the mercy seat, and between man's transgressions against the law and the wrath of God, is the grace of separation,
division, and mediation. Christ interposes himself as separator and
divider.

Another of Milton's contemporaries, Gervase Babington, extends
the application of the same theme to Hebrews 12:29, "For our God is
a consuming fire." His comment on Exodus 25:17 begins as does Diodati's:

> How notable a Figure again this was of Christ, I pray you see: for first,
> it was the cover of the *Arke* where the law of *Moses* lay; and who hideth
> and covereth us from the wrath of God, and from the accusation of the
> Law but Jesus Christ?

Next comes his compounding of Hebrews 9:15 and Hebrews 12:29:

> He is like a coole shadow to flie unto in the scorching heat of Gods
> deserved displeasure, which is a *consuming fire*.[13]

The Satan of *Paradise Regained* knows, or at least senses, the value of
such interposition. Willingly or not, he foretells the fulfillment of
Christ's propitiatory role; and he does so almost precisely in Babington's terms:

> to that gentle brow<br>
> Willingly I could fly, and hope thy reign,<br>
> From that placid aspect and meek regard,<br>
> Rather than aggravate my evil state,<br>
> Would stand between me and thy Father's ire<br>
> (Whose ire I dread more than the fire of Hell)<br>
> A shelter and a kind of shading cool<br>
> Interposition, as a summer's cloud.          [III. 215–22]

Carey is right to object to Northrop Frye's assertion that this passage describes "the direct opposite of Christ's true nature." As a possible source that is also a familar text for the explication of Christ's
soteriology, Carey cites Isaiah 25:4–5, "For thou hast been . . . a
shadow from the heat . . . even the heat with the shadow of a cloud."[14]
This is surely germane. But I must go further. The interposition described by Milton in these images very likely prefigures Christ's fulfillment of his mercy-seat office as separator and mediator. This was
the office described in Hebrews in connection with Exodus 25 and
frequently elaborated in the manner of Diodati or Babington.

What else could the same exegetical milieu, especially the parts
that Milton showed himself particularly drawn to, provide with regard
to these biblical places? Milton and his contemporaries were surely
well aware that the theme of divine separation or division is characteristic of more than one passage in Hebrews. David Berkeley has
pointed out, for example, that the opening phrases of *Lycidas* almost
certainly allude to the following formula for separation of things tran-
sitory from things eternal in Hebrews 12:26–27:

> . . . now he hath promised, saying, *Yet once more* I shake not the
> earth only, but also heaven.
> And this word, *Yet once more*, signifieth the removing of those
> things that are shaken, as of things that are made, that those things
> which cannot be shaken may remain [emphases added].[15]

Seventeenth-century awareness of extensive themes of separation in

Hebrews was often not only broad and deep but even minutely focused. But I am concerned here only with the most striking of the relevant texts and with two of the richest forms of that awareness.

For the description of a divine agency or process of division, the most significant and best known figure in Hebrews is undoubtedly verse 12 of chapter 4, which I will cite whole:

> For the word of God is quick, and powerful, and sharper than any twoedged sword, piercing even to the dividing asunder of soul and spirit, and of the joints and marrow, and is a discerner of the thoughts and intents of the heart.

In this declaration (which has repeatedly been put forth as a possible component of the background for the mysterious two-handed engine of *Lycidas*)[16] some readers of Milton's time believed they could find a warrant for understanding God's Word as being analytic or even dichotomizing in function. The Cambridge of Milton's time, which served as the principal host of Ramist thought in England, and which nurtured Milton's own substantial interest in Ramist logic, was fertile ground for such interpretation.

In discussing Ramist method, Rosemond Tuve emphasized the ways in which the logic and rhetoric of Ramus and his followers could extend the realm of poetic imagery to include novel kinds of verse argumentation. One of her principal assumptions was that Ramism could explain how the tendency to abstraction in much sixteenth and seventeenth century verse could be brought home to roost in one obviously valid criterion of poetic value: the concrete and the visual. But Frances Yates has shown that the drift of Ramist method is usually quite different from, even opposite to, the implications proposed by Tuve. Tuve consciously and completely ignored the schematization of dichotomies that was conventionally identified as the programmatic core of Ramist method.[17] She did so, one may suppose, because she considered it totally lacking in philosophical meaning or because she could not see how it might form a part of the influence of Ramism on poetic practice.

Before bringing Yates's more comprehensive account to bear, I should acknowledge that, indeed, Ramist dichotomization was in itself without significant or distinctive philosophical content. The totally general, almost banal, nature of that content is usefully characterized by Father Ong:

> The Ramist dichotomies have little, if any real theoretical foundation. There is a bipolarity in being, which echoes everywhere through phil-

osophical history; form and matter, act and potency, Yang and Yin, thesis and antithesis, the one and the many, and so on through an indefinite number of epiphanies. This includes perhaps the Neo-Platonic teaching, well known to Aquinas, that from any given unity only one other unity can be generated, further generation requiring the combination of these two originals. The Ramist dichotomy can be regarded as a reflection or correlative of this bipolarity. But it does not arise from any penetrating insight on Ramus' part into the principles of the bipolarity. . . . There is simply no one ground on which we can account for Ramus' dichotomies.[18]

Yet, as Ong is the first to acknowledge, all this does not detract from the fact that, as he says, "the cult of dichotomies which reaches its peak development" with Ramus and his highly dedicated followers had an immense influence on the day to day thinking and writing of countless educated Europeans from the middle of the sixteenth century to at least the end of the seventeenth.[19] By themselves the Ramist dichotomies may *mean* virtually nothing. But there can be no doubt that they expressed a contemporary general tendency to heavily schematized thought of a binary kind; and when they were joined to a structure of thought or belief that did have a distinctive poetic, philosophical, or theological content the result could be powerfully and deeply meaningful.

Yates has shown that the place of Ramist method within the historical development of the art of memory (which is its parent) bestowed upon it an identifiable antagonist and polemical meaning, even a sectarian religious character. Yates explains:

> Though many surviving influences of the old art of memory may be detected in the Ramist "method" of memorising through dialectical order, yet he deliberately gets rid of its most characteristic feature, the use of the imagination. And, above all, gone in the Ramist system are the images, the emotionally striking and stimulating images the uses of which had come down through the centuries from the art of classical rhetoric. The "natural" stimulus for memory is now not the emotionally exciting memory image; it is the abstract order of dialectical analysis which is yet, for Ramus, "natural," since dialectical order is natural to the mind. . . .
>
> The extraordinary success of Ramism, in itself rather a superficial pedagogic method, in Protestant countries like England may perhaps be partly accounted for by the fact that it provided a kind of inner iconoclasm, corresponding to the outer iconoclasm. . . .
>
> Ramism cannot be entirely identified with Protestantism for it seems

to have been popular with some French Catholics. . . . Nevertheless, Ramus became a Protestant martyr after his death in the Massacre of St. Bartholomew, a fact which certainly had much to do with the popularity of Ramism in England. And there can be no doubt that an art of memory based on imageless dialectical order as the true natural order of the mind goes well with Calvinist theology.[20]

As vivid evidence, Yates cites the dicta of the Ramist Puritan William Perkins: "So soone as the minde frames unto it selfe any forme of God (as when he is popishly conceiued to be like an old man sitting in heauen in a throne with a sceptre in his hand) an idol is set up in the minde. . . . A thing faigned in the mind by imagination is an idol."[21] Clearly the imageless dialectical order of Ramism was to be achieved by an iconoclastic purgation of the iconographic arts of memory.

But from Perkins's pronouncements and Yates's commentary it is not clear how, short of simply ignoring the idols spawned by degenerate imagination, the Ramist method was to attack the images themselves— how it was to convert the image of God as an old man sitting on a throne (with a scepter in his hand) into a manifestation of an imageless dialectic. Ong remarks in this connection that by the use of the "dichotomized branching outline" instead of the iconographic arts, the inner iconoclasm described by Yates was in effect already accomplished: "The images were annihilated and the visualism of the age was redirected to a text, to visualizable words."[22] But I would like to suggest that the attempt to subdue the rampagings of imagination was by some Ramists conceived to be far more direct than this.

Returning now to Hebrews 4:12 and the exegetical undercurrents of Milton's age, there are clear indications that, indeed, for at least some Ramists the Word of God offered itself as the great instrument of aggressive dichotomization. The Word was the dividing sword that was to be used in the mind's rational battle against mystification, confusion, and self-deluding emotionalism. William Gouge (1578–1653), fellow of King's College, Cambridge, and one of the best known English defenders of Ramus in the early part of the century,[23] expressed what was after all the inevitable Ramist view of Hebrews 4:12. In two of his principal works Gouge expatiated upon the sword-like dividing Word, wielded by God and man, waging an incessant warfare of divinely willed dichotomization. In his posthumous *Commentary on the Whole Epistle to the Hebrews*, published in 1655, Gouge explains the key phrases in Hebrews—the "word of God . . . quick, and powerful and sharper than any twoedged sword, piercing even to the dividing asun-

der of soul and spirit"—as circumstantial description of the means
"whereby Christ exerciseth his Propheticall Office." Soul for Gouge is
"will and affections"; spirit is "understanding or mind . . . the highest
faculty." The two must not be confused: "the severall Metaphors
whereby the power of the word is set out, may most fitly be applied,"
he says, "to Gods Word preached," by Christ the arch-preacher and
by the generations of his apostle preachers.[24] The work of all such
preachers is to cut the knot that ties the rational faculty to the will and
affections.

As part of his Calvinist understanding of our fallen condition Gouge
envisions a universal mental enslavement to the sensory and sensual
manifestations of the will and affections. He does not explicitly call this
enslavement imagination, but the equivalent of that power is clearly
his concern when he describes the need to separate will and mind as
well as to weed out the growth of will and affections in pure mind:

> The soul and spirit are as nearly and firmly knit together as any parts
> of the body can be: yet the Word can divide them asunder, and that
> not only by distinguishing the one from the other, but also by discov-
> ering the severall desires and delights, or dislikings and loathings of the
> soul; and likewise of the castings, plottings, and contrivances of the
> spirit; and all these both in good and evil things.

The preaching or use of God's Word in this way, says Gouge, must
be pursued aggressively: "As with a two-edged sword a man may defend
and offend, so with the Word. Verity and virtue may be maintained
and defended, and errour and every enormity may be refelled and
repelled. See *The whole armour of God.* . . ."[25] By offend Gouge
means take the offensive by attacking directly the confusion of sensory
and rational faculties. How the divisions of the Word are to manage
this work Gouge does not say here. He comes closest to an explicit
description of the procedures for achieving this in the work to which
he refers us, his own *The Whole Armour of God* (1619).[26] Here the
dividing functions of the Word detailed in Hebrews 4:12 are said to be
directly expressed by Ramist method incorporated into public preaching, as well as private prayer or meditation. One of mankind's principal
ways of wielding God's dividing Word, Gouge explains, is to apply it
reflexively in "dividing the Word aright." In saying this, it is clear that
Gouge intends exegetical as well as polemical uses of the method:

> In laying downe this doctrine of Prayer, the Apostle doth so skilfully
> couch together many severall and distinct points, as every word almost

affordeth a severall Doctrine: he contenteth not himselfe in generall to exhort unto the duty of prayer, but also declareth divers circumstances appertaining thereunto: Whence observe, that

> *It is a warrantable course of teaching, to set forth Principles*
> *of Religion in their severall and particular branches. This is*
> *one kinde of dividing the Word aright.*

Thus will the understanding of hearers be much informed with a distinct knowledge of the mysteries of godliness, and thus shall they much better discerne the great depth of those mysteries, and the rich treasure that is contained in them. Yea, thus also shall their memory be much helped in retaining them: for severall branches distinctly and in order set downe are a great means to strengthen memory.

This iustifieth that manner of teaching, which is (as we speake) *Common-place-wise*: by particular defining, dividing, subdividing, and distinct handling of particular branches of the Principles of Religion.

Gouge shows himself well aware of the monomania to which Ramist dichotomization could lead and therefore warns preachers not to be "over-curious in multiplying their divisions, or over-tedious in amplifying them."[27] But his commitment is clear. The divisions of the Word described in Hebrews signal for him a "distinct" process of attaining divine truth, as well as a structure for embodying it.

The Oxford anti-Ramist, Thomas Jackson, president of Corpus Christi, shows us that the view of Hebrews 4:12 expressed by Gouge was familiar fare in mid-seventeenth-century England. And of course Jackson's demurrer extended its currency. In the final sermons of his *Commentaries upon these Articles of the Creed,* completed before his death in 1640 and published in 1657, Jackson had this to say about the Ramist capitalization on Hebrews 4:12:

> Some Late Writers . . . there be, which doubt, whether by *The Word of God* in the Text, the Son of God be punctually meant: who yet grant, That those *Attributes* ver. 13 (*Neither is there any Creature which is not manifested in his sight, but all things are naked and open unto the eyes of him with whom we have to do*) can be meant of none, but the Son of God, and the ever-living Judge of quick and dead.
>
> But this Interpretation doth contradict it self, doth divide and separate those things which the Spirit of God hath conjoyned; and if it were true, would rend asunder the *very Subject of all the Propositions* in my Text, which is Indivisibly One; it cannot abide the touch or test of any Logick, unless it be of his Logick who opposeth *Invention* unto *Judgment,* unto whose followers nothing more usual than to turn the greatest *Mysteries* in Divinitie into bare *Metaphors* or *Rhetorical*

> *Tropes*: Nothing more familiar, than to interpret those Prophetical Pas-
> sages by which the Holy Ghost doth delineat [sic] the Incarnation of the
> *Word*, to be meant of God only . . . in a common vulgar, not in any
> mystical sense. [28]

If Jackson is not thinking of Gouge's *Whole Armour* and of his *Commentary* (first preached in almost a thousand sermons at Blackfriars),
he surely has in mind Gouge's intellectual twins. What Gouge thinks
of as informing the understanding "with a distinct knowledge of the
mysteries of godliness" is precisely for Jackson the perverse analytic
process of turning "the greatest *Mysteries* in Divinitie into bare *Metaphors* or *Rhetorical Tropes*." On Hebrews 4:12–13 Gouge's *Commentary* offers fourteen pages of metaphorical and rhetorical analysis,
folio!

Jackson has clearly not distorted or focused on a side issue by ac-
cusing the analytic Ramists of denying that the dividing Word is one
and the same with the mysterious Son of God. In discussing the word
*discerner* of 4:12, Gouge carefully disagrees with "they who interpret
the Word of God to be the *Sonne of God*" and exploits for purposes
of disagreement the conventional gloss that "we in English according
to the notation of the Greek call such a one a *Critick*."[29] It was important for Gouge to think of the Word of God as an analytic instrument
distinct from Christ. Jackson was vexed by the analytic impulse that
required such a separation. As Jackson may have sensed, the deeper
motive of this impulse was related to a newly emerging zeitgeist that
was to be extremely dangerous for organized religion of all kinds. The
nature of that zeitgeist was very difficult to talk about. The terms for
describing it were only just then being crystallized in rudimentary form
by the harbinger philosophers of the Enlightenment. But the reasoning
immediately behind Gouge's manifestation of the analytic impulse was
easily located. As Jackson aptly noted, it represented something virtually identical to the Ramist program of opposing *inventio* to *dispos-
itio* or *iudicium* as the binary parts or antitheses of Ramist logic. In
the Ramist universe any kind of creativity can be reduced to its sep-
arable components.

Something of real significance was indeed at stake in the tense
difference of opinion registered by Gouge and Jackson in their disparate
ways of understanding God's dividing Word. In his important essay
"Logic and the Epic Muse: Reflections on Noetic Structures in Milton's
Milieu," Ong has illuminated the background issues that philosophical

and historical retrospection has since identified in the Ramist controversies. Viewed contextually within the history of man's successive attempts to organize his understanding of reality, logic of all kinds, Ong explains, is deeply "antithetical" to its "antecedent rhetorical stage." In its every gesture it proclaims antagonism to the rotund, unrigorous emotionalism that is easily (not always justly) associated with rhetoric. In addition, Ong points out, logic is antithetical "in its very being":

> Logic is polarized in one way toward negativity and violent destruction. It moves toward greater and greater explicitation, typified especially by stress on definition. But, since definition (*de-finire*, to mark off the limits) manifests what a thing is by making clear what it is not, logic proceeds by setting up greater and greater antitheses, typified by stress on division and distinctions—in the case of Ramist logic dichotomies, the most divisive of divisions, modeled on the difference between yes and no, and featured today in the binary structures of computer operations.[30]

Like the Enlightenment world view it helped usher in, Ramist method "symbolized and fostered the aggressive, no-quarter given, intently analytic habits of mind which are at the base of modern science and technology."[31]

It is clear that whether or not Gouge fully understood the implications of his commentary, his elaboration of the meaning of God's dividing Word expressed a large philosophical and religious shift. Jackson felt it in his pulse and cried out. He knew that men like Gouge were giving voice to a powerful need to find a center of rationality—conceived in contemporary logical, dialectical terms—within religion and within the scriptural texts themselves. Jackson saw the growing need and feared the delimiting, reductive consequences of an analytic process that would transform the greatest mysteries in divinity into what Gouge called a distinct knowledge. He foresaw or intuited that the mystical, transcendent principle symbolized by the Incarnation of the Word could easily be squeezed out and discarded in such a process. Jackson particularly stressed the Ramists' unwillingness to identify the Son with the Word of God because he understood that with this point he had snared them in their own den. Gouge was visibly nervous about identifying the Son with the Word as analytic procedure, as Ramist method, because the equation limited and defined the Redeemer too strictly. There must be an escape clause. The Son must be let be in the next verse. Let him remain outside and above the two-edged system.

Without referring to Hebrews or Gouge or Jackson, Ong explains beautifully the larger Ramist issue that lies behind such exclusions and relates it to important questions in Milton's poetry. The exclusiveness of the Ramist dialectical procedures and structures Ong calls a radical form of closure:

> Closure marks Ramist thought conspicuously. Ramist "arts" are to-talities, purportedly embracing all there is of their subjects, and doing so in a way which admits readily of being diagrammed. This sense of closure—which can be identified more or less with the rationalism ma-turing in the Enlightenment—certainly plagued Milton in his effort to pack the reality of Christian revelation into *Paradise Lost.* . . .
>
> Milton's place in the long-range development of the epic and of logic can . . . be described rather neatly, if not with full inclusiveness, in terms of open and closed existence. The epic, which came into being as (among other things) a massive knowledge-storage creation of the prephilosophic world, projected an open cosmology, one in which ex-planation is at best partial and incompleteness is a permanent quality of mortal life. Epic was based on *agonia*, struggle, typically between persons, which is never-ending, but continues generation after genera-tion. . . .
>
> Logic, on the other hand, the paradigmatic knowledge-storage de-vice of the post-philosophical or rationalist world, symbolizes closed existence: the logical universe, certainly as conceived by Ramus and Milton's age generally, purports to carry within itself a full explanation of itself. . . . In actuality Milton's commitment to a closed system of existence was less than total. No man can live or write by method alone. But the rational didactic aim in *Paradise Lost*—"to justifie the wayes of God to men"—and his attraction to Ramist logic (which led him in his own *Logic* to suggest that the divine Trinity was illogical), with much else in his writings and career, suggest how strongly Milton was attracted to ultimate closure.[32]

All this is extremely pertinent and illuminating. Yet we must consider the possibility that, having faced the implications of this ultimate clo-sure, Milton and others in his age may have sought a way to open it significantly. They may have turned to an instrumentality, in other words, that was deeply systematic and authoritative, yet not at all a reversion to a nonrational position, Trinitarian (in Ong's terms), mys-tical (in Jackson's), or otherwise.

A means of this sort would optimally represent a further intensifi-cation of the analytic interpretation of God's dividing Word, even while it placed at the center of reality the Christian deity and revelation that had to be packed into a Christian epic. Ideally it would also open the epic to a never-ending struggle ruled by the transcendent principle itself. And, lastly, it would offer a finely balanced environment for a Christian poet whose commitment to a closed system of existence was great indeed, but, in principle, dramatically less than total.

A list of such conditions constitutes a very tall order. It is unlikely that any one investigation will provide the one true key that answers to all these needs. But we can, I think, hope to find a single, integral grouping of seventeenth-century conceptions that will satisfy—or at least point the way in which an imaginative writer might on good authority satisfy—most of the requirements mentioned. The Ramists who explicated Hebrews with logic in mind were not the most advanced purveyors of a sacred analytic image. Even while they labored, an image of this kind was made available that was from many points of view far more intensely and extensively analytic than the Ramist variety. And this image too had profound Reformation affiliations with the dividing topoi of Hebrews.

## PHILO, GROTIUS, AND THE DIVIDING WORD OF HEBREWS 4:12

Through a different but related access I now return, therefore, to Hebrews. It is time to attempt to explain to ourselves—especially since Milton's age was the first to explain to itself—the immediate philosophical origins of the general patterns of division in Hebrews and, in particular, of the images controlled by the dividing Word of God. I should first leap ahead from Milton's epoch and note that since the publication of Johann Benedict Carpzov's voluminous *Sacrae Exercitationes in S. Paulli Epistolam ad Hebraeos ex Philone Alexandrino* at Helmstadt in 1750, biblical scholars of all schools and creeds have recognized that the Epistle to the Hebrews derives significantly from the Alexandrianism of Philo. Carpzov insisted upon an immensely detailed philological and conceptual relationship between Hebrews and Philo's texts. At the end of the nineteenth century, F. W. Farrar summed up the view of the matter that has remained standard to the present day: "the most marked feature of the Epistle to the Hebrews is its Alexandrian character, and the resemblances which it contains to the writings of Philo." On the other hand, notes Farrar, despite the many obvious borrowings from Philo, such as the images of Hebrews 4:12 and of Hebrews 9, in its general theology and in its way of relating to the Old Testament, Hebrews is worlds apart from Philo's

Judaism. It is Philo's imagery, then, especially the structure of that imagery, that exercised a pervasive influence on Hebrews.[33] Much of this was circumstantially understood in Milton's own time.

Moffatt has remarked that the Philonic and Alexandrian traditions behind Hebrews were in effect suppressed until the Reformation, when the revival of Greek learning made it possible to bring the necessary Hellenistic knowledge to bear.[34] Perhaps the most notable of all the Philo-oriented investigations of the later Renaissance was the Hebrews commentary of Milton's friend, Hugo Grotius, whose *Adamus Exul* served Milton as a model for important elements of *Paradise Lost*.[35] Grotius's and other Protestants' interest in the Alexandrian aspects of early Christianity, like the interest in Ante-Nicene Christianity, expressed part of a Reformation hope (Milton devoutly shared it)[36] of diminishing or even bypassing reliance on Roman Catholic learning. Considering the early date of Grotius's *Bibelwissenschaft* (a full generation before the highly controversial work of Richard Simon), it is clear that there is more than a little of the avant-garde in his lengthy citations of parallel passages from Philo.

Grotius's long extracts from Philo proclaim a self-evident and unique relationship to verses of unquestioned sacred authority. The exegetical case was a rare one indeed. For a Christian of the mid-seventeenth century there could be no difference in scriptural status between verses in Exodus 25 and Hebrews 9, or Genesis 15 and Hebrews 4. They were all the Scriptures. Since, in this case, they were inevitably seen as treating of the same subject they even came together as the same text. If anything, the later exemplars of the text contained aspects of divine value that had not yet emerged in the earlier ones. Here, therefore, was an instance in which an exegesis (Philo's cited by Grotius) was absolutely authoritative, for it had preceded the text in one of its sacred forms and had actually helped to create it. So it must have struck an intelligent contemporary. Indeed, this may have been one of the reasons for placing Grotius in the final position of the *Critici Sacri*, the highly popular multiple commentary published in London in 1660. Grotius's Philonic glosses may not have been viewed by Milton's contemporaries as the final word, but they were surely seen as being among the very latest and most exciting.

On the dividing Word of God in Hebrews 4:12 Grotius quoted extensively from Philo's commentary on Genesis 15. It was this exegetical occasion that Philo had used to elaborate one of his most vivid and most central symbols, that of the logos severer or dividing Word who disposes the parts or opposites of reality. Grotius quotes as follows from the *Quis Rerum Divinarum Heres*:

> He wishes you to think of God who cannot be shewn, as severing through the Severer of all things, that is his Word, the whole succession of things material and immaterial whose natures appear to us to be knitted together and united. That severing Word whetted to an edge of utmost sharpness never ceases to divide. (xxvi.130)[37]

As the rest of his Hebrews commentary shows, Grotius is well aware both of the conceptual significance of Philo's logos severer and of the detailed correspondence between Philo's symbols and the themes and images of Hebrews.

For a seventeenth-century Ramist who had a special interest in Hebrews and its thematics of division, and who yet sought to escape the most extreme consequences of Ramist closure, few representations of divine power could have been more congenial. The image of the logos severer not only obviated the need for excluding the transcendent principle from the analytic acts of the dividing Word; it actually placed that very principle at the center of universal division. Here the logos creator is seen as the logos analyzer who keeps himself at the center of division. Around that center, Philo repeatedly explains, the dichotomies or opposites of reality contend in a struggle that is not only never-ending but that is the key to grasping the fact that the divine nature is beyond boundaries or definition. The logos center of division divides and defines but is itself infinite. The opposites were divided and set into motion by the logos. The logos stands between, unmoved: he is the great interposer who mediates the peace of the cosmos. Emplaced within creation he expresses the form of the divine office. Indeed, in Philo's view we mortals can expect no higher knowledge of divinity. Philo explains that this is the image projected from the tabernacle, the holiest of holies, the propitiatory, the wings of the cherubim, and the imageless voice or logos that speaks from above and between the cherubim.[38] This was the explanation that had contributed significantly to forming the images and themes of divine division in the Epistle to the Hebrews. Indeed, as Grotius's quotations from Philo suggest, the explanation of the meaning of those images had become part of the sacred images themselves.

THE WORD, THE TOWER, AND THE MERCY SEAT

Seventeenth-century commentators on the biblical archetypes of Milton's images of divine division help make us aware of the structural individuality of these images. But in addition to highlighting the structures, the same commentators suggest how the place or activity of separation in these particular dialectical images could be associated with a densely interrelated set of theological values. These values may explain a good deal about the meanings of Milton's poems. For one thing, they suggest that when we find ourselves in the nighborhood of recurring images of this kind we are very likely face to face with a special form of rational Christian theology. This species of images and conceptions dramatically shifts the writer's theological emphasis from the deferred eschatological materialization of Christ's redemption to the immediate realization of Christian meanings in the renewal of a particular divine dialectic. In the events of his life, Christ the logos fulfills the propitiatory image of mediating division or separation. The word is the iconoclast that divides the images of reality to produce an "imageless" dialectical ordering. Taken together, the agent, the activity, and the objects of that activity are the divine image redeemed. For writers with such convictions, creating and recognizing that unique image can serve as a theological end in itself.

A complex of dividing imagination redeems the divine image in Milton's epics. In the creation of his vast poetic forms, Milton does not work emblematically. Nevertheless his largest structures significantly project the image of divine division described in this chapter; and at climactic moments in the epics, Milton even focuses his work of image redemption in what may justifiably be called poetic emblems.

One such emblem is offered in the tower scene of *Paradise Regained.* I noted before that the tower scene provides a final instance of the mercy-seat pattern in explicit relation to Christ the voice or Word of God. The poem's concluding action is thus played out on the geographical site of the historical mercy seat. If it did nothing more than establish this connection between mercy seat and triumphant logos, the moment would be a dramatic one for the story of Milton's sacred images. But the tower scene is vital in still another way. For Milton does not simply re-create an image that, for him, had immense historical and theological significance. He re-forms that image and redefines it, making it consonant with his most deeply Christian feelings about the difference between the Old Covenant and the New.

As I observed earlier, in this scene Satan believes that he has forced Christ into a posture of presumption against the Father. Inadvertently, of course, he has only succeeded in expediting Christ's fulfillment as God's Word. That fulfillment includes the emplacement of Christ as ordained, dividing Word on an enlarged mercy seat. In other words, Christ is able to perfect the propitiatory design so crucial to the divine structure of the world only by standing on the highest pinnacle and speaking—or being—the Word: "Also it is written, / Tempt not the Lord thy God."

But this is not all. Milton gives the Pauline idea of edification its largest possible dimensions by opening it infinitely, yet preserving for it an integral form. In the Old Covenant, the place of the logos was above the midpoint of the mercy seat within the temple edifice. Milton's representation of the New Covenant preserves and enlarges the supervenient relation—but with a substantial Christian difference. Now the floating mercy seat (IV.585) is sent throughout the world as a pattern of universal logos division. The redeemed image of a dividing dialectic is no longer localized and restricted in a particular place, but is made infinitely accessible in the mercy of Christ's intervention. In Milton's specific terms, the grace of the Word's mediatorial division against Satan, on the enlarged mercy seat, is the temple made available to the minds and hearts of all humankind. In the Nativity Ode, immediately after prophesying the fulfillment of the propitiatory pattern, with "Mercy set between," the poet had stepped back and said, "But wisest Fate says no, / This must not yet be so" (149–50). At the close of his career, Milton continued to view Christ the logos as the central part of a permanently established serviceable design. But if in 1629 his conception of the required instauration was of a historical and eschatological nature and required a delayed fulfillment ("This must not yet be so"), in his later years he came to conceive of individual spiritual life as a panorama sufficient for the enactment of the largest Christian revolutions, in every present moment.

The implications of setting afloat the mercy seat and its dividing dialectic are enormous, not only for *Paradise Regained*, but for *Paradise Lost* as well. In both *Paradise Lost* and *Paradise Regained*, Milton projects the time and space not only of history but of the individual Christian mind. In the climaxes of both epics, he celebrates privately, for every man, the feast of dividing mercy postponed from the Nativity Ode—that which *must now be so.*

# 5

❁

# *Paradise Lost*:
# The Divested Image

In the foregoing chapters I have suggested how Milton came to identify a principle of division as a key component of the divine universe; how he built upon a tradition of conceptualizing and representing this cosmic interruption by expanding upon the image of the mercy seat; and how, finally, he interpreted Christ, the logos, as an inherent feature of this scheme of divided relations. What has not yet been considered is how Milton's theological assumptions helped determine the form of his aesthetic expression. Specifically, I have not described how his rational or analytic images could promote a view of imagination and symbolic consciousness that he believed capable of yielding a true perception of divine reality.

## BLINDNESS AND VISION

I should now, therefore, like to claim as one of the many reasons for regarding *Paradise Lost* as Milton's magnum opus that Milton here represents the theological and psychological bases of a muse which recreates the structure of the propitiatory cosmos in the very conditions of human consciousness and which thereby accedes to an image of that cosmos which is both theologically reverent and humanly potent. In *Paradise Lost*, the acceptance of loss, the reconciliation to the necessary deficits in the totality of our perception and knowledge, functions as a subjective correlative to the divisions of the self-sacrificing logos. It also becomes the basis for a revised image of reality that can finally recover what the history of humankind's mistaken images has caused to be lost.

In Milton's theodicy, the mind's relation to knowledge is represented as the struggle to attain a truthful image. Imaging, therefore, features as an unusually prominent and self-conscious activity of the poem. Indeed, the world watched over by Milton's God is an empire of mirrors: reflections come perilously close to being everything in *Paradise Lost*. Not only is Christ the accurate reflection of the Father ("in whom my glory I behold," "in whose face invisible is beheld / Visibly, what by Deity I am"—V.719 and VI.681–82), man the image of God ("God's latest Image"—IV.567), and Eve the image of man; but Satan is an inverted image of highest divinity, Satan's sacrifice of Christ's sacrifice, Sin, Death, and Satan of a divine trinity, Hell of Heaven. That heroic man is also, in some sense, the image of epic Satan, man's fall a reenactment of Satan's fall, and the poet's flight into Satan's mind a subtle mimesis of Satan's diabolical journey are perhaps the most troubling replications of all. Why, after all, is the activity of image reproduction given such prominence in the poem?

Obviously there is no single answer to a question that embraces so many elements of so large a poem. But part of the answer, I believe, lies in Milton's understanding of the fact that human knowledge, including even the knowledge of the divine, which we call faith, lies in the right perception and comprehension of images. On the one hand, Milton's poem dramatizes an event of image violation, of the "coveting . . . Eye" (see IX.923–24), that is "inductive mainly to the sin of Eve." This sin is critically responsible for humankind's loss of paradise and of the image of God that resided therein:

> Thir Maker's Image, answerd *Michael,* then
> Forsook them, when themselves they vilifi'd
> To serve ungovern'd appetite, and took
> His Image whom they served, a brutish vice,
> Inductive mainly to the sin of *Eve*.      [XI.515–19]

And on the other, the poem embodies a process of image formation that attends to that loss and, in accepting it, works to repair it.

The images of Milton's blind muse embody a vision of reality that is not less, but more true for being partially occluded. The poet's lament for his blindness should not deceive us into believing that we stand in a country where perception counts for nothing. The poet has images to spare; only the return or possession of his images is inter-

dicted and that interdiction will turn out to be a significant part of his
visionary capital:

> Thus with the Year
> Seasons return, but not to me returns
> Day, or the sweet approach of Ev'n or Morn,
> Or sight of vernal bloom, or Summer's Rose,
> Or flocks, or herds, or human face divine.      [III.40–44]

The poet only seems to be alone, as if he is standing and waiting,
isolated and inactive. The poem suggests, in fact, that his loss, particularly of the human face divine, is really the condition of all humanity.
Furthermore, the poet's inactivity is more apparent than real. Through
the process of the poem itself he shows that his loss and ours can
become a vital part of the imagination's redemptive activity.

Here I can try to follow out Frank Kermode's brilliant suggestion
that the materials of *Paradise Lost* incorporate "the sensuous import
of the myth of the lost Eden." The main business of the poem, he says,
is to display life in "some great symbolic attitude and not by the poet's
explanations of the how and the why." Recently, Louis Martz has in
effect helped us along the same path of inquiry by emphasizing that
*Paradise Lost* is not simply "a lament for loss," but that "it is written
to sustain true hope amid a sense of loss." Martz points toward the
poetic function of Miltonic loss by calling it a condition of imaginative
exile. Adapting a phrase from St.-John Perse, he observes that *Paradise
Lost* is "a great and delible" poem in which continual erasures figure
at the heart of Milton's activity. [1]

The warrant for Kermode's and Martz's comments appears greater
still when one sees that in Milton's poem acknowledgment of loss is
integrated into the fullest, most circumstantial consciousness of reality.
This loss-centered knowledge or "sensuous import" is presented by
Milton in vast structures that will be examined in some detail below.
But to begin glimpsing its universal necessities, notice how Eve, for
example, after her dream of temptation, mistakenly reassures herself
that her experience of loss is only momentary and that she still retains
vision without deficit:

> O Sole [she says to Adam] in whom my thoughts find all repose,
> My Glory, my Perfection, glad I see
> Thy face, and Morn return'd.                    [V.28–30]

It is not long before Adam realizes that she, and he—very much like the poet—have in fact lost the divine beholding of the human face and the human of the divine:

> How art thou lost, how on a sudden lost,
> *Defac't*, deflow'r'd, and now to Death devote?
>
> [IX.900–901, emphasis added]

They are both, we hear, "in face / Confounded" (IX.1063–64), "discount'nanc't both" (X.110).[2] "This most afflicts me," Adam says, as he stands on the outermost verge of exile,

> that departing hence,
> As from his face I shall be hid, depriv'd
> His blessed count'nance.                    [XI.315–17]

In other words, the poet's acknowledgment of his own carefully specified blindness describes his non-returning or continually dispossessed imagination, and this special imagination somehow corresponds to a model of redeemable or even redeemed perception. Self-knowledge acquired by means of this kind of perception expresses, in God's words, "the spirit within thee free, / My Image" (VIII.440–41).

Until we reach the end of the poem and have examined the range of its symbolic content, we cannot know what this reformed and liberated imagination is. But Michael forthrightly assures Adam that he, and we, will yet learn to see again, in God's signs, "his Face / Express, and of his steps the track Divine" (XI.353–54). Even as they leave Eden, Adam and Eve gain the austere comfort of seeing the gate of Paradise with "dreadful Faces throng'd" (XII.644). The tragic experience of Adam and Eve is somehow itself the stuff of redemption.

## IMAGE PHASES, IMAGE CHOICES

In *Paradise Lost*, I suggest, the idea that a degree of image failure is necessary for imaginative success is itself part of a constructive critique of at least one kind of imagination. Clearly, the meaning of such a critique must be based upon an implicit theory of the imagination's several phases and distinct alternatives, but, as Kermode says, the poet himself declines to give us the hypothetical hows and whys. Milton's Adam, however, offers some fertile propositions when he observes that "of all external things, / Which the five watchful Senses represent," Fancy "forms Imaginations," which Reason must further form—by "joining or disjoining"—into a true "knowledge" (V.103ff.). Ultimately, it turns out, the imagination's higher obedience has to do with disjoining, while its disobedience has to do with joining of the wrong kind. In *Paradise Lost* the first disobedience is defined as it is in the opening prohibitions of the Decalogue: as seeking Godhead in other putative gods (see IX.790), particularly in the construction of self-serving images, images made "unto" ourselves, in the biblical formulation.

Milton, in other words, sees the potential for idolatry even in the first fully necessary stages of creating our awareness of the world. He finds the seeds of self-worship in all the most ordinary interrelations of the ego and its objects. Milton will depict this self-worship as the intercourse of ego and object that degrades and imprisons life itself. Indeed, in the *De Doctrina* he cites the verse in James that was to help inspire his sexual allegory of that very intercourse: "when lust hath conceived, it bringeth forth sin; and sin, when it is finished, bringeth forth death" (1:15). To Milton this suggests that original sin is a predisposition toward sin in which the evil deed is already implicit in the faulty conception or evil desire.

Martz's emphasis on the centrality of Ovid in Milton's thought is well borne out when Milton further illustrates his doctrinal point with a line from Ovid in which volition and action are presented as mere automatic extensions of the all powerful act of perception: "Mars videt hanc, visamque cupit, potiturque cupita"; "Mars sees her; seeing desires her; desiring enjoys her."[3] In *Paradise Lost* original sin is more specifically defined as a disposition to tarry in a state of perception that sets and hardens into hypnoid lust, adoring materialism, or monumental self-divinization. Adam, intent on fornication, gently but maniacally fuses a similar gerundive continuity of perception when he says to likeminded Eve,

> Much pleasure we have lost, while we abstain'd
> From this delightful Fruit, nor known till now
> True relish, tasting  .    .    .    .    .    .    .    .    .    .    .
>
> .    .    .    .    .    .    .    .    .    .    .    .    .    .    .    .
> For never did thy Beauty since the day
> I saw thee first and wedded thee, adorn'd
> With all perfections, so inflame my sense
> With ardor to enjoy thee.                    [IX.1022–32]

*Paradise Lost* is composed of a series of imaginative or perceptual events that not only reflect but, as Milton puts it, chiefly *induce* the narrative events of the plot. The poem tells a story only in a very special sense. When Adam says to Raphael, "now hear mee relate / My Story" (VIII.204–205), we feel painfully that our forebear, who has listened to Raphael's "lik'ning [of] spiritual to corporal forms" (V.573) as if entranced by a story (see VIII.51), cannot fully rise to the occasion. Rather, the poem as a whole describes how Satan, in Milton's words, dared "attempt the mind / Of Man" (X.8–9). It tells of the struggles between two arch modes of imagination, of the recurring battle for the supremacy of man's perception of reality, and of the need, finally, to reform rather than to eliminate the wrong kind of imagination.

In Milton's view both modes were present and active in man even before the fall. This is clear, for example, in Eve's magnificent account of her birth into consciousness. I quote the passage at some length because it contains many elements that are of great interest for the present discussion:

> That day I oft remember, when from sleep
> I first awak't, and found myself repos'd
> Under a shade on flow'rs, much wond'ring where
> And what I was, whence thither brought, and how.
> Not distant far from thence a murmuring sound
> Of waters issu'd from a Cave and spread
> Into a liquid Plain, then stood unmov'd
> Pure as th'expanse of Heav'n; I thither went
> With unexperienc't thought, and laid me down
> On the green bank, to look into the clear
> Smooth Lake, that to me seem'd another Sky.
> As I bent down to look, just opposite,
> A Shape within the wat'ry gleam appear'd
> Bending to look on me, I started back,
> It started back, but pleas'd I soon return'd,
> Pleas'd it return'd as soon with answering looks
> Of sympathy and love; there I had fixt
> Mine eyes till now, and pin'd with vain desire,
> Had not a voice thus warn'd me, What thou seest,
> What there thou seest fair Creature is thyself,
> With thee it came and goes: but follow me,
> And I will bring thee where no shadow stays
> Thy coming, and thy soft imbraces, hee
> Whose image thou art, him thou shalt enjoy
> Inseparably thine, to him shalt bear
> Multitudes like thyself, and thence be call'd
> Mother of human Race: what could I do,
> But follow straight, invisibly thus led?

> Till I espi'd thee, fair indeed and tall,
> Under a Platan, yet methought less fair,
> Less winning soft, less amiably mild,
> Than that smooth wat'ry image.                          [IV.449–80]

Milton, no doubt, expects us to learn many kinds of truth from this account: perhaps among the most interesting of these are that love of others necessarily begins in a form of self-love and that the propagation of what we call our self as well as knowledge of that self can only be achieved, in their turn, through relations with others. But in the evolution of the poem's argument about the nature of imagination, what the passage principally records is not incipient narcissism or self-love or maturing heterosexual love, but rather the immense power of the image experience itself.

Milton achieves two separate but related goals in the passage. First, he dramatizes the natural evolution of Eve's deepest symbolic consciousness; and second, he describes how that consciousness can become no less than overwhelming. Thus, Eve tells us that she at first thought the liquid plain was another sky,[4] that she was, in other words, initially hostage to a perception of universal identity in which plain, water, and sky were grasped as interchangeable counters for an undifferentiated reality. When she tells us that, peering into the mirror surface, she then gradually became fixated on the "answering looks / Of sympathy and love," what she reveals, and half understands, is that she then embarked upon the complex process of recognizing the special category of represented reality and representational image; correlatively, she commenced the task of deepening and binding her objective perceptions with the ligature of emerging self.

This secondary stage she attained in short order, and it is from this new vantage point that she memorially refers to her earliest thought as "unexperienc't." At this point in her intellectual birth the warning voice urgently directed her to note the distant separateness of the image. This distance is paradoxically a prime ingredient in the compounding of self-related consciousness: "What thou seest, / What *there* thou seest . . . is thyself." According to her own narrative, Eve was thus made at least partially aware that she had seized upon a sensory object and organized it as a possession of self. She had subjected the light and surface out *there* to the determinations of her own inner perceptions. These steps could not be avoided. Without them there could be no inception to creating her uniquely human consciousness.

But for Milton this cannot be the whole story. According to the moral and aesthetic categories evolved within *Paradise Lost*, what Eve must next, and finally, achieve—and what she has not yet succeeded in achieving in this entire world-creating moment—is an image life in which she relinquishes control of representational distancing. This ultimate stage is not simply regressive, for the elements of emerging self and representational distance are not to be abandoned totally in Milton's view. Rather the component or shadow of reflected self must become "delible." It must cease to be the autocratic organizer of reality when the idea of self is acknowledged to be, in part, the palimpsest of another partial perceiver, "hee / Whose image thou art."

The redefined, dynamic image, which is thus to be constituted by an inter-determinate and therefore unfixable intercourse of image perceivers, must live within her and grow from her, inseparably hers as well as inseparably Adam's. It is an image code of variable "like"-ness. It leads forward and backward to the "Face Express" that precisely is and meaningfully expresses the "track Divine" or divine trace. This is so, because, as Milton's revised definition of the human image gradually leads one to recognize, the law of imaginative interdependency includes dependency on the image-making power of God Himself. It is a binding law, however, in which the right to essential separateness or self-determination or freedom is in different ways guaranteed to all objects of imagination, God's as well as man's.

It is in this vein that, later, the "gracious voice Divine" finds Adam "knowing not of Beasts alone" but of himself, when he fulfills the essential condition of being "My Image," the condition of "expressing well the spirit within thee free" (VIII.436–41). This condition of spiritual expression is what Milton means by being a true image. The nature and significance of this freedom will be considered in the next chapter. But here it is already evident that for Milton, human consciousness is only temporarily dependent on perception of sensuous objects and on self-regard. It must finally be interrupted to produce a still higher consciousness. Here the so-called image comes to be not self-determined but, so to speak, self-divested. It constitutes providentially determined knowledge of God's will.

By such a will Eve is "invisibly thus led" away from mere visibility, beyond images of mere self. Her active departure and erasure of self helps make possible her vague comprehension of Adam's description of their relationship as spiritual counterparts: "Part of my Soul I seek thee, and thee claim / My other half" (IV.487–88). The living whole that she seeks is not in her own gift, she begins to realize, any more than it is in Adam's. Their consciousnesses are both parts of a larger law of consciousness that their activity of perception and consciousness expresses.

All this would bode fair weather indeed, except that, unfortunately, Eve cannot yet grasp these truths fully. For her, the smooth watery image is not something ephemeral. Rather it is the perfectly controlled, perfectly correspondent, fixed, separated, and stable image. Paradoxically, to her the image in the water seems inherently more winning than the truer knowledge won from a constantly dissolving, constantly reforming consciousness of reality. Her attraction to her own reflection is perhaps caused in small part, in this one instance, by Milton's conventional belief that the female form was created inherently more beautiful than the male. But the crux of the entire passage is Eve's continuous susceptibility to the magnetism of the represented object, the object formed and identified by her own consciousness. Adam does manage to seize her hand and to convince her to go with him. But it is not clear what, precisely, persuades her and, indeed, she closes her account with words of clipped, insubstantial conviction:

> with that thy gentle hand
> Seiz'd mine, I yielded, and from that time see
> How beauty is excell'd by manly grace
> And wisdom, which alone is truly fair.          [IV.488–91]

Satan, who has been listening all the while, well understands Eve's image relish. The dream he hastens to prepare represents a hypnotizing ghost of the very reformed image that was divinely offered to Eve as the means of eluding shadow images. After the Satanic voice has called her forth to a quest for Adam, Eve finds a manlike figure standing, as before, beside a tree. And the key effect achieved once more is that the smooth watery image, the dream-wrapped object—the tree in this case—seems "Much fairer to my Fancy than by day" (V.53). This is the etherealized moment of symbolic lingering, of aesthetic consciousness, in which the world exists only for our private imaginations. Eve has been visually thus induced to regress from the highest level of symbol activity, in which representational distance has been reasserted and mimetic fixation has been discounted, back to a stage of self-absorption in which the mind dizzily spirals inward.

Some readers may be tempted to isolate this phenomenon in Milton's poem as a peculiarly female weakness. Milton does, after all, say,

"Hee for God only, shee for God in him" (IV.299). But this is hardly a full description of the processes of their respective imaginations. Adam's reality is also generated along a track of images (including the image of partnership with Eve) that he, for a time, similarly misunderstands and misdirects. Eve's imagination is undoubtedly more active and more humanly involved than Adam's. When Satan addresses her with human voice the intensity of that involvement becomes the immediate occasion of mankind's fall, as it is also the distant cause, later, of its redemption. But it is in Adam's mind that Milton locates the alternative forms of consciousness between which humankind must choose and, having chosen, follow what Milton calls death or life.

When "*Adam* first of men / To first of women *Eve*" speaks humankind's first words in *Paradise Lost*, "Sole partner and sole part of all these joys, / Dearer thyself than all" (IV.408–12), the chief problems and potentialities of human consciousness are suggestively laid out before us. Adam begins to achieve continuity of consciousness, of "all" twice uttered, by fixing on a part of the all, "sole" twice uttered, which is posited as being identical with self. For a moment one is seriously in doubt concerning the disposition of Adam's mind. He seems to regard Eve as a mere center of object fixation. But then, just as Eve is led away from her image in the water, so Adam's mind is invisibly led away from mere images by his intervening consciousness of an unseen presence:

> needs must the Power
> That made us, and for us this ample World
> Be infinitely good, and of his good
> As liberal and free as infinite,
> That rais'd us from the dust and plac't us here
> In all this happiness.                    [IV.412–17]

His sense of all this happiness has been raised from the dust of created form toward an understanding of the ways in which individual consciousness is an aspect of the infinite and invisible.

The prevailing prelapsarian condition of man's imagination, which Milton here elaborates, furnishes a kind of paradigm of continued image interruption. Though unfallen man begins with a momentarily fixated center of perception, God has provided a mechanism whereby the watery all of entrancing symbol will not totally engulf human consciousness. God externalizes that mechanism in an image of his own. In the paradisal field of vision there is "that only Tree" which he has excluded from man's "Dominion giv'n / Over all other Creatures" (IV.423–31). Man is given to understand clearly that he would provoke "peril great" by even "coveting to Eye / That sacred Fruit, sacred to abstinence" (IX.922–24). The absention from total image control—from coveting to eye and then taste and ingest—is the preservative mechanism of a sanctifying imagination. For Milton, I believe, this is a large part of the meaning of the forbidden fruit.

## MILTON, COLERIDGE, AND CASSIRER

In order to clarify certain aspects of Milton's constructive critique of human imagination, I should like to turn to one of the most articulate philosophers of symbolic consciousness, Ernst Cassirer. Meditating upon the similarities and differences between Cassirer's and Milton's views can, I believe, help us understand *Paradise Lost*'s special program for the imagination. The elements of similarity between Milton's and Cassirer's views of the imagination are not surprising, distant though they are in some respects. For Cassirer shares with Milton, and with Coleridge, who will also figure in my discussion, the tradition of Platonic thought that describes consciousness as an evolving, multistage process that is akin to conception, gestation, delivery, and birth. Indeed, Cassirer's systematic expositions shed light on Coleridge's valuable but unsystematic insights into Milton's rendering of the imagination's multiple activity. The usefulness of the parallelisms among the three writers emerges quite clearly even from the mere juxtaposition of Cassirer's formulations to Milton's and Coleridge's. Of even greater significance, however, is that almost against his will Cassirer highlights a serious inadequacy in the creation of ordinary symbolic consciousness, particularly in the realm of art; and it is the identification of something very like this inadequacy that is one important goal of Milton's larger critique. Only in the last stage of imaginative activity, as it is described by Milton, can this insufficiency be made up.

"All perception as conscious perception," writes Cassirer, "must always and necessarily be *formed* perception. Perception could be conceived neither as belonging to an ego, nor as relating to a 'something,' a perceived object, if both modes of relationship were not subject to universal and necessary laws."[5] Offering a sustained parallel to Coleridge's "infinite I AM," and to Coleridge's theory of non-dissected co-presence, Cassirer argues that

the analytic unity of apperception, the dissection of perception as a whole into particular elements, is only possible if we presuppose some sort of synthetic unity. The fact that they stand in those characteristic sense-relationships, expressible through . . . several categories—that is what makes the perception into a definite perception, into the expression of an "I" and into the appearance of an object, an object of experience.[6]

Cassirer observes that the unique life of the human mind is foremost in representation, in "specific *consciousness* of the image." We inevitably think of Eve's discovery of the separateness of the mirror image when he explains that "wherever the function of representation stands out *as such*, where, instead of giving himself wholly to the actuality, the simple presence of a sensuous content, man succeeds in taking it as a representative of another, he has achieved an entirely new level of consciousness."[7]

Cassirer thus presents, in effect, a more fully developed version of Coleridge's theory of symbols. He makes possible an Idealist extension of that aspect of Coleridge's thought which Eliot chose to reissue as the sensationalist objective correlative, and he explains the rich relevance of that thought to a poetry like Milton's. Milton describes Eve's vain desire fixed on a "shape within the wat'ry gleam," which prompts the warning and the recognition that "What thou seest, / What there thou seest fair Creature is thyself." Here is Cassirer:

Only where we succeed, as it were, in compressing a total phenomenon into one of its factors, in concentrating it symbolically, in "having" it in a state of "pregnance" in the particular factor—only then do we raise it out of the stream of temporal change. . . . Such attributes may be viewed in a purely material sense; they may be of an entirely sensuous nature; but to posit them as attributes nevertheless signifies a pure act of abstraction, or rather of determination. . . . Transcending objective time and experienced time, [consciousness] must seize upon a permanent and stable content and posit it as identical with self.[8]

For Milton, of course, this must not be the end of the process. And we need not, in any case, insist on perfect equivalence between any one aspect of Cassirer's and Milton's views. But Cassirer's description of the birth of human consciousness is deeply suggestive of the overall meanings embedded in Milton's unfolding of the mind of Eve, "Mother of human Race." The day that Eve often remembers was not merely the occasion on which she received her first intellectual stimuli, inscribed as it were upon a tabula rasa. It marked, rather, the emergence of her soul into the world. Motivated by a desire to explain a similar progression from sensory experience to vision, Cassirer attempts to locate the bridge, much sought after by Coleridge, between image perception and the spiritual work of pure reason:

> It is with a view to expressing this mutual determination [between representing and represented] that we introduce the concept and the term "symbolic pregnance." By symbolic pregnance we mean the way in which a perception as a sensory experience contains at the same time a certain nonintuitive meaning which it immediately and concretely represents. Here we are not dealing with bare perceptive data, on which some sort of apperceptive acts are later grafted, through which they are interpreted, judged, transformed. Rather, it is the perception itself which by virtue of its own immanent organization, takes on a kind of spiritual articulation—which, being ordered in itself, also belongs to a determinate order of meaning. In its full actuality, its living totality, it is at the same time a life "in" meaning. It is not only subsequently received into this sphere but is, one might say, born into it.[9]

Cassirer's life in meaning closely corresponds to the realm of Coleridge's combined primary and secondary phases of imagination;[10] and, more important, it is also a clear description of the penultimate phase of imagination that is subjected to austere revision in *Paradise Lost.*

In "The Foundations of Scientific Knowledge," the concluding chapter of his *Philosophy of Symbolic Forms,* Cassirer distinguishes three "steps" or "dimensions" in the process of symbol formation. After expression, he explains, comes representation, and then, for science,

> a third sphere comes into being; for just as the world of representation disengaged itself from that of mere expression and set up a new principle in opposition to it, so ultimately a world of pure meaning grows out of the world of representation. It is through this transition . . . that the form of scientific knowledge is first truly constituted, that its concept of truth and reality definitively breaks away from that of the naïve world view.[11]

In effect, by advancing the cause of scientific knowledge in this way, Cassirer abandons art and imagination by the wayside and relegates them to the realm of imperfect truths. He sees no particular danger in thus leaving them behind.

In one place, however, Cassirer does note the existence of his final stage of symbolic transformation within a literary artifact, and his procedure for doing so is highly instructive. His text is the tenth chapter of Jeremiah, verse 3ff.: "For the customs of the people are vain. . . .

Be not afraid of them; for they cannot do evil, neither also is it in them to do good. . . . his molten image is falsehood, and there is no breath in them. They are vanity, and the work of errors." On the whole, Cassirer devalues the general religious development of Judaism and Christianity because "the images of the mythical fantasy keep rising to the surface even after they have lost their actual life, even after they have become mere dreams and shadows." In the representational "development of all symbolic forms, light and shadow go together. The light manifests itself only in the shadow it casts: the purely 'intelligible' [the consciousness of the represented object] has the sensuous [the expressive] as its antithesis, but this antithesis is at the same time its necessary correlate." Yet in Jeremiah, Cassirer acknowledges a totally different phenomenon: "the new divine life that is here proclaimed cannot express itself without declaring everything opposed to it to be absolutely unreal, delusion." In this prophetic view, Cassirer emphasizes, "the sensuous image and the whole sensuous phenomenal world must be divested of their symbolic meaning, for this alone makes possible the new deepening of pure religious subjectivity."[12] In Cassirer's view it is this systematic divestiture that raises Jeremiah's imagination toward the rational symbolic status of scientific thought.

Curiously enough, Cassirer never followed out the implications of this insight by attempting to find for the arts or theology in general the fruition of a symbolic process parallel to that of science. His observations on this point ended with the bare assertion that "only the religious geniuses, the great individuals . . . draw the line radically,"[13] as if in some exclusively private realm of activity.

Fortunately for us, however, there is in Coleridge an exponent of symbolic consciousness and an interpreter of literary texts who was able to identify in Milton a poetic process of the kind fleetingly described by Cassirer. Milton said that poetry must be "more simple, sensuous, and passionate" than rhetoric. Coleridge knew that Milton's words could not be understood simplistically, and he worked to explain Milton's passionate, dynamic handling of sensuous content. Here I must quote again Coleridge's comment on the genius of *Paradise Lost*:

> the imagination is called forth, not to produce a distinct form, but a strong working of the mind, *still offering what is still repelled*, and *again creating what is again rejected*; the result being what the poet wishes to impress, namely, the substitution of *a sublime feeling of the unimaginable for a mere image.*[14]

For Coleridge, as D. G. James has emphasized, the secondary imagination, "the conscious imaginative activity of the artist," has "a necessarily destructive side which the primary imagination has not."[15] In Coleridge's words, the secondary imagination "dissolves, diffuses, dissipates, in order to recreate." In his encounter with Milton, Coleridge became aware of a further phase, a further distinction in which the symbolic creations of secondary imagination are themselves to be continually repelled, continually divested of their recognizable symbolic meaning.

Coleridge's intuition that in Milton we experience an imagination of continuous symbol divestiture may be the closest anyone has ever come to a description of the philosophical scope of Milton's images. He realized that Milton was one of those geniuses who radically draw the line of image rejection; for Milton continually divests sensuous imagery of any appearance of symbolic wholeness. Coleridge recognized that the lingering upon what Cassirer calls the living totality was an important concern in Milton's imaginative world. For Milton, he knew, it is decisively this stage of consciousness that must be finally and continuously abandoned within art and imagination.

## THE EGOISTIC CENTER

With Coleridge's and Cassirer's help, the bare outlines of Milton's project can be reproduced in a series of philosophical propositions. But this does not tell us how the poem's various operations are carried out; how, in particular, the work of image divestiture is finally achieved by Adam and Eve, how it is managed by the poet, and how Milton *finds* it, as it were—invents it—in our theological heritage and in the longings of the mind.

Milton took great pains to impress upon us the imprisoning power of the totalizing imagination. The disastrous implosion latent in Adam's first recorded words threatens to occur each time he describes his perception of his "sole partner and sole part," Eve, and the "all" of his surrounding world. When he first saw Eve, he tells Raphael,

> what seem'd fair in all the World, seem'd now
> Mean, or in her summ'd up, in her contain'd.     [VIII.472–73]

Adam's lingering in the vision of an objectified part, his impulse to contract and sum up, soon leads Raphael to crease his brow in fear for the future and in contempt for inferior imagining. Adam's ill-conceived rapture is an instance of the symbol of self seen as absolute, self-sufficient, all-dominating, all-containing, worship-inspiring.

Adam is proud of the chains of his fixation:

> when I approach
> Her loveliness, so absolute she seems
> And in herself complete, so well to know
> Her own, that what she wills to do or say,
> Seems wisest, virtuousest, discreetest, best;
> All higher knowledge in her presence falls
> Degraded, Wisdom in discourse with her
> Loses discount'nanc't, and like folly shows;
> Authority and Reason on her wait,
> As one intended first, not after made
> Occasionally; and to consummate all,
> Greatness of mind and nobleness thir seat
> Build in her loveliest, and create an awe
> About her, as a guard Angelic plac't.                    [VIII.546–59]

One reason for Raphael's response is surely his sense of déjà vu. He and the whole heavenly host have already seen in Satan the manifestations of the perception that Adam fancies is his own advance in the life of the mind, and Satan's example of image-abuse sharply sets off the errors of the sinning Adam. Viewed from Raphael's perspective, modern attempts to see in Satan's "fixt mind" (I.97) Milton's suppressed ideal of mental freedom seem wide of the mark. We may feel momentarily attracted by the idea of "a mind not to be chang'd by Place or Time" (I.253), a mind willing to voyage "th' unreal, vast, unbounded deep" (X.471), a self-preserved continuity of consciousness, an "intellectual being," as Belial puts it, forever wandering "through Eternity" (II.147–48). But we must remember that all this does not really represent philosophical courage. Satan well knows the cogency of cosmic goodness. His motive is far from purely intellectual. He is driven by despair, by hatred, and by a frustrated desire for absolute control. "The mind is its own place," Satan wants to believe, "and in itself / Can make a Heav'n of Hell, a Hell of Heav'n" (I.254–55). But God's real world, he knows, continues to impinge. He is soon reduced to silly lies about the reality he says he does not acknowledge:

> What matter where, if I be still the same,
> And what I should be, all but less than hee
> Whom Thunder hath made greater?                    [I.256–58]

Satan the arch-deceiver is also the arch-victim of the same mode of imagination that he works so hard to inflict on mankind. His curse is ever with him, even in his most spontaneous acts of perception, as when he gazes on heaven and earth and addresses the sun:

> Sometimes towards *Eden* which now in his view
> Lay pleasant, his griev'd look he fixes sad,
> Sometimes towards Heav'n and the full-blazing Sun,
> Which now sat high in his Meridian Tow'r:
> Then much revolving, thus in sighs began.
>   O thou that with surpassing Glory crown'd,
> Look'st from thy sole Dominion like the God
> Of this new World; at whose sight all the Stars
> Hide their diminisht heads; to thee I call.          [IV.27–35]

Satan is capable only of fixed perception of the sole, singled-out factor—in this case, the sun—which is necessarily seen as a version of his imperious self, and which is assigned absorptive dominion over all that inhabits his consciousness. By the time we reach Satan's final mental preparations for involving humankind in the fullest possible extent of his own doom, he has reduced the principles of his afflicted perception virtually to a science. When he fixes his gaze on the earth, everything else must be diminished to it, as everything else was earlier diminished to the sun when it occupied the dead center of his attention. All the heavenly bodies must now be seen as pointing to earth, and as existing purposefully for earth, into which they are further and further collapsed, until finally they are concentrated in a focus of dominion that is, for Satan, necessarily a reflection or projection of his all-reflecting self:

> Light above Light, for thee alone [for earth], as seems,
> In thee concentring all thir precious beams
> Of sacred influence: As God in Heav'n
> Is Centre, yet extends to all, so thou
> Centring receiv'st from all those Orbs; in thee,
> Not in themselves, all thir known virtue appears
> Productive in Herb, Plant, and nobler birth
> Of Creatures animate with gradual life
> Of Growth, Sense, Reason, all summ'd up in Man.     [IX.105–13]

Satan's own perceptual activities of concentering and centering become his systematic way of annihilating reality, and of demi-deifying man in the process of totally deifying his own fixed mind. When Satan in his grand seduction speech says to Eve, "Thee all things living gaze on, all things thine / By gift" (IX.539–40), we sense that he is as much self-abused as abusing. What interests Milton is not, as has sometimes been suggested, Satan's strategies of the big lie, but rather the inevitable failure of the imagination that has become oblivious to the transcendent structure of creation.

As Milton conceives it, Satan's mind is a coil of self-representations in which the quest for a surpassing first principle, the track of the divine, has been forever abandoned. If Satan is a tragic figure, his tragedy is that of a consciousness so totally enthralled by the images of objective correlation that he has lost the freedom of his reason. He is totally engrossed by the objects that occupy his thinking. When, in the opening of the second book, he convenes the council of ways and means to insult the invisible throne of God, we see that his proud imaginations (II.10) have already been made crude and vulgar by the automatic gestures of a materialistic, self-worshipping imagination. In Milton's description, the personified gorgeous East that showers with richest hand is effectively without a brain. Inasmuch as Satan has been bereft of what Milton considers a truly rational imagination, this is also Satan's condition:

> High on a Throne of Royal State, which far
> Outshone the wealth of *Ormus* and of *Ind*,
> Or where the gorgeous East with richest hand
> Show'rs on her Kings *Barbaric* Pearl and Gold,
> Satan exalted sat.                                    [II.1–5]

When, similarly, in the first book, he looks toward the flaming shore to call forth his entranced legions, he spontaneously arranges himself into the carefully framed, rigidly focused image of an Eastern icon, complete with crosier:

> his ponderous shield
> Ethereal temper, massy, large and round,
> Behind him cast; the broad circumference
> Hung on his shoulders like the Moon, whose Orb
> Through Optic Glass the *Tuscan* Artist views
> At Ev'ning from the top of *Fesole*.

Satan carries a spear,

> to equal which the tallest Pine
> Hewn on *Norwegian* hills, to be the Mast
> Of some great Ammiral, were but a wand.          [I.284–94]

Satan has made himself into an insensate object, or even only part
of an object. A rational distinguishing component is as far from the
object into which he has assmbled himself as is the intelligence of
Galileo from the moon. Galileo is an artist because his mind labors to
comprehend form and distinction. His optic glass is a counterweapon
to Satan's hypnotic, orb-like arms because the glass refracts the pure
image, magnifies its distinct components, and captures it at a safe distance. Understood in this way the lines may also suggest that the artist
who views at evening aims at a contemplative understanding of God's
universe. Evening is not only his astronomical window for lunar observations, it is also his time for hallowed meditation.

By contrast, Satan's attractiveness is not that of a protagonist who
exemplifies qualities that are extendible into the world of our moral
activity. Rather his magnetism is that of an aesthetic objectification,
mesmerizing in its apparent completeness and autonomy. He is the
incarnation of our representational consciousness of an inadequate
bookish ideal, rather than of idealized life. It is difficult to know the
extent to which the epic heroes of Homer or Virgil were even by their
authors meant to represent ideal types of living men or whether Milton
perceived them as such, or whether the figure of Satan is a satiric
comment on Homer's or Virgil's pagan heroism. But these issues are
ultimately less important for Milton than the falsification of epic aesthetic consciousness itself, that which annihilates all to an epic thought
in an epic shade. Indeed, his presentation of Death's celestial bridge-
building, its entry into life, is among other things an allegory of this
special rigor mortis of one kind of imagination:

> The aggregated Soil
> Death with his Mace petrific, cold and dry,
> As with a Trident smote, and fix't as firm
> As *Delos* floating once; the rest his look
> Bound with *Gorgonian* rigor not to move.          [X.293–97]

The fixity is that of a Gorgonian seeing. When Eve gazes "Fixt on
the Fruit" (IX.735), the same self-petrifying force has mortally glanced
her imagination. Very like Perseus, Milton holds up the mirror to the
Gorgonian imagination to defeat its deadly power by revealing it to its
users. But as pointed out earlier, he also provides an affirmative model

for the exercise of a redeemed imagination. Part of this exercise is undoubtedly to be sought within ourselves and in the affective dispositions engendered by reading the poem.[16] But within the dramatic structure of *Paradise Lost* everything, I believe, that has significant validity for the reader's responding imagination already exists as an accomplished fact of cause and effect, and redeemed effect, in the imaginative life of the poem's protagonists. In Milton's descriptions of the diseases of imaging, there are implicit instructions for purging the visual nerve (see XI.414–15). He is excruciatingly clear about just where Adam and Eve misstep. And the same descriptions point onwards to the rediscovery of a viable imagination in which an obedience of omission is vitally functional. The two imaginations are obverses of each other. At the crucial moment, Milton turns the coin.

THE WAY OF EXCLUSION

From the very beginning of the poem's cosmic history, both over-categories of mind, God's and Satan's, show us the inevitability of self-imaging. God desires to externalize his image in Christ and universal life; Satan involuntarily lusts to bring forth his self-image in Sin and universal Death. For Milton, what is the essential difference between these imaginative minds? As image-maker, what does Satan do wrong that God does right? And how might the differences be related to the sin that loses Paradise for man?

The answer to these questions, I suggest, is to be found in the history of image-making embedded in the poem. The time sequence of *Paradise Lost* begins with the creation of an image and with the wrong perception of that image. Satan's catastrophic self-imaging takes its inception, that is, from the moment he casts glances of dominion at God's newly created self-image. God sets the scene. "Hear all ye Angels, Progeny of Light," He announces,

> This day I have begot whom I declare
> My only Son, and on this holy Hill
> Him have anointed, whom ye now behold
> At my right hand; your Head I him appoint;
>
> . . . . . . . . . . . . . . . . .
> . . . . . him who disobeys
> Mee disobeys, breaks union, and that day
> Cast out from God and blessed vision, falls
> Into utter darkness, deep ingulft. [V.600–614]

This for Milton is the first imaginable moment in the existence of the universe. In this moment of self-imaging God creates the germinal impulse not only of all creativity but of all further imagining as well. That there was some stage of godhead anterior even to this self-imaging Milton did not doubt. But as he wrote of the general problem of understanding the generation of Christ, "Anyone who wants to be wiser that this ['that God imparted to the Son as much as he wished of the divine nature, and indeed of the divine substance also'] is really not wise at all. Lured on by empty philosophy or sophistry, he becomes hopelessly entangled and loses himself in the dark."[17] Milton was content to date the cosmos from the commencement of God's image creation. He needed no more explicit source.

At this prime moment, Satan looks outward and sees only himself, himself displaced, his place projected but unrecognized, his own existence diminished by the forced recognition of a perceptible existent that stands outside and above his sovereignty. In heaven and in the earthly Paradise, "blessed vision" is dependent upon the recognition of an image component that is excluded from our imaginative control, which stands as a sign of our incomplete cognitive power. Satan, in Milton's words, "could not bear / Through pride that sight, and thought himself impair'd . . . Deep malice thence conceiving" (V.664–66). In his envy (V.662) or possessiveness of that sight—a possessiveness that Milton understood to be constantly potential in the creation of consciousness—he violates the abstinence and obedience that is requisite for the integrity, the stratified union, of that consciousness. In typical Ovidian fashion, his punishment is psychologically implicit in his encroachment, in his collapsing of blessed vision into utter darkness, deeply engulfed. The malice thence conceived and gestated stands for Milton's intuition of the monstrousness of endlessly protracted perception.

Milton had diagnosed the disease described in James's words and Ovid's before he represented it in the allegory of Sin and Death. If one interprets that allegory according to the perceptual categories that elsewhere inform the poem, Satan's fierce projection of his self into the place of God's image, his refusal to abide by exclusion, results in an attempt to invade God's image with a mere image of self. Since he knows no image abstinence, knows nothing but the total embrace of all image life within his ken, his mental intercourse with his self-image retains no recognition of a reality that is not self. As Sin tells it,

> Thyself in me thy perfect image viewing
> Becam'st enamor'd, and such joy thou took'st
> With me in secret, that my womb conceiv'd
> A growing burden.                               [II. 764–67]

Sin's words confirm allegorically what we have already guessed: Satan's consciousness is self-condemned to inward, downward spiralling, more and more deeply engulfed in moribund fixation.

In Milton's view, the antagonist imagination is chiefly determined by its inability to admit exclusion, its failure to internalize loss as an element in vision itself. The keynote of Satan's proud imaginations at the beginning of the second book is his refusal to recognize that the glories of heaven are forever outside his scope: "I give not Heav'n for lost" (II.14), he says. His mind, indeed, cannot abide the idea of consciousness interrupted, of good beyond reach. The acceptance of incomplete control as a condition of existence and of thought is for him impossible. He must fill the gap with a denial that he has, in sum, lost anything: "all Good to me is lost," he says, "Evil be thou my Good" (IV.109–10).

Milton's God, by contrast, he "from whom / All things proceed, and up to him return" (V.469–70), is characterized by his Abraham-like willingness to see his self-image depart from him, to see his Son lost. "I spare / Thee from my bosom," God tells Christ, "to save, / By losing thee a while, the whole Race lost" (III.278–80). This in Milton's view is the distinctive feature of the conjoined godhead of Father and Isaac-like Son. This special relation or, more technically, prolation is what makes Christ, as the Father explains, "by Merit more than Birthright Son of God" (III.309).

Furthermore, the necessity of loss is implicit even within the eternal fixedness of the perceived cosmos. Even divine consciousness, fully blessed vision, is apparently characterized by the cessation of some aspects of continuous being. In Milton's account of creation, the Son's departure from and return to the Father serve as a mysterious suggestion of the self-sacrificial requirements of the continually creative cosmos. Indeed, the description of these necessities constitutes a Miltonic version of Spenser's Sabbath-Sabbaoth sight at the conclusion of the *Cantoes of Mutabilitie*. In *Paradise Lost* we hear the following:

> And now on Earth the Seventh
> Ev'ning arose in *Eden*, for the Sun
> Was set, and twilight from the East came on,

> Forerunning Night; when at the holy mount
> Of Heav'n's high-seated top, th' Imperial Throne
> Of Godhead, fixt for ever firm and sure,
> The Filial Power arriv'd, and sat him down
> With his great Father, for he also went
> Invisible, yet stay'd (such privilege
> Hath Omnipresence) and the work ordain'd,
> Author and end of all things, and from work
> Now resting, bless'd and hallow'd the Sev'nth day. [VII.581-92]

Divine, dynamic fixedness, a truly stable imagining, is for Milton the
product of an imagination of loss. For him it means the creation of an
independent, free, entity that is decidedly a version of self—in this
case, an invisible reflection or image—but one that is placed beyond
the requirement of return to self. True imaging, in this sense, must
involve loss for the subject, loss of the object. For Adam, as for God
the Father, the essence of creation from self must be the freely given
separateness of the being with whom they associate as self-image. True
perception of reality is thus privative perception. It results from
achieved recognition of the independence of the image from obsessional
subjective continuities. Without recognition of continual loss, perception, in Milton's view, soon collapses into deathly rigor.

In the light of Milton's attempt to achieve a kind of poetic vision
that would set loss or exclusion at its very heart, I believe it is inaccurate to claim, as do Hanford and Taaffe, that *Paradise Lost* was
composed in two radically different styles, "corresponding to two different kinds of object or two qualities of poetic inspiration. The one . . .
abundant, highly colored, pictorial, figurative; the other direct, closely
woven, and relatively plain. The first . . . the language of Milton's
impassioned visual imagination, the second, of his ethical and intellectual intensity."[18] The first, says Rajan, is the infernal style of books one
and two; there, it would seem, we may find a genuine Miltonic visual
imagination. The second is said to be the celestial style of most of the
rest of the poem. On this basis it may be too easily concluded that
*Paradise Lost* lacks ultimate unity because the two styles are not com-
mensurate or fully cooperative.[19] I propose to the contrary that at their
root and in their law of growth both styles are radically the same.
Although in *Paradise Lost* no one style of imaging dominates, the
poem's variety of styles is controlled by a single image life seen at
different metamorphic stages, all of which conduct us toward an image

interruption. *Paradise Lost*, in this view, offers a poetry of loss that is produced by an imagination of freely accepted, partial exclusion.

This is the high dividend finally paid by R. M. Frye's invaluable researches.[20] We may think that we can fully see Milton's hell, even if he does not allow us to see his heaven. But after we have supped half full on the horrors there offered to us, the images of hell and of Satan in books I and II turn out to be just as inaccessible to the mind's attempts to grasp a whole image, just as disintegrative, as is the devil's apprehension of the fruit of soot and cinders in book X. To what depth do we focus our eyes, in the first book, to see "bottomless perdition"? Whoever saw or will see "Adamantine Chains"? How do we set bounds to the "fiery Gulf" or manage to gaze upon its ferocious blaze? How can we blink away the heavy unspecified blur of "sights of woe," or expand our pupils wide enough to see in "utter darkness"? The Satan who is memorable as the Leviathan on whom

> haply slumb'ring on the *Norway* foam
> The Pilot of some small night-founder'd Skiff,
> Deeming some Island, oft, as Seamen tell,
> With fixed Anchor in his scaly rind
> Moors by his side under the Lee,                    [I. 203–207]

is not so much an image as an interruption of image, a massive intervention meant to head off the dangers of encumbering fixation.

The poet's imagination does not rest or linger in infernal images. It flees across the imagined analogical landscape of hell as the ground beneath quakes and fumes and splits, as if in a tortured rhythm of image creation and image rejection. Moloch

> made his Grove
> The pleasant Valley of *Hinnom, Tophet* thence
> And black *Gehenna* call'd, the Type of Hell.
> Next *Chemos*, th' obscene dread of *Moab's* Sons,
> From *Aroar* to *Nebo*, and the wild
> Of Southmost *Abarim*; in *Hesebon*
> And *Horonaim, Seon's* Realm, beyond
> The flow'ry Dale of *Sibma* clad with Vines,
> And *Eleale* to th' *Asphaltic* Pool.                    [I. 403–11]

What the poet seems to constitute hopefully as valleys full of pleasantness, dales shimmering with flowers, cities edged with fruitful vineyards, all crumbles in a trice into the Valley of Death, into cities doomed (as Isaiah and Jeremiah were to record)[21] to sere destruction,

into the Sea of Death itself. This is the "dead Sea of subversion" of
*Church-Government* wreaked on the types of prelatical corruption.
There is no cause for visual wonder when the fallen angels look beyond
Lethe with "eyes aghast' (II.616), with eyes affrighted, immobilized.
What they see is the very dissolution or interdiction of perceptibility:

> Beyond this flood a frozen Continent
> Lies dark and wild, beat with perpetual storms
> Of Whirlwind and dire Hail, which on firm land
> Thaws not, but gathers heap, and ruin seems
> Of ancient pile; all else deep snow and ice,
> A gulf profound as that *Serbonian* Bog
> Betwixt *Damiata* and Mount *Casius* old,
> Where Armies whole have sunk.                    [II.587–94]

The apparently different landscape of Paradise, with its intensively
cultivated growth of proleptic stylization and negative comparison, is
also rendered insusceptible to stable visualization. Its prospects are
elegiac percepts, theaters of mind that are characterized by recession
and retreat:

> Groves whose rich Trees wept odorous Gums and Balm,
> Others whose fruit burnisht with Golden Rind
> Hung amiable, *Hesperian* Fables true,
> If true, here only, and of delicious taste:
> Betwixt them Lawns, or level Downs, and Flocks
> Grazing the tender herb, were interpos'd,
> Or palmy hillock, or the flow'ry lap
> Of some irriguous Valley spread her store,
> Flow'rs of all hue, and without Thorn the Rose.    [IV.248–56]

A passage such as this is evidence that forces of visual exclusion are at
work in *Paradise Lost* even and especially at the moment when we
believe we have landed in the lap of visibility itself. What could seem
more accessible to sight than a prospect that shifts naturally from large
grove to smaller tree to detailed gums and balms? For suspicious minds,
the visual tranquility is perhaps ruffled slightly by the word "rich,"
which may suggest a lamination of narrative judgment rather than
something seen. With the word "wept" we dissolve into a world of
personified objects. When we "see" that the fruit has the capacity of
hanging amiable and that its surfaces burn with the light of faery ore,
we must altogether give up the quest for any merely visual fulfillment.
Even the vague images of distant fable are shivered into uncertainty

and ambiguity: "Hesperian Fables true, / If true, here only." Only the taste, curiously enough, is somehow fully offered. The next five lines employ a simpler technique of exclusion, of taking away with the right hand what has been offered with the left: we end with a spectrum of infinite gradation, beyond conceiving, and with a rose beyond belief.

To decry such descriptions as evidence of sensuous poverty, as did F. R. Leavis,[22] is to remain oblivious to the central progression in the imaginative life of the poem. Milton's great similes are most typically anti-similes. They declare themselves as counterforces to image involvement. "*Not* that fair field / Of *Enna*" (first emphasis added), Milton tells us,

> where *Proserpin* gath'ring flow'rs
> Herself a fairer Flow'r by gloomy *Dis*
> Was gather'd, which cost *Ceres* all that pain
> To seek her through the world. . . . . .
>
>       . . . . . . . . . . . . . . .
> . . . might with this Paradise
> Of *Eden* strive.                                    [IV.268–75]

For Milton virtually no part of the perceptual legacy that flows into our symbolic constructs can be totally sacred, or if sacred, sacred only to the renovations of a controlling abstinence. Inherited, divine images, such as those of the mercy seat, pointed the way to such a view.

Milton's goal, unembarrassed even by blindness, was to undo the imagination's images. *Paradise Lost* teaches "mental sight" (XI.418) in which the ravenous appetite of perceptual consciousness has been inured to a reorganized mental discipline. Here no image is ever to be ingested whole. So important is this lesson for the work of the poem, that already in the opening lines of book one the ground is carefully prepared for the poet's own ultimate claim to moral vision, his disciplined sight. The lines serve as ethical proof of an imagination resisting all mere images of what is in the heavens above or the earth below or the waters below the earth. The familiar images are framed by an averted imagination, by reason bent on differentiation and categorization:

> Of Man's First Disobedience, and the Fruit
> Of that Forbidden Tree, whose mortal taste
> Brought Death into the World, and all our woe,
> With loss of *Eden*, till one greater Man
> Restore us, and regain the blissful Seat,

> Sing Heav'nly Muse, that on the secret top
> Of *Oreb,* or of *Sinai,* didst inspire
> That Shepherd, who first taught the chosen Seed,
> In the Beginning how the Heav'ns and Earth
> Rose out of *Chaos.*

The phrases of Milton's poetic fiat are full of shifting, dislodged quantities: generalized "Man" for Adam; abstract "Fruit" for a perceptible temptation, now tragically removed; "that Forbidden Tree" for a sight that should never have been sought, now must never more be seen; "all our woe" for the movable phantasmagoria of human pain, unlocatable; "loss of Eden" for an antecedent that always succeeds the present, never to be completed; "one greater Man" who is a god; and a "Heav'nly Muse" who far outstrips the pagan muses who are themselves only empty dreams. This is more than learned or epical periphrasis. This rather is a consciousness of heaven and earth born of image disestablishment. In the beginning, the poet works to banish moral-symbolic chaos by the imaginative obedience to exclusion.

In *Paradise Lost* the way to apprehend the process of reality, to know it categorically as law, is to employ an imagination of loss that issues from (or *is*) symbol divestiture. The image life of the poem may be thought of as an infinitesimal calculus of image abnegations, each drawing us onward, in a discipline of symbolic elision, to Paradise well lost and Paradise reformed. Perhaps nowhere else in the poem is this discipline from shadowy type to truth more beautifully expressed than in Eve's love song to Adam in the fourth book.[23] That song is suspended as a magnificent parenthesis between Eve's perfunctory acknowledgment to Adam, that

> God is thy Law, thou mine: to know no more
> Is woman's happiest knowledge                    [IV.637–38]

and her speaking of what is really on her conscious mind: "But wherefore all night long," she asks, "shine these [heavenly lights], for whom / This glorious sight, when sleep hath shut all eyes?" (IV.657–58). This simple, untechnical question, which I shall examine in some detail in chapter six, is echoed and reechoed by Adam and Satan. It is the question that will ultimately pry humankind from Paradise. Howard Schultz sees in it an impugning of God's wisdom and an aberrant desire for knowledge in and for itself.[24] Its intrinsic significance and its importance for *Paradise Lost* as a whole are also, I believe, directly related to the poem's most characteristic image patterns, for it brings together the central issues of a loss-centered consciousness and of a divinely wrought symbolism that, according to the poet, everywhere dominates the forms of God's universe. The question and the parenthetical love song are placed in a very special relationship.

Eve's inset speech is always one of the celestial moments in any reading of *Paradise Lost*. It is a rare and intriguing balance of passionate feeling and cool, tenacious thought:

> With thee conversing I forget all time,
> All seasons and thir change, all please alike.
> Sweet is the breath of morn, her rising sweet,
> With charm of earliest Birds; pleasant the Sun
> When first on this delightful Land he spreads
> His orient Beams, on herb, tree, fruit, and flow'r,
> Glist'ring with dew; fragrant the fertile earth
> After soft showers; and sweet the coming on
> Of grateful Ev'ning mild, then silent Night
> With this her solemn Bird and this fair Moon,
> And these the Gems of Heav'n, her starry train:
> But neither breath of Morn when she ascends
> With charm of earliest Birds, nor rising Sun
> On this delightful land, nor herb, fruit, flow'r,
> Glist'ring with dew, nor fragrance after showers,
> Nor grateful Ev'ning mild, nor silent Night
> With this her solemn Bird, nor walk by Moon,
> Or glittering Star-light without thee is sweet.

Ironically, Eve does not realize that she has spontaneously enunciated the answer to her Paradise-perturbing question concerning the celestial lights. Even in a state of dynamic perfection where death and permanent loss are yet unimaginable, Eve has applied a principle of perception analogous to the obedience of omission. By locating her appreciation of all earthly being around an imagination of "without thee"—of imagined loss of an organizing center—she has, in effect, made her way toward the creation of a higher order of consciousness. Temporarily at least, she has discovered the essential condition of sustained "sweet" consciousness; and thereby she has fulfilled the conditions of blessed vision that are a prime motive of divine creation.

What Eve cannot yet understand is how and why this spontaneous organization of her consciousness around an acknowledgment of the possibility of loss corresponds, and therefore can function as an implicit answer, to the terms of her question: wherefore shine these heavenly lights when sleep hath shut all eyes? She and Adam will have to learn that God has created an unending series of disjunctive correlatives for a human consciousness centered in loss.

In *Paradise Lost* Milton repeatedly presents these same heavenly lights as objects that interrupt or divide the field of human consciousness. On one perceptual level, of course, the heavenly lights are fully accessible to human vision; so is the evening scene; and so are the forbidden tree and the Paradise of which Adam and Eve must lose sight. But within the imaginative discipline embodied by the poem, all of these entities must be sanctified as objects of a distinct kind. All of them must be acknowledged to be occluded and elided, translated to a realm of signification in which they create image loss and image discontinuity. All of them, in other words, function as interruptive centers of a unique symbolism. Yet we should not hurry to conclude that the product of this imaginative process is mere skepticism or even nihilistic obscurantism. Lee Jacobus has well said that for Milton God's "interdiction is not an interdiction against acquiring knowledge," but "against losing" it.[25] Against losing *all of it,* I might add. Here we can see the practical steps that Milton takes to insure a constructive view of God's prohibitions. To be sure, the knowledge promised to man is not of a simple variety. It is conditional knowledge, conditioned by the implicit recognition that a part of each datum of reality remains unavailable to the dialectical consciousness that has located it. One aspect of this process may appropriately be thought of as a "consuming," in Stanley Fish's terms. But such consuming or obliteration is contained within a structure that remains thoroughly stable and intact.

Eve, and Adam with her, will yet forget the obedience of omission that makes all this possible in their prelapsarian world. As redress, the interdiction of death will become integral to all human experience. In book ten, Eve shows the first glimmerings of a life consciousness renewed in loss. She begins to revive the human imagination of loss, of bereavement, and in this manner she initiates the process of humankind's regeneration. Even the rhythms of her appeal seem to suggest necessitated, unavoidable loss. The worst fears of her earlier love song are about to materialize, by her own hand:

> Forsake me not thus, *Adam,* witness Heav'n
> What love sincere, and reverence in my heart
> I bear thee, and unweeting have offended,
> Unhappily deceiv'd; thy suppliant
> I beg, and clasp thy knees; bereave me not,

> Whereon I live, thy gentle looks, thy aid,
> Thy counsel in this uttermost distress,
> My only strength and stay: forlorn of thee,
> Whither shall I betake me, where subsist?
> While yet we live, scarce one short hour perhaps,
> Between us two let there be peace.                    [X.914–24]

Eve's offer to take all of God's wrath on herself alone, and, subsequently, her alternative suggestion that she and Adam destroy themselves before they produce a posterity of suffering, awakens in Adam more than pity. It reminds him, and he then reminds Eve, that the human intellect contains "something more sublime" (X.1014) than hunger for life. He retrieves the discipline that can renew their consciousness of earthly and transcendent being.

# 6

❀

## *Paradise Lost*:
## Reason, Interpretation,
## and the
## Structure of Sacrifice

The discipline "From shadowy Types to Truth, from Flesh to Spirit" (XII.302–03) suggests a progression from sacrifical ritual toward a more purely intellectual worship. But the fact that it is one continuous discipline implies that certain conceptions or formal elements of the initial religious perception remain in force all along the route of the Christian's journey. As a result, although our own translations of Milton's narrative can provide relevant philosophical or psychological explanations of Adam's and Eve's experience, we should not miss the theological traces that for Milton necessarily inform every stage of mankind's religious development. More specifically, we cannot forget that from the beginning of the poem to the end the poet's redeemed activity of rational imagination is bound up with the salvation of mankind brought about by the sacrifice of "one greater Man."

Indeed, it would be surprising if, for a poet of such thoroughgoing decorum as Milton, the idea of sacrifice, which is so large a part of his subject, were not functionally related to rational imagination itself. Milton, in fact, creates this relation by interknitting the causalities of his narrative with images of divine division and by offering his own implicit interpretation of the meanings of those images. In order to identify the religious perception traced out in Milton's discipline, I shall proceed from the psychological and philosophical dimensions of Eve's and Adam's experience to the theological factors in which they constantly originate.

## EVE'S MATRIX QUESTION

"Can we suppose, gentlemen, that the sweep of so vast a sky, which is marked and illuminated by eternal lights, sustains so many swiftly and intricately revolving bodies, merely to give light to ignorant and sluggish men, and to be torch-bearers to us below, the lazy and slothful?"[1] These portentous words were uttered, half in jest, by Milton the young man of nineteen. Decades later he reared an epic that was to give monumental form to essentially the same question. As I have pointed out, Eve is perplexed by the lazy and slothful nighttime phase of earthly existence. "But wherefore all night long shine these," she asks, "for whom / This glorious sight, when sleep hath shut all eyes?" (IV.657–58). And it is this question, too, that leaves Adam dissatisfied with Raphael's instruction, so that even after the angel has already rounded off the ample body of his discourse, Adam feels impelled to offer a professorial reformulation of his best student's heart-of-the-matter question:

> When I behold this goodly Frame, this World
> Of Heav'n and Earth consisting, and compute
> Thir magnitudes, this Earth a spot, a grain,
> An Atom, with the Firmament compar'd
> And all her number'd Stars, that seem to roll
> Spaces incomprehensible (for such
> Thir distance argues and thir swift return
> Diurnal) merely to officiate light
> Round this opacous Earth, this punctual spot,
> One day and night; in all thir vast survey
> Useless besides; reasoning I oft admire,
> How Nature wise and frugal could commit
> Such disproportions.                    [VIII.15–27]

The unstated logic that is the cause of setting forth this reasoning can be stated as follows: why should there be a part of the cosmic field of vision that is excluded from our sight; who else but man could be at the center of all earthly perceptual organization, of all symbolic consciousness; why should any part of universal knowledge be excluded in any way; and why, after all, should it be necessary to create firm interdictions in the very structure of the universe, "to divide / The Day from Night," as the angel says; "merely to officiate light . . . One day and night," as Adam puts it? Indeed, considering the implicit intent of what is really being asked, it is not surprising that once Eve has heard Adam repeat *her* question, she rises "With lowliness Majestic from her seat" (VIII.42). The moment is a proud one for Eve. She knows that she will later receive a private account of Raphael's answer from Adam, and she departs with the intoxicating realization that her thoughts are to crown—or unsettle—the entire divine colloquy.

Satan immediately senses the intellectual leverage of the question Eve has posed. Already in book five, just hours after she has voiced her perplexity, Satan attacks her with a nightmarish rejoinder that is a version both of her own words and of what he intuits is the real spur to her questioning: her unwillingness to accept incomplete perceptual dominion of her world, her reluctance or inability to abide by a context of consciousness in which all elements are not reducible to a privately organized symbol. She would like to return, he knows, to her own image on the watery surface. Satan plays upon her. He knows her stops, as Hamlet would say, and sounds her from her lowest note to the top of her compass:

> now reigns
> Full Orb'd the Moon, and with more pleasing light
> Shadowy sets off the face of things; in vain,
> If none regard; Heav'n wakes with all his eyes,
> Whom to behold but thee, Nature's desire,
> In whose sight all things joy, with ravishment
> Attracted by thy beauty still to gaze.          [V.41–47]

Satan's tempting answer to the very question Eve has raised is initially plausible only in the ego-rampant world of dreams. But after Adam has ponderously given his stamp of approval to very much the same questioning, it is no wonder that Satan dares speak again in the same vein, this time with lethal, waking success.

In a syntactical construction that emanates from the word "Thee," the night lights of the heavens are now described as pulsating with cosmic desire to adore Eve, who continually ravishes them. "Thee" becomes for Eve and Satan the controlling object that undermines ordinary subject-object relations and itself becomes the sentence's (and the world's) displacing subject:

> Thee all things living gaze on, all things thine
> By gift, and thy Celestial Beauty adore

> With ravishment beheld, there best beheld
> Where universally admir'd.                                    [IX.539–42]

Satan tempts Eve by appealing to her repressed desire for universal centrality and to her secret inclination to believe in her own power to bestow reality on the objects around her. This is the desire that can monopolize the center of humankind's symbolic self-consciousness and that is the cause of her fall and Adam's.

Satan, of course, makes explicit claims to original research that, by pure accident, happens to run parallel to Eve's and Adam's special perturbation. His alleged discoveries are a pretense to unified perception of all reality, of the transcendent One. But his representations are in fact no more than fixation on one fragment of the derivative Many:

> to Speculations high or deep
> I turn'd my thoughts, and with capacious mind
> Consider'd all things visible in Heav'n,
> Or Earth, or Middle, all things fair and good;
> But all that fair and good in thy Divine
> Semblance, and in thy Beauty's heav'nly Ray
> United I beheld.                                             [IX.602–608]

As I suggested earlier, what is most remarkable about these careful preyings on Eve's self-afflicted consciousness is that they stem, by uncontrollable necessity, from Satan's own inner affliction fully as much as, or more than, they represent contrived stratagems of exploitation. Here the drug pusher mercilessly victimizes his mark, but he is himself a helpless addict. Eve's and Adam's question concerning a disproportionate, immeasurable "divide" inevitably reawakens in Satan's mind all the old impossibilities. It drags in its wake his memory of the inviolable centers of divine exclusion. These are the divides that require not only full and resigned attention to divine being, but that signify the reduction in the status of his own self. These exclusions require the construction of the essence of consciousness around their acknowledged centrality. For Satan, this is the impossible, unbounded debt of fidelity and of "endless gratitude" that he can never fully pay and therefore would rather not pay at all (see IV.50ff.). That debt functions, for humankind and for Satan both, as a center of exception and obedience that can help sustain infinite happiness, but that, once repudiated, carries the penalty of "endless woes" (see X.752ff.).

In addition to serving as a vivid correlative to these problems of consciousness, Eve's question directs us to one of the greatest of human

challenges: how to maintain the integrity of our mental lives in the face
of dramatically incomplete knowledge, knowledge that must itself include the recognition of an unknowable, incorporeal first cause. When
in the privacy of his own mind Satan tries to take direct hold of Eve's
question, he can only muster a response that is built around his sense
of a fully tangible cosmic center, analogous to a pantheistic or emana-
tionist conception of God as the great credit-extender of the universe.
In the context of the present discussion, the form of his response merits
a second reading:

> O Earth, how like to Heav'n, if not preferr'd
> More justly, Seat worthier of Gods . . . .
> . . . . . . . . . . . . . . . . . . . .
> Terrestrial Heav'n, danc't round by other Heav'ns
> That shine, yet bear thir bright officious Lamps,
> Light above Light, for thee alone, as seems,
> In thee concentring all thir precious beams
> Of sacred influence: As God in Heav'n
> Is Centre, yet extends to all, so thou
> Centring receiv'st from all those Orbs.          [IX.99–109]

With this model in mind, Satan imagines that he should be able to
contemplate the full extensiveness and vitality of creation, the "sweet
interchange / Of Hill and Valley, Rivers, Woods and Plains" (IX.115–
16). But his consciousness of that reality, as of all realities, is doomed
to painful collapse because, as he himself seems to realize, his perceptions lack a center of repose. The divine center of exclusion that he
cannot acknowledge is a prerequisite for any sustained contemplation
of reality. His hatred of "contraries" implies his recognition of God's
dialectic of opposites throughout His creation. Satan's mind is not admitted to the repose within that dialectic:

> but I in none of these
> Find place or refuge; and the more I see
> Pleasures about me, so much more I feel
> Torment within me, as from the hateful siege
> Of contraries.          [IX.118–22]

## EVE, EVENING, AND THE MATRIX SCENE

The image of interminably assaulting contraries, and of a center of
repose endlessly denied, represents Satan's accursed being. A search
for sanctuary of a very different sort comes to represent Adam's and

Eve's blessed being. It is not surprising that the construction of this alternative habitat is closely linked to Eve's question. In order to understand the architectural significance of this other scene, note that Eve's unease is itself generated by her confrontation with a variety of scenic elements that have been detailed by the poet himself.

This poet is well qualified to sing of just such a sanctuary place, hovered over by a singing bird, for he earlier took upon himself the poetic charge of singing in a shadiest covert, a dove-like inner sanctum—

> as the wakeful Bird
> Sings darkling, and in shadiest Covert hid
> Tunes her nocturnal Note.          [III.38–40]

There the bird can reveal darkling knowledge, "through a glass darkly," as Paul has it. The poet who places the bird in this scene labors to recreate a conceptual temple preferable to all visible ones, to see "face to face." He is the same dramatized persona who first introduces the zone of silent evening that functions in the poem as the unquantifiable divide separating day from night. Like the heavenly lights, in other words, evening represents the peace that intervenes between contraries, for it not only denotes the recessional time of still prayer, between day and night, but it puts us in mind of the veiled center of creative repose:

> Now came still Ev'ning on, and Twilight gray
> Had in her sober Livery all things clad;
> Silence accompanied, for Beast and Bird,
> They to thir grassy Couch, these to thir Nests
> Were slunk, all but the wakeful Nightingale;
> She all night long her amorous descant sung;
> Silence was pleas'd: now glow'd the Firmament
> With living Sapphires: *Hesperus* that led
> The starry Host, rode brightest, till the Moon
> Rising in clouded Majesty, at length
> Apparent Queen unveil'd her peerless light,
> And o'er the dark her Silver Mantle threw.          [IV.598–609]

Adam's physical and spiritual instincts tell him to hasten to the cover of night and to the mysteries of wedded love and retirement. "Fair Consort," he says,

> th' hour
> Of night, and all things now retir'd to rest

> Mind us of like repose. . . .
> . . . . . . . . . . . . . . . .
> . . . . . . Night bids us rest.                    [IV.610–33]

But Eve still longs to understand evening, almost as if she believes that the extent of evening is in part a function of her own mental powers. Her mind lingers, not merely because she finds it delicious to vibrate to a mood of quickened, independent consciousness, but because she senses that the evening scene harbors a precious mystery. She senses that it is a mystery of some enormous intercession, some sacrifice or loss or absence, that she yearns to summon up as a presence. She must know, as she puts it, the gigantic "wherefore."

We know that Eve's intuitions have fixed on something significant, even if she is misusing them; for the space of evening that extends from the grassy couch below to the nests and firmament above is only one instance of a multiplying pattern. It calls forth memories, for example, of sanctuaries hovered over by the bird-like spirit whose activity is also to "mantle" a protected space (the term is from falconry as much as from the prophets).[2] The poet would himself be bird-like, as he invokes the flying light that first brooded the cosmos:

> Before the Heavens thou wert, and at the voice
> Of God, as with a Mantle didst invest
> The rising world of waters dark and deep,
> Won from the void and formless infinite.
> Thee I revisit now with bolder wing.                    [III.9–13]

Eve's effort, therefore, to reconstitute and fill in the evening disjunction expresses a desire to close the divinely wrought gap of intercession, and in this way to make the scene wholly hers. She longs to integrate its infinitely divided details into a symbol of totality that represents or that *is* her self-determined consciousness. In this instance she fails virtuously, and, because of her love for Adam, she continues to enjoy a sustained vision of reality. This love for Adam provides the privative recognition that is the best answer to her egocentric question. The same love rehabilitates her perception of surrounding reality. It becomes a scenography of saving knowledge, a movable sanctuary of recession-centered apprehension.

As Milton presents it, the harmony of consciousness that Eve will soon attain grows out of the scene itself. The amorous notes of the wakeful bird play counterpoint to the harmony created by recessive evening, for in this special harmony, the poet tells us, "Silence accompanied" and "Silence was pleas'd." The intercession within nature is matched by the bird's art of silence. Whatever Eve's perplexity may be, her restless plainsong entirely matches the disjoined scene that she is engaged in tracing. Her harmony too is built on a principle of "Silence." Hers is a love song of "without thee" consciousness. Without fully realizing it, she has been put in mind of a kind of knowledge that is informed by acceptance of her own incompleteness.

The shape of this incipient realization beautifully prefigures the knowledge that she will regain at the end of the poem, when she quietly recognizes the necessity for losing the scene of Paradise altogether. There she acknowledges that she must do so in order to attain, one day, a wandering habitation of perpetual blessing. Her final declaration of perceived harmony reproduces the concinnity of her earlier apprehension:

> with thee to go,
> Is to stay here; without thee here to stay,
> Is to go hence unwilling; thou to mee
> Art all things under Heav'n, all places thou.
>
> . . . . . . . . . . . . . . . .
> . . . . . though all by mee is lost,
> Such favor I unworthy am voutsaf't,
> By mee the Promis'd Seed shall all restore.     [XII.615–23]

Not surprisingly, in this moment of muted triumph, when the signal of remove (XII.593) has been given, the vision of evening is suggestively reattained. It is re-created in a world in which the hopeful laborer, representative of a scattered and fragmented humankind, is forever seeking the center of repose that he might call home. He hurries to the place that he may in all allowable ways apprehend as *his*, as the possession of humankind in a world judged to universal bereavement:

> from the other Hill
> To thir fixt Station, all in bright array
> The Cherubim descended; on the ground
> Gliding meteorous, as Ev'ning Mist
> Ris'n from a River o'er the marish glides,
> And gathers ground fast at the Laborer's heel
> Homeward returning.     [XII.626–32]

## THE TEMPLE OF COSMIC REPOSE

The image of sanctuary repose suggested by Eve's and Adam's intellectual experience has a large function in the life of the poem as a whole. Even before I explore the overall significance of the image, its centrality may be indicated by recalling that the leading topological features of the first book figure the fallen state of the angels in the profanation of a highly similar sanctuary, while the twelfth book prophesies humankind's restoration as the replacement of the eternal ark with a temple that has been cleansed and restored. Right at the beginning Milton locates his muse on what he believed to be the site of the sanctuary on Sion Hill, near "Siloa's Brook that flow'd / Fast by the Oracle of God."

Similarly, even our first views of Satan's earthly depredations are foregrounded, more than we may at first be aware, by the violations of that same sacred enclosure. Satan's cohorts are described as preying on God's creatures, as in the grisly rites of Gehenna, adjacent to Mount Zion. Correlatively, they invade with material images the innermost space of God "thron'd / Between the Cherubim":

> The chief were those who from the Pit of Hell
> Roaming to seek thir prey on earth, durst fix
> Thir Seats long after next the Seat of God,
> Thir Altars by his Altar, Gods ador'd
> Among the Nations round, and durst abide
> *Jehovah* thund'ring out of *Sion*, thron'd
> Between the Cherubim; yea, often plac'd
> Within his Sanctuary itself thir Shrines.          [I.381–88]

The description of Satan's realm culminates in an architectural object that is, like the idolatrous "Temple right against the Temple of God" (I.402), a "Fabric huge . . . Built like a Temple" (I.710ff.). The invader's anti-temple is filled with a predatory "hiss of rustling wings" (I.768), in ghastly imitation of the heavenly porch described by Ezekiel, and it is fully equipped with its own *sanctum sanctorum,* where instead of God's golden mercy seat is a violent breed of seraphim and cherubim. Their golden seats are frequent and full rather than respectfully separated in adoring attitudes:

>                              far within
> And in thir own dimensions like themselves
> The great Seraphic Lords and Cherubim
> In close recess and secret conclave sat
> A thousand Demi-Gods on golden seats,
> Frequent and full.          [I.792–97]

Their agenda is not mercy, but revenge and death.

When at last, after the tale of intervaling woe, we somehow reach the twelfth book, the book of recomfort, Milton re-creates the image of divine intervention. Here the interspace by which God chooses to represent himself is set forth in the incontrovertible language of chronicle:

> he voutsafes
> Among them to set up his Tabernacle,
> The holy One with mortal Men to dwell:
> By his prescript a Sanctuary is fram'd
> Of Cedar, overlaid with Gold, therein
> An Ark, and in the Ark his Testimony,
> The Records of his Cov'nant, over these
> A Mercy-seat of Gold between the wings
> Of two bright Cherubim.          [XII.246–54]

By the steady rhythms of Michael's narrative, Adam is assured that though the decreed place of God's presence will often be besieged and may be removed from place to place, it can never be abolished. This locus, which is the promise both of the perdurability of creation and of humankind's consciousness of creation, will never be invaded at the core that is circumscribed by Tabernacle, Sanctuary, Ark, and cherubic wings. At that core resides the focus of the intervening mercy that inheres in all creation.

Milton further expresses the continuity of the divine promise in parallelisms between the cedar Ark of the Covenant and the "wondrous Ark" entrusted to the first custodian of God's covenant, Noah, gathered to a place of exception "amidst / A World devote to universal rack" (XI.819–21). Indeed, the Ark built by Noah, long "Wand'ring that wat'ry Desert" (XI.779) and guided by the wings of the dove, foreshadows a train of examples of the winged and "clouded Ark of God" in tents long "Wand'ring" (XII.333–34). The divine image of mercy will always persist.

The reappearance and disappearance of God's sanctuary, Michael shows Adam, corresponds strictly to the wavering of God's covenantal partners:

> foul Idolatries, and other faults
> Heapt to the popular sum, will so incense
> God, as to leave them, and expose thir Land,
> Thir City, his Temple, and his holy Ark

until, Michael continues,

> the house of God
> They first re-edify, and for a while
> In mean estate live moderate

until

> thir strife pollution brings
> Upon the Temple itself.                    [XII.337–56][3]

Adam cannot be told in what form the image of God will yet again be made manifest. But Michael is able to suggest that even though there will inevitably be those who will come to "unbuild / His living Temples, built by Faith to stand" (XII.526–27)—much as the earthly Paradise itself will be lost, despoiled, its center-holding trees set adrift (XI.829ff.)—it will still be possible to inhabit a paradise within (XII.587).

This regained paradise will be a mysterious continuation of the disjoined design that is at the heart of the created universe as a whole and that was stipulated at the focus of the original paradise. In *Paradise Lost* Milton employs a variety of counterplots.[4] While the discipline from shadowy types to truth is embodied by increasingly abstract realizations of God's meaning, it also results in more explicitly delineated images of the holy temple. By the end of the twelfth book, we have been given both the retrieved images and the retrieved knowledge gained from a disciplined presentation of those images. Milton does not allow himself to dispense with any part of the disciplinary cycle. As if in full and direct confirmation of the poet's exordial declaration of faith, the historical redispositions of the temple are themselves offered as confirmations of the fact that God does prefer, as Milton states at the very beginning of the poem, "Before all Temples th' upright heart and pure" (I.18). (There is a similar historical circling back at the end of *Paradise Regained*.)

Just how these disciplines are effected and what their meaning may be can best be understood, as I have suggested, by observing the same pattern of circumscription and abeyance in the landscape of the redeemed mind, in the paradise within. In the language that conjures the all-seeing eye of the whirlwind Chariot of Paternal Deity, this pattern is one of wheel whirling within wheel, powerfully "instinct" with spirit (see VI.749ff.).[5] Very much as in *The Reason of Church-Government*, each of the many passages that describe this pattern represents an attempt to locate a recessional center of extraordinary efficacy within the disciplines of self. They present an image (far too highly refracted to be conceived as an ordinary image) of the intermingling of what for Milton were the deity's two arch self-presentations in the material universe: first, the brooding emplacement of the holy spirit on the face of the abyss, on the eve of the first evening; second, the delimitation of presiding mercy between the wings of the cherubim.

Already in his first invocation to the muse the poet suggests the nature of the special creativity that will be made increasingly explicit in the rest of the poem:

> And chiefly Thou O Spirit, that dost prefer
> Before all Temples th' upright heart and pure,
> Instruct me, for Thou know'st; Thou from the first
> Wast present, and with mighty wings outspread
> Dove-like satst brooding on the vast Abyss
> And mad'st it pregnant: What in me is dark
> Illumine, what is low raise and support;
> That to the highth of this great Argument
> I may assert Eternal Providence,
> And justify the ways of God to men.          [I.17–26]

The surrounding wings of creative deity and the temple wings that enclose divine mercy suggest an essential part of the poet's edification. They symbolize the disjunction that brings about and preserves the created cosmos and that, so symbolized, can sustain an interrupted but extensive knowledge of that cosmos.

In his struggle to escape the world of false images associated with the Aonian mount, the poet hopes to apply the instruction that he is even now learning from the Spirit of the circumscriptive wings. Beginning here, he attempts to build in the body of his poem an immaterial temple, a carefully reared high argument corresponding, somehow, to the conceptions of the upright heart. What this architecture of the immaterial amounts to is reflected in the construction of the passage itself. The configuration of the lines seems to suggest the model of the temple mercy seat, with its two wings of earthly compass (I.17–19, 22–26) tightly surrounding the median agent of the unseen deity. And that agent, whose very presence cannot be addressed without an interjection ("O Spirit"), implying recession from immediate or intuitive knowledge, is itself the great exemplar of creation by exclusion.

The meaning of such exclusion may be better understood if contrasted to the following passage from Martin Foss's critique of what he believes are the reductive liabilities of all symbol usage. Building on

Cassirer's and Usener's reminders that in its philological origins "*templum* signified nothing other than bisection, intersection," Foss writes,

> Ritual is a reduction as all symbolic transformation is. The holy process, unique, incomparable, and infinite, is pressed into a part and worshipped in its fixed, exact, and reputable limitation. The limit, the frame, the symbolic order is holy in itself. All emphasis is concentrated on the limitation, the demarcation or stereotype formula. Out of the World a small piece of space is cut out . . . and sanctified as "templum," as a holy place and spatial circumscription, holy because of its symbolic reduction and closed totality.[6]

In the temple circumscriptions of *Paradise Lost* it is precisely such bisection and intersection, such fixed closedness of symbolic reduction, that the disjoined form attempts to elude.

## DIVINE RETIREMENT, LOGOS LIBERATION

Indeed, it may be that at the deepest level of Milton's discipline of temple images divine creativity is equated with God's and the Word's bestowal of liberty upon the very objects of creation. Evidence of this equation is perhaps most dramatically offered when the Father explains to the Son that he will now "bid the Deep / Within appointed bounds be Heav'n and Earth":

> Boundless the Deep, because I am who fill
> Infinitude, nor vacuous the space.
> Though I uncircumscrib'd myself retire,
> And put not forth my goodness, which is free
> To act or not, Necessity and Chance
> Approach not mee, and what I will is Fate.          [VII.166–73]

This act of exclusion suggests the poet's most precise definition of God's bequest to the cosmos. For the earthly auditor, no less than for the heavenly, these convoluted phrases imply an immense burden of deific self-revelation. Robins has suggested that even in *De Doctrina Christiana* Milton may have glanced momentarily at the metaphysical possibilities of a doctrine of divine kenosis, a concept of self-emptying elaborated from the description by Paul in Philippians 2:7.[7] But even if we are convinced that there is no meaningful suggestion of a so-called retraction theory anywhere in the *De Doctrina*, we cannot ignore the possibllity that in his theological epic Milton hoped to put into practice something fully as complex as this.

Denis Saurat was fundamentally correct in asserting that these difficult lines are God's account of his creative retirement from a portion of the universe. Errors in Saurat's formulation, and unfounded objections raised against it, have been well taken care of by Robins's careful work, while R. J. Z. Werblowsky's persuasive refutation of Saurat's contention that Milton's immediate source for the phraseology of his lines was the *Zohar* has incidentally served to buttress Saurat's larger argument by adducing a whole host of other available sources for the doctrine of divine retraction.[8] Robins has cogently restated Saurat's main point as follows:

> Milton's lines picture one action and one action only: God's creation of unformed matter by the withdrawal of himself from a portion of infinity. The withdrawal [God's] is not repeated; by this single act God has brought into being all the materials subsequently to be used by the creating Logos in fashioning the universe.[9]

Saurat's own lean and Gallic formulation of the ensuing interpretative implications cannot easily be improved upon:

> Had therefore God not withdrawn from being, there would have been in the Universe nothing but God.
>     This is the central part of Milton's doctrine, the instrument of his justification of God, for man's responsibility is derived from it. Therefore Milton has carried as high upwards as he can that principle of liberty, implanting it in God himself, "which is free to act or not," and of all creation he has made a liberation.[10]

What Saurat and Robins did not observe, however, is that in *Paradise Lost* God's retirement initiates a pattern of other analogous acts and patterns of exception. These latter exclusions, taken together, represent the larger poetic application of Milton's grand principle. They also help solve a problem not dealt with by Saurat and Robins: how the world of created beings, having been given their fully specified form by the logos, can be free. By a perusal of the poem from the perspective of this and the previous chapter, we can more readily see that Milton's poetic universe is ruled by a series of linked propositions that all derive from God's intitial self-exclusion, itself a kind of kenosis. As matter (the *materia* of creation) is the subtrahend that remains after God's retiring, so the logos gives form to matter by compelling it to a further withdrawal and separation. "I saw," Uriel tells Satan,

> when at his Word the formless Mass,
> This world's material mould, came to a heap:

> Confusion heard his voice, and wild uproar
> Stood rul'd, stood vast infinitude confin'd;
> Till at his second bidding darkness fled,
> Light shone, and order from disorder sprung:
> Swift to thir several Quarters hasted then
> The cumbrous Elements, Earth, Flood, Air, Fire.   [III.708–15]

Robins states that in *Paradise Lost* "after God withdraws himself, leaving invisible and formless material in the void, he does no more. The Word, as his agent, from this time forward fulfills the great plan of creation."[11] This is undoubtedly correct, but in Milton's account the logos perpetually creates the freedom that God has willed by being the agent, most specifically, of infinite harmonious separation. To use Clement's phrase, the Word "discriminates all things."[12]

Very much in this vein, correlations between creation and separation or withdrawal (or separation *as* withdrawal) are particularly notable in the account of creation that follows soon after God's mysterious words. As noted earlier, here the Son, the instrumentality of creation, rides on Ezekiel's movable mercy seat, "on the Wings of Cherubim / Uplifted, in Paternal Glory" (VII.218–19). From within this harmony the Son as logos decrees a species of creation that is the very opposite of *discordia concors*:

> Silence, ye troubl'd waves, and thou Deep, peace,
> Said then th' Omnific Word, your discord end.   [VII.216–17]

Just as the deity's creativity revolves around an act of circumscription that culminates in exclusion, so the sustaining virtue of creation is its ability to maintain a space of *in*-coincidentia oppositorum, an interval of unmerged opposition.[13] This interval must be rigorously maintained, lest the universe collapse upon itself; lest "fierce extremes / Contiguous might distemper the whole frame" (VII.272–73). The effects of Miltonic inversion serve the purposes of Miltonic intervention when they help to circumscribe an intervening spirit center: "His brooding wings *the Spirit of God* outspread" (VII.235; emphasis added).

An analogous cosmic syntax may obtain in the logos's use of golden compasses in order to locate and circumscribe the extent of creation—"from centre to circumference," as Adam is given to understand (V.510). The compasses are plural in function as well as in name. They may thus be integrally related to the particular kind of creation that takes place upon the moment of the logos's temporary immobili-

zation of the undrawn wheels-within-wheels, as if a massive communication of pattern and power is about to be effected:

>                       him all his Train
> Follow'd in bright procession to behold
> Creation, and the wonders of his might.
> Then stay'd the fervid Wheels, and in his hand
> He took the golden Compasses, prepar'd
> In God's Eternal store, to circumscribe
> This Universe, and all created things:
> One foot he centred, and the other turn'd
> Round through the vast profundity obscure.          [VII.221–29]

The logos, in other words, defines cosmic reality with regard to the
undefinable space that circumscribes it, as if by the agency of one outer
compass. It also locates and delimits that reality with the other, inner
compass, which is no less a provision from "God's Eternal store." In
*Paradise Lost,* as in Donne's other-purposed hands, the commonplace
conceit acquires a multiple and microscopically exact meaning. Here
the logos's emplacement of the centered foot, which silently turns in
perfect congruency with its partner, supplies the recognition that the
inadequacies of our spatial conceptualizations may too easily allow us
to ignore that God's separating being is within creation as well as
around it.

In their best moments Adam and Eve achieve vivid consciousness
of precisely that dividing being.

### PRAYER, SACRIFICE, INTERPRETATION

Eve's love song is addressed, for example, to the Adam whose com-
panionship gives her the sweet savor of all the other elements of God's
creation. In this sense she addresses herself to God in him rather than
to God only. Yet her song strongly suggests the form and function of
prayer to God himself. Her activity is grateful enumeration of God's
blessings, including Adam as one among many, and she expresses heart-
felt hope for the continuance of those blessings. The devotional function
of her song is also apparent from the fact that it serves as introduction
to Adam's and Eve's evensong. In that prayer they specify the awareness of God's being toward which Eve's thoughts have been migrating,
as to a further blessing, unawares. The poet makes clear that the love
song and the evensong take their rise in the sanctuary scene of evening.
That hallowed scene serves as antechapel to the "sacred . . . close

recess" (IV.706–708) where the "Rites / Mysterious of connubial Love" (IV.742–43) are celebrated. There love "lights / His constant Lamp, and waves his purple wings," suggesting the eternal light and cherubic wings of the tabernacle (IV.763–44). The waving purple and constant light describe an innermost recess of creative retirement. The scene of recession and the song are one. Together with the "Celestial voices . . . Singing thir great Creator," Adam and Eve's songs "divide the night" and lift their "thoughts to Heaven" (IV.682–88).

The poet strongly suggests that prayer is closely related to the forms of temple rite. Here the discipline "From shadowy Types to Truth, from Flesh to Spirit," and to spiritualized body, appears as a fact of the poem's imaginative life. But the meaning of the relationship between prayer and temple rite, most especially to the types of fleshly sacrifice, is not at all obvious. An act of interpretation is required to make the meaning functional in the poem. That interpretation is supplied by the poem itself, which at the same time gives interpretation its own symbolic meaning with regard to the arch images of sacrifice and prayer. Before turning to these matters, it will be useful to peruse the prayer that Adam and Eve offer when they reach the "close recess" that is the cleansing counter-image to the close recess (I.795) of Satan's murderous conclave. They offer a prayer to divide the night in the evening moment between day and night:

> Thou also mad'st the Night,
> Maker Omnipotent, and thou the Day,
> Which we in our appointed work imploy'd
> Have finisht happy in our mutual help
> And mutual love, the Crown of all our bliss
> Ordain'd by thee, and this delicious place
> For us too large, where thy abundance wants
> Partakers, and uncropt falls to the ground.
> But thou hast promis'd from us two a Race
> To fill the Earth, who shall with us extol
> Thy goodness infinite, both when we wake,
> And when we seek, as now, thy gift of sleep.      [IV.724–35]

This prayer is closely analogous to Eve's and Adam's unsettling question about the celestial lights. Here too they realize that by themselves they are inadequate objects for "goodness infinite." But here their perturbation immediately gives birth to a new equilibrium. Praying together, they acknowledge that reality is a scene that they cannot hope or wish to engross by themselves. Their realization that the extent of God's goodness is forever ungraspable is the essence of their achievement in prayer. Their evensong, like Eve's harmony of "without thee," re-creates the music of silence and retirement that they have apprehended in evening. They have won their way toward meaningful exclusion, so that their consciousness of the plenitudinous "delicious place" is interleaved by God's unknowable being.

Perhaps more than anywhere else in the poem, the relationship of prayer to sacrifice is established and interpreted in the climactic opening of book eleven. In that passage the "Prevenient Grace" that makes possible redeeming human prayer is imagined as a scene of the highest temple rite. Here the highest sacrifice of all is described as an intellectual exchange that is simply called *interpretation*. At this moment of greatest simplification, Milton's identity as a Christian poet becomes most integral to his task. Now it becomes apparent that the web of recessional imagination spun by *Paradise Lost* is a function of Christian consciousness made possible by Christian grace.

For Milton, Christ's sacrificial redemption not only saves the physical creation from corruption. It also bestows on man the condition of rational being, since only the intellectual imitation of Christ's retirement can redeem human consciousness. For Milton every right gesture of the mind is thus a Christian emulation. Its Christian nature is not only a matter of following a particular formula that may be abstracted from Christ's activity of self-sacrifice. Rather, its location in the universe of meaning is its relation to its bestower. The thread or vestigium, therefore, which carries through the discipline from shadowy type to truth is the endlessly renewed sacrifice of Christ's self: the structures of both temple rite and prayer are, for Milton, reflections of Christ's crucifixion. In this view, rational imagination is itself the practical working of prevenient grace.

All of this is shown when the doom of the species hangs in the balance and the Word as "great Intercessor" re-creates the universal harmony of exclusion. By sacrificing himself he restores the hearts of Adam and Eve to their upright, sanctuary state. In the discipline of prayer that unbuilds the shadowy type of temple rite, they remove the "stony" from their hearts. They regain the condition of "before all Temples" by incorporating the sacrificial structure in their minds:

> Thus they in lowliest plight repentant stood
> Praying, for from the Mercy-seat above
> Prevenient Grace descending had remov'd
> The stony from thir hearts, and made new flesh

Regenerate grow instead, that sighs now breath'd
Unutterable, which the Spirit of prayer
Inspir'd, and wing'd for Heav'n with speedier flight
Than loudest Oratory: yet thir port
Not of mean suitors, nor important less
Seem'd thir Petition, than when th' ancient Pair
In Fables old, less ancient yet than these,
*Deucalion* and chaste *Pyrrha* to restore
The Race of Mankind drown'd, before the Shrine
Of *Themis* stood devout.                    [XI.1–14]

Appropriately enough for the issue being decided, the controlling image of the entire passage is the mercy seat, situated in the "high Temple" that is the precedent Idea of all temples (see VII.148). Once again the temple structure suggests the creative paragon of what Milton in *Areopagitica* calls "spirituall architecture." Now the cosmos as a whole becomes an embracing temple. In this passage and the related lines on God's retiring, Milton takes us close to a direct imaging of the divine nature. The archetypical harmony of exclusion or silence is supplied by the "sighs . . . breath'd / Unutterable," the "mute" sighs (see XI.31) that the Word asks the Father to accept as "wing'd for Heav'n":

To Heav'n thir prayers
Flew up, nor miss'd the way, by envious winds
Blown vagabond or frustrate: in they pass'd
Dimensionless through Heav'nly doors: then clad
With incense, where the Golden Altar fum'd,
By thir great Intercessor, came in sight
Before the Father's Throne: Then the glad Son
Presenting, thus to intercede began.          [XI.14–21]

The Son's "presenting'" has the quality of a charade. It inverts the usual order of linguistic activity by making abstract concepts the unitary building blocks of expressive structures. The Son's aim is to reassemble a dialectical emblem around the center of "implanted Grace": between the heavenly doors of God's accepting presence and before the cherubic wings of the mercy seat. The logos thus re-creates the pattern of sacrificial dissection that stands for renewed covenant, even while it disciplines fleshly impulses by singling out incense offering from among the range of sacrificial alternatives prescribed for the temple:

> See Father, what first fruits on Earth are sprung
> From thy implanted Grace in Man, these Sighs
> And Prayers, which in this Golden Censer, mixt
> With Incense, I thy Priest before thee bring.          [XI.22–25]

In his form of a servant or priest, the Son postpones to the last the immediate cause and effect of prevenient grace itself. He delays all mention of the logos medium that is even now restoring humankind to the temple of recession. Crucifixional sacrifice is the second highest of all recessions, after the *primum mobile* retirement that is creation itself. It is offered up simply as the Word's interpretation of mankind's words:

> hear his sighs though mute;
> Unskilful with what words to pray, let mee
> Interpret for him, mee his Advocate
> And propitiation, all his works on mee
> Good or not good ingraft, my Merit those
> Shall perfet, and for these my Death shall pay.          [XI.31–36]

The Son links his sacrifice to the clarification of human reason. Set before us as on an altar is the suggestion that there is a kind of reason that can itself become a self-sacrificial act, a rational enactment that can sustain spiritual being. At this critical juncture of the epistemological love story, we are shown more clearly than ever before the disjunctive pattern that Adam and Eve have been observing all along, and to which they have learned to respond. At the atonement moment of abeyance and second brooding, all mankind's experience of loss will either hurry them into the gulf of oblivion or, with the help of a knowledge made available by the divine logos, it will enable them to pass on toward a more stable knowing.

For Milton this knowing is a condition far happier and much preferable to any other paradise or temple, for it constitutes a movable sanctuary, an Ezekiel chariot, that is forever accessible to any mind attuned to Christ's meanings. We end where we began when we discover that the final stage of knowledge has been stored up in the human mind from the very beginning. Without the rational awareness of our incomplete consciousness, no impulse to gain true knowledge would ever have existed. Man and woman would not have been the questioning beings that the poem, in its central four books, shows us that they are. The Son's self-sacrifice and the Father's willingness to lose him "a while" (III.280ff.) are the dissolving objective correlatives for Christian awareness of creation and repose. In emulating the divine example, man becomes critically aware of the elements of life and loss that make up his world. He learns that he must exist as a creature of interpretation.

To interpret and redeem his world, man must provide an island of disinterest, a consciousness that is disengaged from space and time. He must create self-exclusion. Interpretation of this kind necessitates loss for the interpreter. Susan Sontag has argued that a self-aggrandizing impulse underlies the tradition of Western hermeneutics.[14] But in *Paradise Lost*, interpretation is the avoidance of just such aggrandizement. It seeks rather to reinstate the gulf of the unknown that subjectivity tends to deny. It locates unknowing and cessation of knowing at the center of perceivable reality and at the center of consciousness of that reality. William K. Wimsatt has written that "For all the objects of our manifold experience, for every unity, there is an action of the mind which cuts off roots, melts away context—or indeed we should never have objects or ideas or anything to talk about."[15] Milton shows us a life of imagination in which the mind also cuts deep into the object so that it may divest itself of totalizing perceptions. The same mind then reintegrates consciousness around acknowledged exclusion. In this kind of theological knowledge the world is apprehended as unresolved, separated by a "high Injunction" at its heart (X.13).

We misread the poem's so-called autobiographical passages if we try to find in them the poet's attempt to set loose his imprisoned subjectivity. The poet who revisits "with bolder wing" the dwelling of the creator who was "Before the Heavens" (III.9ff.) is not in search of self. His hope is to understand the innermost chamber of reality, the place of rest and divine exclusion. There he offers himself as Christian co-partner, virtually as sacrificial victim: blind, outcast, on the verge of extinction. His blindness helps create the special condition of his consciousness:

> ever-during dark
> Surrounds me, from the cheerful ways of men
> Cut off, and for the Book of knowledge fair
> Presented with a Universal blanc
> Of Nature's works to me expung'd and ras'd.        [III.45–49]

It is just this vantage point of exile that grants him the interpretative capacity to "see and tell / Of things invisible to mortal sight" (III.54–55).

The poet of *Paradise Lost* locates himself at a kind of sabbatic centerpoint at the beginning of book seven. He rests between halves of the poem, very much as Milton pauses to speak of his own hopes and frustrations halfway through *The Reason of Church-Government.* "Half yet remains unsung" (VII.21). By locating his outcast being at a point of suspended activity, he imitates the Son's solitary withdrawal from human life:

> though fall'n on evil days,
> On evil days though fall'n, and evil tongues;
> In darkness, and with dangers compast round,
> And solitude.                    [VII.25–28]

Unlike Satan, who cannot elude the hateful siege of contraries, he has found a place to stand within the "barbarous dissonance" (VII.32). Thus he too has become a medium and interpreter of redemptive knowledge. His interpretation "Of Man's First Disobedience, and the Fruit / Of that Forbidden Tree" is made possible by his acceptance of the loss entailed by that disobedience. The loss focused in his exile is quintessentially represented by Christ's sacrifice of himself for mankind. The poet too interprets from the center of loss so that humankind may proceed to its providential retirement, its "place of rest." The internalization of this rest is a "paradise within . . . happier far" (XII.575ff.).

Adam's and Eve's new beginning is their obedience to the cherubim's "signal of remove" (XII.593). The exclusion from paradise that they first apprehend as penitential type can become, in its entirety, the line of distinction in a world that is otherwise all before them. Interpreted within the matrix of Christian consciousness, the recognition that paradise is indeed lost can itself restore paradise.

# 7

❋

# *Paradise Regained*
# and the Language of
# Christian Experience

The representation of reality offered in *Paradise Lost* is so embracing
that it is at first difficult to imagine what another poem about paradise
could possibly add. Having shown "Prevenient Grace descending," Milton has presumably shown it all. But the title of the later poem seems
to blazon a totally new dimension of the unfolding story: *Paradise Regained!* And its opening lines assert that the poet is taking on a significantly new role:

> I who erewhile the happy Garden sung,
> By one man's disobedience lost, now sing
> Recover'd Paradise to all mankind,
> By one man's firm obedience fully tried
> Through all temptation, and the Tempter foil'd
> In all his wiles, defeated and repuls't,
> And *Eden* rais'd in the waste Wilderness.

Clearly what is new in this projected account is the manifestation of
Christ's earthly existence. Here, for all mankind, is the sequel to the
story already told. But this is not all the newness offered.

According to Milton, the redemption Christ brings is a part of a
scheme of things that is changing before our eyes; it is a paradise
recovered *now* to (or for) all mankind, both in Christ's protracted presence in the world and in Milton's singing of it. Like most other Christians of his time, Milton believed that Christ's experience in human

form thenceforth continuously altered human existence throughout history, down to and including the present moment. In some sense, therefore, Christ is even "now" being fully tried; all of Satan's wiles are now and forever being foiled, defeated, and repulsed; the waste wilderness, which is as much our wasted world as it is the Judean desert, is being transformed into Eden, even now.

In *Paradise Regained*, one of Milton's goals, I would suggest, is to represent this continued life of Christ's experience. But, as another feature of the newness of his enterprise, Milton also claims to want to sing now that which in Christ's experience has remained unrecorded and hence unsung. We hear this in the address to his muse immediately following the commencement of the poem:

> Thou Spirit who led'st this glorious Eremite
> Into the Desert, his Victorious Field
> Against the Spiritual Foe, and brought'st him thence
> By proof th'undoubted Son of God, inspire,
> As thou art wont, my prompted Song, else mute,
> And bear through height or depth of nature's bounds
> With prosperous wing full summ'd to tell of deeds
> Above Heroic, though in secret done,
> And unrecorded left through many an Age,
> Worthy t' have not remain'd so long unsung.          [I.8–17]

Since we know that Milton is not speaking of newly discovered documents, we must understand his aspiration to mean that he will attempt to recover from the known events of paradise regained, new, secret, meanings that heretofore have not been understood. He will attempt, in other words, to discover in the known written record new definitions of the theological terms that we may have thought were already fully explicated. In the triple account of Christ's baptism as the son of God, the poem itself emphasizes the special importance of a correct application of recorded language:

> And last the sum of all, my Father's voice,
> Audibly heard from Heav'n, pronounc'd me his,
> Mee his beloved Son, in whom alone
> He was well pleas'd; by which I knew the time
> Now full, that I no more should live obscure,
> But openly begin, as best becomes
> The Authority which I deriv'd from Heaven.
>                          [I.283–89; cf. I.29–32, I.79–85]

The two innovations or kinds of newness that Milton proposes to introduce in his poem are not unrelated. What I would like to argue is that, in singing Christ's obedience, Milton records not only the baptizing and subsequent life of Christ, but the christening of the Christlike elements of human awareness that make an inward paradise available "to all mankind." The key to the realization of Milton's objectives is his unfolding or further revelation of the hidden valences of revealed language. Stanley Fish has suggested that in *Paradise Regained* Milton works to lose language and poetry in silence.[1] But, while silence is one of the key effects achieved by the poem, it is, I believe, only one component in the fully formed language of Christian experience that Milton is attempting to re-create. Milton's own achievement in the poem is to restate Christian redemption in a changing definition of the terms of human existence. The recovery of paradise, he shows, is "now" effected in the renewal of Christ's sacrifice in the minds of men. This is the secret, unrecorded, and unsung story that he will sing, because it is a story that has heretofore been locked in a language we have not fully spoken.[2]

## MEANING AND POSTPONED DEFINITION

I can begin to trace the special language of *Paradise Regained* by noting a stark fact: the key terms of the poem are by and large kept inaccessible to definition, even of an ironic variety. Of course, some such inaccessibility is not surprising, because the poem is a self-declared exploration of christological mystery, "in secret done." In a poem of this kind we do not expect revelation of the meanings of Christ's redemption without a Christian struggle. But what is surprising is that the obscurity is not cleared up right through the end of the poem. Recurring terms such as *now, deeds, ends, means, time, due time, retiring, waiting, fulfilling,* seem to imply continuity, transferability, and augmentation of meaning. Individually and collectively they give the impression that a world of related meanings is gradually reaching a stage where it can be stated fully and openly. Yet the meanings do not emerge with the telling of the story. Instead, not only do *begin* and *end, act* and *wait,* and so forth, not have their usual meanings, but the poet repeatedly suggests that they remain withdrawn from referentiality as we know it.

In the very last moment of the poem, for example, the angels beckon Christ onward: "on thy glorious work / Now enter, and begin to save mankind." Nothing could seem clearer. But the action that follows on the angels' triumphal hymn immediately withdraws or displaces the ostensible meaning of their invocation:

> Thus they the Son of God our Savior meek
> Sung Victor, and from Heavenly feast refresht
> Brought on his way with joy; hee unobserv'd
> Home to his Mother's house private return'd.     [IV.634–39]

The full circle of Christ's experience in the poem begins and ends here: not with his beginning, nor with the recognition or epiphany on the tower that some critics wish to see as the poem's fitting conclusion,[3] but rather with the reconfirmation of the obscurity of Christ's existence. Clearly, *beginning* does not mean what we think it means.

A large part of the poem's materials undoubtedly creates the expectation that the moment of ripeness for Christ's beginning to act will indeed be reached, even if at the end of the poem it is postponed. The prefigured fulfillment, we feel, will be achieved, and within the measurable time of human history. Christ himself seems to say as much, and his reminders on this subject may easily be regarded as a kind of homing device that gives the poem its most obvious trajectory:

> When I was yet a child, no childish play
> To me was pleasing, all my mind was set
> Serious to learn and know, and thence to do
> What might be public good.     [I.201–204]

It is true that in the lines that follow these Christ makes clear that his "victorious deeds" (I.215) will not be of a conventional sort. Yet their public and active character, based on a process of decisive learning, never seems to be in doubt, an impression that is reinforced when the poet calls them Christ's way to begin to "publish his Godlike office now mature" (I.186–88). Indeed, Christ himself anticipates the angels' concluding hymn when, after the descent of the baptismal dove, he suggests that he

> knew the time
> Now full, that I no more should live obscure,
> But openly begin.     [I.286–88]

But what is implied by Christ's unobserved, private return home in the final lines of the poem directly contradicts the suggestions of public meaning and public beginning that punctuate the poem. The withdrawal into obscurity, we begin to realize, far from being a state that

Christ must leave behind him when he begins, is in fact the essential condition of Christ's being and his beginning both.

This protracted redefinition of *beginning* draws a coil of circular and apparently regressive meanings around the whole of Christ's enterprise. He is engaged in discovering that being in this world, even for the son of God, is somehow also withdrawal from being, withdrawal into obscurity.[4] In Milton's telling of the story, the Father avoids saying that Christ has anything at all to learn in the wilderness or from the temptations. Christ's experience, therefore, may well constitute not incremental progress toward a clearly delineated goal, but the postponement of action, the deferral of completion, which will, ultimately, in itself, somehow yield a fulfillment of the divine intention. "First I mean," the Father says,

> to exercise him in the Wilderness;
> There he shall first lay down the rudiments
> Of his great warfare, ere I send him forth
> To conquer Sin and Death the two grand foes,
> By Humiliation and strong Sufferance:
> His weakness shall o'ercome Satanic strength
> And all the world, and mass of sinful flesh.          [I.155–62]

The creative phrase here is, I think, *lay down*. This laying down, which constitutes, as it were, Christ's education in the wilderness and the beginning of his career as savior, describes a very special form of activity. It combines the determinate action of an independent agent with the passive acceptance of another's higher direction; it embodies kinetic actuality within static potentiality, the particular relation of passive to active being which seems to me to express the poem's most startling perception about human-divine relations in the Christian universe.

Christ further articulates the meaning of *to lay down* when he explains the higher virtue of regal being:

> to give a Kingdom hath been thought
> Greater and nobler done, and to *lay down*
> Far more magnanimous than to assume.
> [II.481–83; emphasis added]

There are many possible classical and Christian sources suggested by "hath been thought,"[5] but of at least equal significance with these is the form of the assertion created by its bordering alternatives. What is recommended here is not passivity as an isolated phenomenon.

Rather, what the form as a whole sets forth is withdrawal from action within a setting of active choices. The context transmutes inaction into a new kind of expressive action by enlisting it in a syntax that is its own fulfillment.

Andrew and Simon's unwitting emulation of Christ's laying down signifies a conformity to God's ways comparable to Christ's and further explicates the relationship between passive acceptance, withdrawal, or waiting, and the ultimate comprehension and serving of divine will:

> But let us wait; thus far he hath perform'd,
> Sent his Anointed, and to us reveal'd him,
> By his great Prophet, pointed at and shown,
> In public, and with him we have convers'd;
> Let us be glad of this, and all our fears
> Lay on his Providence. [II.49–54]

The context here performs the significance of *lay on* without defining it. Since the time of Christ's public appearance at the Jordan, Andrew and Simon have been actively searching for Christ everywhere,

> in each place these
> Nigh to *Bethabara*; in *Jericho*
> The City of Palms, *Aenon*, and *Salem* Old,
> *Machaerus* and each Town or City wall'd
> On this side the broad lake *Genezaret*,
> Or in *Peraea*, but return'd in vain. [II.19–24]

They have been seeking his appearance in public (II.41); expecting him to be shown again (II.13). Yet their own return to the place of Christ's showing of himself at the Jordan provides an implicit solution to their dilemma. After searching in vain, they return to the place of baptism where Christ was "so lately found, and so abruptly gone" (II.10). There they re-experience the sensations of repose that are bonded to other conditions of withdrawal and waiting and that are necessary for discovering Christ for themselves:

> Then on the bank of *Jordan*, by a Creek
> Where winds with Reeds and Osiers whisp'ring play,
>
> . . . . . . . . . . . . . . . . . . . . . .
> Thir unexpected loss and plaints outbreath'd. [II.25–29]

Without realizing it they have found an inlet moment that is simultaneously part of the continuity of time, space, and event and yet lateral to it. They have come to rest in the pause in meaning where the revelation they seek can be whispered to their inner mind. In other words, when they cease to seek Christ's public appearance, they begin to discover his coming, in themselves, in the retirement and withdrawal that spontaneously emulates Christ's movements (see II.40, 55).

What precedes the interruption of Andrew and Simon's active pursuit of Christ is their condition of intense doubt. They

> Began to doubt, and doubted many days,
> And as the days increas'd, increas'd thir doubt.    [II.11–12]

These lines surely have a straightforward psychological meaning. In the circumstances their doubt is totally natural. But the convoluted and self-referential repetition of doubt and redoubled increase of doubt suggest an accretion that goes beyond simple perplexity. It begins to point to a system of apprehension different from the one they initially comprehend. Given the subsequent course of their experience, doubting, it would seem, can be a meaningful activity in and of itself, not only intransitive and self-sustaining, but quantifiable, measurable, and capable of incremental value. Andrew and Simon's spiralling doubt comes to represent, in other words, a state of suspension from the expectation of total knowledge, an intermission from absolute comprehension that yet contributes to a sum of apprehension of a different kind. The striking parallel between their doubting and Satan's a hundred and twenty lines later—"So spake th'old Serpent doubting" (II.147)—is a hint that in some as yet unexplained way Satan's own activities involuntarily reinforce this same pattern of interrupted intellectual control, the break in mental domination that Satan, in fact, is striving to foil.

Milton gives a name to this discontinuous way of thinking about Christ's being. He calls it "thoughts / Meekly compos'd" awaiting "the fulfilling" (II.107–108). He applies this phrase to the resolution of Mary's anguish:

> But where delays he now? some great intent
> Conceals him: when twelve years he scarce had seen,
> I lost him, but so found, as well I saw
> He could not lose himself; but went about
> His Father's business; what he meant I mus'd,
> Since understand; much more his absence now
> Thus long to some great purpose he obscures.
> But I to wait with patience am inur'd;

> My heart hath been a storehouse long of things
> And sayings laid up, portending strange events.    [II.95–104][6]

Just as Christ's going about his Father's business and what it meant involve his becoming lost or absent, Mary's expectations of the prophecied fulfillment must be organized around a mental suspension, an awaiting, that is also a virtual act of mental organization, of composition or composure. Her knowledge is laid *up,* as Andrew and Simon's is laid *on* and Christ's is laid *down.* Her plaint implies the structuring of thoughts in which waiting—"But I to wait" (like Andrew and Simon's "But let us wait")—forms the indeterminate center of a meaning that is systematically located.

### DIALECTIC WITHOUT MEANS

This syntax of suspension is purposive rather than purposeful. Christ's agency is repeatedly associated with a special form of dialectic, but we do not know, as a fact, what that agency and dialectic produce. We feel this most powerfully, perhaps, when we contemplate the means whereby events occur in this story. During the course of the poem, the term *means* is gradually made to lose the sense of concrete action generally associated with it, until it seems to refer only to the instruments or means of abstract dialectic. But even in this usage of the term, there seems to be a declared absence of specified or bridged meaning.

In Milton's poem, in other words, we seem to be dealing with a language, and with a form of cosmic agency, that none of the protagonists fully comprehend. Least of all Satan: "Great acts require great means of enterprise" (II.412), he says, confident that he is stating a truism both of all action as dialectical form and of all dialectical description of reality:

> prediction still
> In all things, and all men, supposes means,
> Without means us'd, what it predicts revokes.    [III.354–56]

Satan cannot imagine any process or experience that is not tied to cause and effect. Applying to the Aristotelian rules of heroic or tragic meaning derived from Greek drama, Satan concludes that Christ must necessarily be a failure unless his purpose issues in significant *action,* unless he finds a means to his end:

> the lofty grave Tragedians taught
> In *Chorus* or *Iambic*, teachers best
> Of moral prudence, . . . . . . . . . . .
>
> . . . . . . . . . . . . . . . . . . . . . .
> Of fate, and chance, and change in human life,
> High actions, and high passions best describing.    [IV.261–66]

To which Christ answers by lauding Hebrew poetry as the purest form of literary expression, corresponding not to action, but to the static depicting of the highest conception of human life. Greek poetry, he says,

> Will far be found unworthy to compare
> With *Sion's* songs, to all true tastes excelling,
> Where God is prais'd aright, and Godlike men,
> The Holiest of Holies, and his Saints.    [IV.346–49]

The proper subject of poetry, according to Christ, is not high actions or means to ends at all. Rather, it is God's being and God's being reflected in godlike human beings, his holiest of holies. The suggested model for the superiority of the saints over the classical heroes is the holy of holies: the withdrawal (in specified ways) from high actions and high passions that bestows a Christian peace and tranquility, a Sabbath rest, on the fate, chance, and change of the pagan world.

We need not feel subversive, I think, if for a moment we wonder whether when Christ says, "but what the means, / Is not for thee to know, nor me to tell" (IV.152–53), he is engaged in a kind of divine hocus-pocus, as if his hand is quicker than Satan's eye. In Milton's account, if Christ may be said to learn or confirm anything, it is that he has nothing to learn because he somehow is or represents the knowledge he would gain. His mode of being is itself a form of knowledge, and it is inaccessible to ordinary dialectics. He is in and of himself the indescribable means that he refuses to describe. According to the terms of knowledge that the poem works to establish, Christ both bypasses action and knowledge and enacts them—in being.

In *De Doctrina* Milton wrote that "the Son . . . does not know absolutely everything, for there are some secrets [the purpose of] which the Father has kept to himself alone."[7] The Christ of *Paradise Regained* does not say whether he himself knows the Father's means. Indeed he need not, since his sacrifice of himself is the means. He saves mankind by descending into earthly body, by living obscurely and becoming lost or absent, and perhaps even by foregoing self-knowledge, as we usually conceive it. But in *Paradise Regained,* very much unlike *De Doctrina,* Milton engages in illuminating the Father's secret purposes, in quite an explicit way. The language of his Christian poem, formed according to the language of Christ's sacrificial experience, declares and tells the story that has not yet been recorded and sung. Most particularly, the poem takes the linguistic data or givens of continuous space and time and recasts them in a sacrificial form that reinterprets Christ's experience and makes it available to the theological understanding of all mankind.

### THE LANGUAGE OF DISCONTINUOUS SPACE AND TIME

In *Paradise Regained,* the functional meaning of space and time within the universe can be summoned up in two key words: "wilderness" and "now." That the wilderness is a primary focus of the entire work is obvious. Right from the start of the poem the reader knows that, by the end, Eden is to be "rais'd in the waste Wilderness" (I.7) and that the means to this end (if means there be) will be Christ's sojourn in the same wilderness. From his standpoint in eternity, the Father, as we have seen, has fixed on this wilderness as the essential locale of the narrative: "first I mean / To exercise him in the Wilderness; / There he shall first lay down the rudiments / Of his great warfare." Whereupon the poet, accenting the divine decree, announces, "He enter'd now the bordering Desert wild" (I.193), and Christ, joining in, says, "And now by some strong motion I am led / Into this Wilderness" (I.290–91).

Yet, from the beginning of the poem through to the end, the forty days of that sojourn in the wilderness are already behind Christ. In other words, despite its declared centrality, the focus of the entire narrative is kept anterior to the main body of the narration and therefore, in effect, is excluded from it. Milton's decision to follow Matthew, rather than Luke, in placing the temptations after the forty days' fast, is crucial here. Initially the wilderness interval is dressed up by Milton in all of the paraphernalia of an anticipated there and then passing into an immediate here and now. It is made to constitute the border of becoming that would seem to be dramatic being itself. But then, suddenly, it is withdrawn from us. As a completed action that is also the action of the poem, it is barred off in a grammatical tense which cannot properly be labeled either present or past. Instead, it becomes an elided action, or nonaction, on which Satan's temptations seem to ride as mere anxious footnotes.[8]

Satan, therefore, attempts futilely to draw out meanings that, we are made to understand, have already been rendered unavailable to all but a Christian form of comprehension. Satan tries his damndest to get Christ to play by agreed or at least shareable rules of being. But Christ remains continuously beyond Satan's reach because even his presence is not present. He is already somewhere else, even as he speaks, and always has been.

Christ, for example, implies the denials signified by the space he has traversed when he says to Satan,

> In the Mount
> *Moses* was forty days, nor eat nor drank,
> And forty days *Eliah* without food
> Wander'd this barren waste; the same I now.          [I.351–54]

When is or was Christ's now? Surely it is already past. And just as surely Christ means to suggest that his experience is coextensive with Moses's and Elijah's—or does he? And is it really past?

We may try to distinguish between a just past that was the forty days themselves and an actual now that is the temptations. The poet, after all, speaks of the first period in the simple past: "Full forty days he pass'd. . . . Till those days ended" (I.303–309). And Christ locates "that Fast" in the "four times ten days I have pass'd" in which he had no desire to eat and which were prelude to an important change in his condition: "But now I feel I hunger" (II.245–52). It is tempting to write off the poet's neglect of the first, largest phase of Christ's wilderness experience as a practical decision to avoid another kind of secret purpose.

But this will not do as an answer because this passage is not an isolated instance of Milton's hedging on the delineation of time and place. Throughout the poem, patterns of duration and fulfillment consistently deny the existence of any solid present. These patterns suggest that every here and now is contained in an anterior place that is the only kind of fulfilled present we can expect to find. The juxtapositions within Christ's own utterances shape a language of a displaced present, even when he himself seems only partially aware of what he is saying:

> I knew the time
> Now full, that I no more should live obscure,
> But openly begin, as best becomes

> The Authority which I deriv'd from Heaven.
> And now by some strong motion I am led
> Into this Wilderness, to what intent
> I learn not yet; perhaps I need not know;
> For what concerns my knowledge God reveals.     [I.286–93]

The time, Christ tells us quite clearly in line 287, is "*Now* full" to "openly begin." And yet, apparently, not quite now: "and *now*," Christ says in lines 290–91, "by some strong motion I am led / Into this Wilderness." "Now," Milton is suggesting, is a moment that is both past and present. Its pastness, we may say, already contained its present, and its presentness draws forward its past, thus displacing any simple present. Similarly, while at first the Father's voice pronouncing Christ his own would seem to be the self-sufficient, final, sum of all, by the end of the soliloquy a new sum has apparently been reached. By ending the first part of the soliloquy with "the Authority which I deriv'd from Heaven," Christ seems to seal off the foregoing six lines as the total datum or *factum* of the Father's voice. Yet the full syntax of the baptismal moment includes God's subsequent calling of Christ into the wilderness. The sum is now a larger sum; yet it is, by definition, still the same infinite and unchangeable sum of all with which we began. The "And now" of line 290, which at first seems to augment and extend the previous moment, melts a solidified present into another more fluid temporality and defines the substance of divine space as a physics not susceptible to the ordinary laws of addition and measurement. The earlier moment is not, finally, augmented and extended. Instead, duration and extension are eclipsed by an anterior now and a perdurable sum.

The interruption of time and space embodied in this soliloquy is pervasive in the poem. Milton may even be suggesting that it is part of the fabric of Christ's mental being. The now of wilderness existence permeates all his movements, all his thoughts, present, past, and future:

> And he still on was led, . . . with . . . thoughts
> Accompanied of things past and to come
> Lodg'd in his breast, . . .
>
> . . . . . . . . . . . . . . . . . .
> Full forty days he pass'd . . . .     [I.299–303]

Again, Christ passes his full time in a present that has already passed. His future passes into the same tense. In the same vein, the poet's adjectival use of the word "full" confirms Christ's use of full and sum to suggest that the now of fulfillment is already behind us rather than to be provided in the present or future. For reasons that are not yet made clear, the future must balk our expectations of a palpable fruition: Christ will not openly begin. He will continue to live obscure. The full forty days that are identified with fulfillment in its most complete form will be allowed no duration in the poem.

Despite this endless deferral, however, Christ need not reject the hypotheses that he will "merit . . . exaltation without . . . end" (III.196–97), that he will "reign in *Israel* without end" (II.442). For by the poem's conclusion, the phrases *without end* or *no end* signify for him not only eternity but also the replacement of dialectical resolution with transcendent stasis. "Means there shall be to this" (IV.152), he will say, thus shifting his sense toward a dialectical mediation in a new key. He does not yet acknowledge that this mediation is a form of inaction. Yet more and more it emerges that the hidden means of his dialectic is not only the wilderness, but also, quite spectacularly, the now which is always before action.

Few other words in English bind us so completely to a sense of a real present as the word *now.* Yet the effect of Milton's repetitions of this word (particularly in book one and at the beginning of book two) is to dislocate the narrative present. The repetitions suggest that the poem's meaningful present exists as a disruption of the narrative life that we take to be unbroken and immediately available.

> I who erewhile the happy Garden sung,
> By one man's disobedience lost, *now* sing
> Recover'd Paradise to all mankind.       [I.1–3]

> *Now* had the great Proclaimer with a voice
> More awful than the sound of Trumpet, cried
> Repentance.       [I.18–20]

Satan says,

> Long the decrees of Heav'n
> Delay, for longest time to him is short;
> And *now* too soon for us the circling hours
> This dreaded time have compast.       [I.55–58]

The poet again: "He enter'd *now* the bordering Desert wild" (I.193). Then Christ: "I knew the time / *Now* full, . . . *now* by some strong motion I am led" (I.286–91).
Christ again:

> In the mount
> *Moses* was forty days, nor eat nor drank,
> And forty days *Eliah* without food
> Wander'd this barren waste; the same I *now*.    [I.351–54]

And then the beautiful ending of book one:

> for *now* began
> Night with her sullen wing to double-shade
> The Desert; Fowls in thir clay nests were couch't;
> And *now* wild Beasts came forth the woods to roam.
>    [all emphases on "now" added]

A collocation of this kind suggests that Milton means to tease us out of fixed thoughts of a fictional present. In *Paradise Regained*, now is the interval of divine ripeness: in that time the poet begins to sing, the baptist proclaims, and Christ enters the wilderness—and remains and waits in the wilderness. Here we do not find the past brought to an issue. Instead, the naming of *now* is an occasion for the sliding away of time. The time that is "now full" is extraneous to the time measured by the story. As Milton uses it here, *now* acquires, instead, a frame of reference that escapes origin. The *now* that denotes the surging of Christ's divine impulse immobilizes event, place, and time. In partnership with its wilderness referent, *now* signals the unraveling of the phenomenal world and suggests the establishment of a realm of mental being independent of act.

Milton's conjuring of the special temporality in the wilderness is not without great analogues. We may think particularly of the Old Testament type of Christ's wilderness phase, Abraham's and Isaac's journey to Moriah, itself preparatory to the Old Testament type of the crucifixion, the binding of Isaac. Indeed, Erich Auerbach's memorable analysis of Abraham's and Isaac's journey in Genesis 22 can usefully be applied to Christ's wilderness sojourn as Milton presents it in *Paradise Regained*:

> The journey is like a silent progress through the indeterminate and the contingent, a holding of the breath, a process which has no present, which is inserted, like a blank duration, between what has passed and what lies ahead, and which yet is measured: three days! Three such days positively demand the symbolic interpretation which they later received.[9]

This presentation of the journey is a vivid instance, says Auerbach, of a principal characteristic of biblical narrative:

> The world of the Scripture stories is not satisfied with claiming to be a historically true reality—it insists that it is the only real world, is destined for autocracy.[10]

We recall Cassirer's statement that in Jeremiah's apparently inimitable example, "the new divine life that is here proclaimed cannot express itself without declaring everything opposed to it to be absolutely unreal."[11] In a similar way, the wilderness sojourn of *Paradise Regained* signifies total reality by a framed absence of meaning.

It would be incorrect to say, I think, that Christ gradually realizes that this is the case. Instead, his choices of action and inaction bespeak his decisive recognition, just as his uses of terms such as end, fulfillment, and due time gradually express a meaningful pattern, rather than conform to a meaning that can be separately defined. The meaning thus symbolized exhausts meaning. It is in effect terminal. Indeed, in Milton's handling of typological relations, the present, I would argue, is emptied rather than fulfilled in the antitypological moment. Christ, therefore, does not define a specific messianic function but rather revolves a series of typological equations that circumscribe it:[12]

> I again revolv'd
> The Law and Prophets, searching what was writ
> Concerning the Messiah.                    [I.259–61]

In my own search of what is here writ it emerges that the sequence of hypotheses presented is its own meaningful referent because it conforms to the Christlike postponement of realized meaning. As if to confirm this circularity in Christ's revolving activity, the poet constructs the segments of his revolutions from a combination of New Testament and Old Testament texts. The returning movement, therefore, is from Testament to Testament as well as within each Testament. On the one hand, for example, the Christ of Galatians 4:4 says he "knew the time / Now full" (I.286–87); on the other, the Christ of John 7:6 says, "My time I told thee . . . is not yet come" (III.396–97). In the combination of his statements Christ suggests that the revolving must go on and on. By implication at least, his being is in deferral. He quotes Ecclesiastes as a way of reassuring himself that he will finally merit "exaltation without change or end" (III.197): "All things are best fulfill'd in their due time, / And time there is for all things" (III.182–83). Yet he also says that due time must be left to providence (III.440). In the mood of Luke 4:8, itself revolving Deuteronomy 6:13, he acknowledges that he must "endure the time" (IV.174) that God has prescribed. This sequencing of statements acquires local meaning in relation to his wilderness journey. His earthly time, whether it is apparently before or after that journey, is of a piece with that excluded interval. Christ refers to his pre-baptismal years as the time prefixed (I.269): "The time prefixt I waited," he says, by way of contrast with "the time / Now full." But he soon discovers that all of his time on earth is a time prefixed, a time without fulfillment.

For in the course of the entire poem, visible fulfillment never comes. Palpable ends earned by palpable means never materialize. Time never falls due. This is so because the means presupposed for such conceptual, active, and temporal fulfillments are carefully excluded from the poem. Instead, all such means and ends are replaced by the wilderness. And the wilderness, in this poem, is a zone of absence.

## PATTERNS OF RETIRING

I noted earlier that in Andrew and Simon's responses to their master's disappearance the poet suggests that Christ's withdrawal into the wilderness is part of a pattern of redemptive retirement. I would now like to explore the same point with regard to the kind of temporality I have been describing. Andrew and Simon ponder:

> whither is he gone, what accident
> Hath rapt him from us? will he *now* retire
> After appearance, and again prolong
> Our expectation? God of *Israel*,
> Send thy Messiah forth, *the time is come*;
>
> . . . . . . . . . . . . . . . . .
> . . . . . he will not fail
> Nor will withdraw him *now*.     [II.39–55; emphases added]

When they ask, "will he now retire / After appearance, and again prolong / Our expectation?" (II.40–42) they have in part taken on the prophetic knowledge of an advent that is paradoxically a withdrawal. By the time they exclaim in anguish, "the time is come," their consciousness has begun to give way to the necessity for a redemptive reappearance of their Messiah in modes beyond their grasp of time. Somehow God must vindicate His glory and free His people (II.47–48). But they know not how. From across the eerie space of this poem without temporal partitions, Christ, refusing Satan in the language he

speaks to his disciples (John 7:6), more gently calls out to them: "My
time I told thee . . . is not yet come" (III.396–97). Their resigned use
of the phrase, "But let us wait" (II.49) suggests that they know as
Christians that the present must be endured. Yet they cannot yet understand that Christ's now is always one of withdrawal. No accident
has rapt him from them. He must and will withdraw him now.

Satan helps us understand the success achieved by Christ's retirement when he mocks the very disengagement from act and phenomenon that will spell his own doom. "Think'st thou," he says, feigning
contempt for the dominance of thought over act,

> to regain
> Thy right by sitting still or thus retiring?
> So did not *Maccabaeus*: he indeed
> Retir'd unto the Desert, but with arms.    [III.163–66]

Again and again he urges upon Christ not only present action but a
view of reality in which a vacuum is the most abhorrent of all things.
Satan becomes the proponent of a kind of Heraclitean fullness that is
apparently the inevitable product of allegedly interpenetrating flux. [13]

He begins this advocacy by expressing his solicitude for Christ in
the wilderness, "Of all things destitute" (II.305), and then elaborates
the idea of all things into a dependency upon the confirmation of one's
own inner being offered by the ministrations of material reality:

> Hast thou not right to all Created things . . . ?
> . . . . . . . . . . . . . . . . . . . . . . .
> Nature asham'd. . . . . . . . . . . . . . .
> . . . . . . . . . . . . hath purvey'd
> From all the Elements her choicest store.
> . . . . . . . . . . . . . . . . . . . . . .
> All these are Spirits of Air, and Woods, and Springs,
> Thy gentle Ministers, who come to pay
> Thee homage, and acknowledge thee thir Lord.    [II.324–76]

The idea of a material plenum becomes the backbone of Satan's conception of fulfillment. He would crown Christ,

> Now at full age, fulness of time, thy season,
> When Prophecies of thee are best fulfill'd.    [IV.380–81]

In the same way he arranges the storm scene not merely to unnerve
Christ by violence but to assault him with the totality of a material

reconciliation of opposites. The image pressed on Christ's flesh appears absolutely continuous:

> and either Tropic now
> 'Gan thunder, and both ends of Heav'n; the Clouds
> From many a horrid rift abortive pour'd
> Fierce rain with lightning mixt, water with fire
> In ruin reconcil'd.                    [IV.409–13]

On this level at least, Satan knows exactly what he is doing. His greeting to Christ the following morning states the thesis of his stage set:

> Fair morning yet betides thee, Son of God,
> After a dismal night; I heard the rack
> As Earth and Sky would mingle.                    [IV.451–53]

Of course, says Satan, the entire raging scene was nothing more than a child's game. But he makes clear that the iconography of his presentation is intended to remain "as a sure foregoing sign" (IV.483). There is no place for withdrawal in the real world, he insists, fearing for his very being.

What Satan senses is that Christ's retiring is at the heart of his power and his mission. He intuits the *kenosis* or self-emptying described in Philippians 2:7. Christ, says Paul, "made himself of no reputation and took upon him the form of a servant." Barbara Lewalski has discussed in detail the place of the kenosis doctrine in Milton's theology. She has also explained that the conception of *kenosis* was very much on Milton's mind when he composed *Paradise Regained*.[14] My interest here is in the formal manifestation of Christ's self-diminishing or retirement, which is clearly the focus of Satan's attention. Almost as if in response to the Pauline linkage of Christ's kenosis with the form of a servant, Satan yearns to know what the form portends. After Christ has said that his destiny is to lay down rather than to assume (II.482–83), Satan grills him to learn "the perfect shape" of his service (III.10–11).

The relation of present inaction to destined service is much on Christ's mind as well. Indeed, the implications of this relation are so much at the fore in *Paradise Regained* that sometimes they seem to leap off the page. Milton may have even consciously chosen to reinforce this impression by more or less directly associating Christ's self-consciousness with the form of a servant represented in his nineteenth

sonnet. This sonnet was discussed in chapter four, but the parallelisms
with *Paradise Regained* in theme and accent are in many ways so
striking that it is worth repeating the lines:

> When I consider how my light is spent,
> Ere half my days, in this dark world and wide,
> And that one Talent which is death to hide,
> Lodg'd with me useless, though my Soul more bent
> To serve therewith my Maker, and present
> My true account, lest he returning chide;
> "Doth God exact day-labor, light denied,"
> I fondly ask; But patience to prevent
> That murmur, soon replies, "God doth not need
> Either man's work or his own gifts; who best
> Bear his mild yoke, they serve him best; his State
> Is Kingly. Thousands at his bidding speed
> And post o'er Land and Ocean without rest:
> They also serve who only stand and wait."

In *Paradise Regained* the predicament stated at the beginning of
Christ's "holy Meditations," when he enters "now the bordering Desert
wild" (I.193–95), is formulated as follows: "O what a multitude of
thoughts at once / Awak'n'd in me swarm,"

>                         while I consider
> What from within I feel myself, and hear
> What from without comes often to my ears,
> Ill sorting with my present state compar'd.
> When I was yet a child, no childish play
> To me was pleasing, all my mind was set
> Serious to learn and know, and thence to do
> What might be public good; myself I thought
> Born to that end, born to promote all truth,
> All righteous things.                         [I.196–206]

In both passages the speaker explains that the orientation of his entire
being has been determined by an idea of divinely informed action. God
seemed to confirm that idea and even to expect a fulfillment in work
or doing or things. On the other hand, the speaker's present state,
which he knows also expresses God's will, commits him to absolute
inaction. Since he cannot believe that God is not consistent, he tries
to discover what his quandary itself can signify. In the sonnet the
answer is produced in fourteen lines. In the epic it is protracted over
some thousands and becomes one of the principal elements in the for-

mation of a universe of Christian meanings. But the formal response provided by both poems is essentially the same. In the sonnet the speaker acknowledges that the shape of divine service is acceptance of enforced retirement from the activity and fulfillment he had imagined to be his identity. The parallelism of the last two lines suggests that a servant of this kind achieves activity within passive acceptance. He achieves fulfillment through interminable postponement of self-fulfillment.

In Christ's analogous meditation the signs of initial frustration are hardly less in evidence. His verbal repetitions and variations—what from within . . . what from without; child, not childish; play, not pleasing; born to that end, born to promote; all truth, all righteous things— suggest the anxiety of a mind held in check against its first will. Coming as it does at the end of the line, "and thence to do" is virtually an outburst of frustration. Indeed, the progression of the entire passage may remind us of Herbert's *Collar.* Christ the child of God must and will conform to a kind of stillness. But at this point at least, he knows not why or when. Surely the end, he thinks, is to promote truth by deeds. Surely the time is now full to begin openly (I.286ff.). For the time being, Christ is not liberated from his perplexity. We seek for clues elsewhere.

Satan knows a good deal about Christ's form of a servant. He senses that it describes Christ's withdrawal from the materialistic plenum and that this withdrawal will somehow entail intercession on behalf of man. But the limitations of his language make it impossible for him to combine his pieces of information. He too is at a loss for answers. Why not intercede for me too, he asks? All you need do is give up your acceptance of inactivity:

> to that gentle brow
> Willingly I could fly, and hope thy reign,
> From that placid aspect and meek regard,
> Rather than aggravate my evil state,
> Would stand between me and thy Father's ire
> (Whose ire I dread more than the fire of Hell)
> A shelter and a kind of shading cool
> Interposition, as a summer's cloud.          [III.215–22]

But Christ will stand and only wait the time prefixed. That will be his action and intercession. Nothing else. When in the storm scene Satan tries to force him to relinquish his static poise and bow to reconciled ruin, Christ remains withdrawn at the eye of the turbulence, "in calm and sinless peace" (IV.424ff.). The pattern of standing (or sitting— IV.425) firm at the center of nothingness is the very form of a servant. The poet confirms this by his apostrophe to the untouchable Christ shrouded in the siege of contraries, "water with fire / In ruin recon- cil'd":

> ill wast thou shrouded then,
> O patient Son of God, yet only stood'st
> Unshaken.                                      [IV.419–21]

And the beautiful lines, "Thus pass'd the night so foul till morning fair / Came forth with Pilgrim steps in amice gray" (IV.426–27) mirror the same intercessive pattern. They insinuate the dividing, twilight moment, between night and day, that corresponds to Christ's peace at the center of Satan's hateful assault. These last lines are strikingly similar to those describing the scene of twilight peace in book four of *Paradise Lost*. There every particle of being is said to be wrapped in immaterial grandeur:

> Now came still Ev'ning on, and Twilight gray
> Had in her sober Livery all things clad.       [IV.598–99]

The moment of universal recuperation projected in both passages is in *Paradise Regained* almost at hand.


## SANCTUARY PATTERN AND HEAVENLY DOORS

The necessities of criticism that force us to build from the relatively simple to the more complex have so far caused us to neglect one of the foundations of Milton's poetic argument. As Milton manages them, the major patterns of *Paradise Regained* take their rise in one extended sacred image or scene that appears three times in book one. Near the poem's conclusion the framework of the same image recurs in a scenic design that encompasses the climax of the poem.

The first image series constitutes one of the most striking instances of repetition in all Milton's poetry. This is the itemized description of Christ's baptism at the Jordan. The first picture is drawn by the poet himself:

> on him baptiz'd
> Heaven open'd, and in likeness of a Dove

> The Spirit descended, while the Father's voice
> From Heav'n pronounc'd him his beloved Son.      [I.29–32]

Hardly fifty lines have passed before the same details are sketched again, this time by Satan. Whether by malicious intent or through ignorance, Satan omits the identity of the dove, but otherwise slightly expands the account. He adds nothing that will not be attested in the third view provided by Christ himself. Satan says,

> I saw
> The Prophet do him reverence; on him rising
> Out of the water, Heav'n above the Clouds
> Unfold her Crystal Doors, thence on his head
> A perfect Dove descend, whate'er it meant,
> And out of Heav'n the Sovran voice I heard,
> This is my Son belov'd, in him am pleas'd.      [I.79–85]

Christ explains that this scene was the naming of the now in which he waits:

> as I rose out of the laving stream,
> Heaven open'd her eternal doors, from whence
> The Spirit descended on me like a Dove;
> And last the sum of all, my Father's voice,
> Audibly heard from Heav'n, pronounc'd me his,
> Mee his beloved Son, in whom alone
> He was well pleas'd; by which I knew the time
> Now full, that I no more should live obscure,
> But openly begin, as best becomes
> The Authority which I deriv'd from Heaven.
> And now by some strong motion I am led
> Into this Wilderness, to what intent
> I learn not yet; perhaps I need not know.      [I.280–92]

What is most distinctive about these passages considered as a series is the growing emphasis on heaven as an identifiable structure that *opens* itself to send out a dove and a voice. "Heaven open'd" becomes "I saw . . . Heav'n above the Clouds / Unfold her Crystal Doors," which is then transformed to "Heaven open'd her eternal doors," whence (as the point of issue well-specified) "The Spirit descended." In the last passage we hear what we have heard before, but we hear it *in situ*: "And last the sum of all, my Father's voice, / Audibly heard from Heav'n." Milton's immediate source for his architectural elaboration upon Matthew are Psalms 24 and 78. But the warrant for his emphasis is distinctly typological. Here again Milton turns to the most typological of New Testament texts, the Epistle to the Hebrews.[15] In Hebrews 9, Christ fulfills the types of the temple ritual by bringing himself as sacrifice and, thereafter, by replacing the earthly temple with the heavenly temple of which it was a figure. Because this chapter of Hebrews was quoted earlier, it will be cited now in somewhat compressed form:

> For there was a tabernacle made . . . And after the second veil, the tabernacle which is called the Holiest of all; Which had the golden censer, and the ark of the covenant overlaid round about with gold . . . And over it the cherubims of glory shadowing the mercyseat; of which we cannot now speak particularly. Now when these things were thus ordained, the priests went always into the first tabernacle, accomplishing the service of God. But into the second went the high priest alone once every year, not without blood, which he offered for himself, and for the errors of the people: The Holy Ghost this signifying, that the way into the holiest of all was not yet made manifest, while as the first tabernacle was yet standing . . . . if the blood of bulls and of goats, and the ashes of an heifer sprinkling the unclean, sanctifieth to the purifying of the flesh: How much more shall the blood of Christ, who through the eternal Spirit offered himself without spot to God, purge your conscience from dead works to serve the living God? And for this cause he is the mediator of the new testament, . . . by means of death, for the redemption of the transgressions that were under the first testament. . . . almost all things are by the law purged with blood; and without shedding of blood is no remission. It was therefore necessary that the patterns of things in the heavens should be purified with these: but the heavenly things themselves with better sacrifices than these. For Christ is not entered into the holy places made with hands, which are the figures of the true; but into heaven itself, now to appear in the presence of God for us.

It is worth recalling Diodati's comment on the mercy seat in Exodus 25 and Hebrews 9: It "signified Christ," he says, "who with his righteousness covereth all our sins, and containeth within himself all the Churches righteousness, as the tables of the Law were inclosed under the cover: and interposeth himself as Mediator, between the Law which accuseth us, and God our Judge, as the cover was between the said Tables, and the maiestie of God which shewed it self present over the Cherubims of this Cover, as sitting upon his throne." As we noted before, Diodati points neatly to the chief structural underpinning of Hebrews 9. The mysterious phrase "of which we cannot now speak

particularly" is part of a figure of *occupatio* or *occultatio*. It is a signal
for the expansion of the mercy seat into an abstract projection of
Christ's office as mediator. Christ, the Word, stands between and above
the Cherubim. He makes "manifest" the "way into the holiest of all"
by standing between the law and the Father. The organizing theological
terms acquire a vast spatial reality: "he is the *mediator* of the new
testament, . . . by the *means* of death, for the redemption of the
*transgressions* that were *under* the first testament" (9:15; emphases
added).[16] In the invisible mediation, expressed by a half-drawn image,
is the means.

Some of the ways in which *Paradise Regained* embodies a language
of retirement, the heart of which is Christ's wilderness waiting, have
now been discussed. Milton presents the baptism and tower scenes as
redefined anticipation and fulfillment of the Christian sanctuary image,
itself a well-established symbol of rest and mediation. Before continuing to the meaning of the baptism parallels, it should be noted that
in the concluding scenes of the poem Christ is said to be the "true
Image of the Father . . . enshrin'd / In fleshly Tabernacle . . . Wan-
d'ring the Wilderness" (IV.596–600). Here, we know, he is the embodiment of the Pauline theme of edification, of transference of the
external temple structures to the inward and heavenly ones. In Milton's
conception of Sion Song, Christ is the fulfillment of the godlike man
as "Holiest of Holies" (IV.348–49). At the center of that holiest of holies,
the author of Hebrews (following Exodus 25) sees the cherubim of glory
shadowing the mercy seat. In Milton's version of the tower temptation,
we note further, the uneasy station that Satan has chosen for Christ
directly over the highest pinnacle of his Father's house (IV.549–52), is
shown to be the fulfillment of the Word's mediation in repose. The
mercy seat is the archetype of this disjoined fulfillment. In Milton's
poem the immovable surfaces of the Old Testament mercy seat become
a three-dimensional floating couch:

> straight a fiery Globe
> Of Angels on full sail of wing flew nigh,
> Who on their plumy Vans receiv'd him soft
> From his uneasy station, and upbore
> As on a floating couch through the blithe Air.    [IV.581–85]

Satan has helped Christ to the preordained place of the Word over the
holy of holies. Christ perfects the sanctuary pattern by serving only as
medium for the already written Word: "Also it is written, / Tempt not

the Lord thy God." His reply is appropriately the Old Testament Word in its New Testament fulfillment. Here the poet finds warrant for his augmentation of the narrative of the divine Word: "And Jesus answering said unto him, / It is said . . ." (Luke 4:12) plus ". . . Ye shall not tempt the Lord your God" (Deuteronomy 6:16):

> To whom thus Jesus. Also it is written,
> Tempt not the Lord thy God. [IV.560–61]

The relationship of supplementarity between the Old and New texts is extended in Milton's delineation of the space of intercession. That space is not now filled or closed. Rather it is opened toward the heavens. The mercy seat pattern is thenceforth represented as floating throughout the world, not tied to building or place.[17]

If we turn back now to the architectural elements of the baptism scene, we can see how they serve as the stimulus for the strong motion that leads Christ into the wilderness (I.290–92). That scene is itself a faithful reflection of the true image of the Father mirrored in the earthly Christ,

> remote from Heaven, enshrin'd
> In fleshly Tabernacle, and human form,
> Wand'ring the Wilderness. [IV.598–600]

In the baptism revelation we already have the first projections of the poem's propitiatory language. The baptism scene already whispers higher affiliations of the wilderness place, for we are there shown Christ in proximate relation to "heaven itself." Here a pattern of divinely ordered polarity, expressed as heavenly opening doors, is already replete with the Word that descends to Christ as his mandate and mission. That the doors are specifically propitiatory is implied by the destiny of sacrifice bound up with the Father's pronouncement. The identification is ultimately made certain in the final segment of Christ's triumph in withdrawal. I turn to that segment now.

We experience a shock of recognition when the globe of angels deposits Christ at the heart of his destined work:

> Then in a flow'ry valley [they] set him down
> On a green bank, and set before him spread
> A table of Celestial Food, Divine,
> Ambrosial, Fruits fetcht from the tree of life,
> And from the fount of life Ambrosial drink. [IV.586–90]

In this penultimate scene of *Paradise Regained* Milton has fused the

soteriological lines of his two epics. The foregoing passage places Christ
right at the center of the scene of prevenient grace described in book
eleven of *Paradise Lost*. There Adam and Eve join Christ in the moment when they begin to repair the losses incurred by their own experience of temptation. There the doors of heaven are immediately
identified with the mercy seat and with the edification of sanctified
hearts:

> Thus they in lowliest plight repentant stood
> Praying, for from the Mercy-seat above
> Prevenient Grace descending had remov'd
> The stony from thir hearts, and made new flesh
> Regenerate grow instead, that sighs now breath'd
> Unutterable, which the Spirit of prayer
> Inspir'd, and wing'd for Heav'n with speedier flight
> Than loudest Oratory . . . . . . . . . . . .
> . . . . . . . . . . . . . . . . . . . . . . .
> . . . . . . . . . . . To Heav'n thir prayers
> Flew up, nor miss'd the way, by envious winds
> Blown vagabond or frustrate: in they pass'd
> Dimensionless through Heav'nly doors.          [XI.1–17]

Christ the mediator or Interposer of *Paradise Regained* is Christ the
"great Intercessor" and Interpreter of *Paradise Lost* (see XI.19, 33).
The ambrosial fruits that are fetched from the tree of life have already
been offered preveniently, in their renewed life, in *Paradise Lost*:

> See Father, what first fruits on Earth are sprung
> From thy implanted Grace in Man, these Sighs
> And Prayers, which in this Golden Censer, mixt
> With Incense, I thy Priest before thee bring,
> Fruits of more pleasing savor from thy seed
> Sown with contrition in his heart, than those
> Which his own hand manuring all the Trees
> Of Paradise could have produc't, ere fall'n
> From innocence.          [XI.22–30]

The fruits of *Paradise Regained* spring from the wilderness of Christ's
journey. Like the life they are brought to support (momentarily) they
furnish dramatic components of a larger sacrifical image. Together they
make up the structure of mediation, sacrifice, retirement, and awaiting,
which is all the meaning, and the only act, that the poem proposes.

In *Paradise Regained* Milton acknowledges the eschatological inev-
itabilities that adhere to Christ's appearance in human form. But it is

the business of his poem to embody the essence of Christ's activity in a form that is improgressive and quietistic. In *Paradise Regained* the logos-divided form emerges as the sum of Christian knowledge. Christ's life and sacrifice are for Milton not only the arch image of that form but the medium of its continuous efficacy in the universe. In the mystery play that opens *Paradise Lost* book eleven, Christ is the shadowy Word of propitiation. In *Paradise Regained* his sacrificial mode of being becomes a propitiatory language of ongoing Christian experience.

During the course of Milton's tragic and extraordinarily coherent career, his representation of a divine intercession became a large part of his rational and imaginative life. In the spirit of his high decorum, nothing could have been more fitting than to provide a living language for this form of forms, even in his final creative hours.

# Philo's Severing Logos

The image of a dividing *logos* is undoubtedly very ancient. On the basis of early shadows cast by such an image, scholars have speculated about the forms it must have taken before its extensive appearance in Philo Judaeus (fl. A.D. 30) and about which ur-forms (reconstructed from fragments in Stoic, Pythagorean, Egyptian, and Jewish writers) may have influenced Philo.[1] For the purpose of understanding the history of a disjunctive imagination, as opposed to a conjunctive kind, the image of the dividing logos in any case takes on particular interest beginning with Philo. As far as we know, Philo is the first writer who explicitly sets this image against the prevailing symbolism of logos resolution associated with Heraclitus. Later writers, like the author of the Epistle to the Hebrews and Clement of Alexandria, found the image of the dividing logos in this antithetical orientation and proceeded, from there, to adapt it to their own uses.[2] I would now like to describe the features of Philo's logos symbolism that are most relevant to the present study.

## PHILO'S COUNTER-HERACLITEAN HARMONY

From a doctrinal point of view there is little doubt that Philo's central contribution to the evolution of Judaism and, in more dramatic ways, of Christianity is his elaborated description of the immanent logos. As the early Church Fathers continually indicated, the development of Trinitarian thought was substantially indebted to this description. In his attempt to describe a symbolism that is distinctly alternative to the symbolism of resolving opposites that he closely identified with Heraclitus, Philo's conception of the immanent logos also plays a principal role. But here the deputation of the logos is not consistently emphasized. Here what is of greatest importance to him is the explication of a pattern of cosmic symbolizing in which our dialectical perception of the present can be made to absorb an undetermined first cause.

For Philo, Heraclitus was a powerful foe who had to be faced squarely and conquered within the stronghold of his system. In the following passage from the *Quis Rerum Divinarum Heres*, Philo, as Burnet notes, gives one of the most authoritative early accounts of the fundamental thought of Heraclitus:[3]

> The two opposites together form a single whole, by the divisions of which the opposites are known. Is not this the truth which according

to the Greeks Heracleitus, whose greatness they celebrate so loudly,
put in the fore front of his philosophy and vaunted it as a new discovery?[4]

Philo's hostility is at this moment aimed at Heraclitus's and the Greeks' pretensions to having made a discovery that, in Philo's view, was long before made
clear in Scripture. That Philo also considered Heraclitus's statements a distor-
tion of this divine truth is emphasized in the *Legum Allegoriae,* in which
Heraclitus is shamefully linked to the bad man who "thinks that God is in a
place, not containing but contained." This sort of bad man, Philo explains, is
like another, "the man with an issue" (for whom "everything flows"), who

> deriving everything from the world, and making it return into the world,
> imagines that nothing has been created by God, associating himself with
> the opinion of Heraclitus in his advocacy of such tenets as "fullness and
> want," "the universe one," and "all things interchange."[5]

Few writers of antiquity lavished upon Heraclitus's formulas the unremit-
ting grain counting that Philo unhesitatingly brings to bear.[6] Nothing else, he
acknowledges, can grant so clear an understanding of the beauty of the universe
as can a consciousness of the structures of created oppositions.[7] Yet in imagining
the intersection of described opposites, Philo senses the vice-like hold of an
apparently total apprehension of reality, a reality that, in terms of human intellect, must after all be seen to revolve around an incomprehensible lacuna.
In the very process of envisioning reality, Philo believes, we must somehow
become aware of the presence, even if not of the essence, of the "God who
cannot be shewn."[8]

In his description of a divine symbolism Philo retains an Heraclitean emphasis on visualized harmony. But in opposition to Heraclitus, he insists that
such harmony is only one aspect of reality.[9] His own view of cosmic harmony
depends upon an evolution of the *logos tomeus,* which, it was believed, in
Heraclitus was not associated with a differentiated monad. Philo's logos is not
only divinely ordered *proportion* or *ratio,*[10] it is also an intervening entity that
exists on a plane of being totally removed from that of the harmonized opposites. His interpretation of sacred symbols thus negates a central aspect of the
Heraclitean world view by breaking the hold of intersective consciousness. His
symbols represent recognition of the incorporeal in the hollowed-out center,
as it were, of the corporeal.[11] The immaterial logos, he explains, stations itself
"to keep these elements apart . . . so that the universe may send forth a harmony like that of a masterpiece of literature. [It] mediates between the opponents amid their threatenings, and reconciles them." As the invisible "bond
of all existence," the logos simultaneously separates and harmonizes all opposing forms.[12] In this *discordia concors,* therefore, the effected concord is eternal
peace rather than, as for Heraclitus, perpetual warfare.

According to Philo, this structure of intervention and harmony is the very
"image of God."[13] In the same harmony, Philo locates the God of sabbatical

rest, the God of his beloved Seven: the Six of materiality plus the One of immateriality. One essential purpose of the Sabbath, he says, is that on that day the visible reality in imposed inaction "should call to mind Him who does all things invisibly."[14] Here the represented opposites do not evaporate at the fringes of mystic transport. Rather, they remain clearly imagined at the impassable borders of intervening invisibility, like the starkness of day and night, he says, at the edge of evening's pure spirit. This is the culmination of "the master art of God"[15] that he would teach. It is an art in which the life of symbolic consciousness, as he believed Heraclitus conceived it, is austerely deferred.

PHILO'S CHOICE OF TEXTS

Philo's presentations of his intervened symbol are set out in his discussions of two principal texts. First is the sacrificial symbolizing of Genesis 15, in which God first seals His covenant with Abram and his seed. This is the so-called Covenant Between the Halves in which the Land is promised to Abram's descendants through Isaac, yet unborn:

> 8   And [Abram] said, Lord God, whereby shall I know that I shall inherit it?
> 9   And he said unto him, Take me an heifer of three years old, and a she goat of three years old, and a ram of three years old, and a turtledove, and a young pigeon.
> 10   And he took unto him all these, and divided them in the midst, and laid each piece one against another: but the birds divided he not.

Here Philo finds the paradigm for inheritance of divine creation and divine knowledge. His treatment of the text makes clear his view that true symbolizing is the arrangement of material reality into the representation of an immaterial truth. Symbolizing of this kind, he believes, is at the heart of God's activity in creation. Israel's fulfillment of divine destiny, in the same view, must also partake of a kind of phenomenal symbolizing, one that always points to an invisible reality. This pattern of presentation, Philo shows us, is projected by God Himself through the intercessory logos sent to Abram. Thus the pattern that governs the relations among earthly existents also governs the relations of Heavenly to earthly: "To His Word, His chief messenger, highest in age and honour, the Father of all has given the special prerogative, to stand on the border and separate the creature from the Creator. This same Word both pleads with the immortal as suppliant for afflicted mortality and acts as ambassador of the ruler to the subject." The "he" of verse ten is for Philo God Himself dividing and harmonizing through His Severer. Here God discloses the symbolism of the physical universe.

This is the explanation that, as we saw in chapter four, Grotius cited liberally in his commentary on Hebrews. In this verse, Philo believes, Scripture wishes us to think of God who cannot be shewn, as severing through the Severer of all things, that is his Word, the whole succession of things material and immaterial whose natures appear to us to be knitted together and united. That severing Word whetted to an edge of utmost sharpness never ceases to divide. . . . So it divided each of the three in the middle, the soul into rational and irrational, speech into true and false, sense into presentations, where the object is real and apprehended, and presentations where it is not. These sections He at once placed "opposite to each other." [But] the birds He left undivided, for incorporeal and divine forms of knowledge cannot be divided into conflicting opposites. . . .

The half-pieces of the three animals . . . . divided into two made six altogether and thus the Severer, the Word, who separates the two sets of three and stationed himself in their midst, was the seventh.[16]

By the bonding of the divine Word, Abram is promised that the in-gathered people will inhabit the Land that must henceforth be whole and sanctified. The fire consecration of the undivided center completes a symbolizing pattern of incorporeal intervention. In that pattern we are meant to identify both the consummation and the preservation of a process of symbolic knowing that is, on one side, as omnipresent as the unknowable nature of the Creator Himself, and, on the other, as universal as the shape of created reality and the highest mode of human intelligence.

That the envisaging and representation of this symbolizing are for Philo the highest of human intellectual activities is made apparent in his discussion of his second principal exemplum of the intervented symbol. This text, in Exodus 25, presents the blueprint for God's specified resting place and framed self-presentation within earthly existence:

20   And the cherubims shall stretch forth their wings on high, covering the mercy seat with their wings, and their faces shall look one to another; toward the mercy seat shall the faces of the cherubims be.

21   And thou shalt put the mercy seat above upon the ark; and in the ark thou shalt put the testimony that I shall give thee.

22   And there I will meet with thee, and I will commune with thee from above the mercy seat, from between the two cherubims.

The symmetry and mediation thus rendered are for Philo starkly vivid. "The divine Logos, inasmuch as it is appropriately in the middle," he says, "fills all things and becomes a mediator and arbitrator for the two sides which seem to be divided from each other . . . for it is always . . . the artisan of peace." One sees this, he says, "if one can accurately view and understand" in the description of the cherubim and "directly above them, in their midst, the voice and the Logos and, above it, the Speaker. . . . He who is elder than the one and the monad and the beginning."[17]

In this passage, as elsewhere, Philo emphasizes the accompaniment of the logos (or of God without the logos) by the two cherubim who represent, as he puts it, "the primary Potencies of the Existent, namely that through which He wrought the world, the beneficent, . . . and that by which He rules and commands what He made, that is the punitive, [both] separated by God Himself standing above and in the midst of them."[18] In this description, and in the similar account of the seraphim in Isaiah 6:1–2, Philo once again distinguishes a way of imagining divine reality in a process that first embraces the cosmic symbol of Heraclitus and then proceeds a bold step further.[19] This, I would suggest, is the symbolic significance of the vision of God separating the Potencies that, as Goodenough notes, dominates all Philo's writings.[20]

Philo's visualizing was a symbolic method in which the comprehension and representation of the divided forces of existence—those embracing earthly "recognition and full knowledge"[21]—were always accompanied by the higher knowledge granted by the intervented symbol as a whole. Philo, like Heraclitus, feels powerfully the fullness of the divine *discordia concors*. But for Philo the central fullness is necessarily a realm beyond imagination. Goodenough points out that where Heraclitus "taught that reality was a unity of underlying opposites," Philo's parallel account differs "always in the essential particular that [the bond between the opposites] was never an inherent aspect of the material opposites or of their common original nature"[22] Whereas for Heraclitus every object, every act of symbolic perception, and every representation of such perception, are apparently all immediate, for Philo they must be both intervented and supermediated, either by God's intellect or our own. For Philo the mercy seat is a true symbol because it represents in the "theological sense, . . . a mind which is gracious to itself and feels the duty of repressing and destroying with the aid of knowledge the conceit which in its love of vanity uplifts it in unreasoning exaltation and puffs it with pride."[23] The conceit that Philo attacks is closely related to an alleged Heraclitean hold on interfused reality.[24] At the center of Philo's symbol there is always the invisible bond of peace or Sabbath Seventh. By the human mind this bond is to be represented as the recession that creates sustained meaning in the continuum of existents.

# APPENDIX B

## The Logos Medium of Bonaventure's *Itinerarium*

In the tradition of religious meditation that informs seventeenth-century poetry, the classic contemplation of the intervented design of the mercy seat is the *Itinerarium Mentis in Deum* of St. Bonaventure. The centrality of the *Itinerarium* among meditative models has long been recognized and its relevance to Milton's intellectual milieu has been suggestively described by Louis Martz.[1] In the following pages I would like to highlight the structural features of the *Itinerarium* that are pertinent to the tradition of thought studied in this book. Specifically, I want to show how Bonaventure creates an extensive symbolism that includes the intervention of a transcendent principle.

### BONAVENTURE AND THE COINCIDENCE OF OPPOSITES

Ewert H. Cousins has recently pointed out that Bonaventure interprets the propitiatory image according to the logos christology that he derived to a great extent from the early Greek Fathers, particularly from Clement of Alexandria and Origen.[2] Cousins's commentary on these matters provides an excellent introduction to our particular concerns. Bonaventure, he explains, sees a reality of universal oppositions in the mercy seat symmetrically watched over by the cherubim and in the symmetrical six wings of the seraph or cherub itself. For all these symmetries or opposites of being, Christ the Word is the mediator, center, or medium. Cousins suggests that the controlling form implied by Bonaventure is a "coincidence of opposites" located in the incarnate Word. Although he applies the Cusanian term to the *Itinerarium*, Cousins differentiates Nicholas of Cusa's *coincidentia oppositorum* from Bonaventure's in a significant way. For the purposes of this differentiation, as well as for our own discussion, Cousins's description of what he calls "three architectonic models of the coincidence of opposites" is extremely helpful:

> In the first, unity swallows up difference; opposites coincide to such an extent that they become one—in a unity where they no longer exist as opposites. This is a monistic view, in which opposites are judged either to be an illusion or to be transcended in an undifferentiated unity. . . .
> In the second class, that of difference, opposition remains; but there is no genuine coincidence. The opposites persist as opposites to such

an extent that they achieve no real union. They coincide only by repel-
ling or opposing each other or at the most by mere juxtaposition. . . .

With regard to this second class, Cousins notes that, "although the Incarnation
affirms a coincidence of God and creation . . . the Christian tradition shares
with the [Jews and Muslims] the basic sense of God's transcendence and the
opposition between God and creation. This theme has been strongly stressed
at times in Christian history, for example in Calvin."

Cousins completes his classification in the following way:

> In the third framework, that of unity and difference, opposites genuinely
> coincide while at the same time continuing to exist as opposites. They
> join in a real union, but one that does not obliterate differences; rather
> it is precisely the union that intensifies the difference. The more inti-
> mately the opposites are united, the more they are differentiated. I call
> this a coincidence of mutually affirming complementarity.[3]

In Nicholas, Cousins finds a combination of "a monistic coincidence and one
of mutual complementarity," while Bonaventure, he believes, falls squarely and
consistently within the class of mutual complementarity. This, he explains, is
because Bonaventure is committed to an emanation model, derived from the
Greek Fathers, that emphasizes "the fecundity and dynamism of the Father in
the Trinitarian processions," whereas Nicholas is "much more interested in the
Trinity as a mystery of unity and diversity. . . . This produces a significant
difference in the coincidence of opposites. In Bonaventure the dynamic coincidence of opposites predominates, that is, the coincidence of emanation and
return; however in Nicholas the more static coincidence of unity and plurality
predominates."[4]

Cousins's distinction between Nicholas's and Bonaventure's ways of envisioning the opposites and their medium leads to an extremely helpful way of
understanding the mercy-seat structure of the *Itinerarium*—a way that Cousins himself does not choose to follow to its full implications. To say that in
Bonaventure's view, as Cousins puts it, the "opposites genuinely coincide" and
"join in a real union" leaves a less accurate impression of the *Itinerarium*, I
believe, than to say that, following the logos christology of Clement and Origen,
Christ the intervening medium serves as the dynamic ground of "emanation
and return." Thus the "real union" in which the opposites "genuinely coincide"
in the logos is both coincidence and non-coincidence, because one aspect of
the dynamic logos exists on a different metaphysical plane from the opposites
it mediates. In that sense the opposition between transcendence and immanence that Cousins restricts to his second class of coincidence of opposites is
also to be found in the usages of the *Itinerarium*. It is significant that an
emphasis on the incarnation which would break down this opposition is not yet
paramount in this, the major work of Bonaventure's middle period. As Cousins
acknowledges, that emphasis belongs to the final phase of Bonaventure's chris-

tology, represented by the *Collationes in Hexaemeron.* The logos who mediates the opposites in the *Itinerarium* is more of the soul than of matter and
history.[5] He is a transcendent center, though his dynamism also implies the
emanation and return of creation. In the *Itinerarium,* therefore, Bonaventure's
logos christology strongly suggests Clement's model of a separating logos which
itself transcends the opposites that it mediates.

Bonaventure by no means shows a Calvinist tendency to differentiate totally
between the transcendent and the immanent; still less does he bypass the
incarnation for the crucifixion after the manner of seventeenth-century Puritanism.[6] But the structure of the *Itinerarium* derives from the same logos
models of the early Greek Fathers that stand behind Calvin and the Puritans.
Indeed, I would now like to show that the final stage of the *Itinerarium* is an
expression of the logos christology that envisions transcendent division between
the opposites.

## THE TRANSCENDENCE WITHIN

"It seemed good to divide this work into seven chapters," Bonaventure remarks
in the Prologue to the *Itinerarium,*[7] yet virtually every commentator has read
it as if it contained, in effect, only six. Because the seventh chapter deals with
"transcending yourself and all things," it has been thought inaccessible to formal
analysis. Its motive force has seemed unconnected with the rational Christian
philosophy of the first six chapters. This impression is undoubtedly reinforced
by the art of the Seraphic Doctor himself. Bonaventure avoids any suggestion
that his journey incorporates in its own duration the equivalent of an *arrival*
in God. If his art does somehow succeed in creating a totality beyond the
structures of the first six chapters, such success, he clearly believed, is in any
case best left unproclaimed, as the border between art and grace is better left
unmarked. And yet the self-described "seventh Minister General" does specify
in the Prologue the discipline that embraces the full seven stages of the *Itinerarium*:

1. In the beginning
I call upon the First Beginning,
from whom
all illuminations descend
as from the *Father of Lights,*
from whom
comes *every good and every perfect gift.*

I call upon the Eternal Father
through his Son, our Lord Jesus Christ,
that through the intercession of the most holy Virgin Mary,
the mother of the same God and Lord Jesus Christ,

and through the intercession of blessed Francis,
                our leader and father,
        he *may enlighten the eyes* of our soul
                *to guide our feet*
            *in the way of* that *peace*
        *which surpasses all understanding.*

            This is the peace
        proclaimed and given to us
          by our Lord Jesus Christ
        and preached again and again
            by our father Francis.

At the beginning and end of every sermon he announced peace;
        in every greeting he wished for peace;
    in every contemplation he sighed for ecstatic peace—
        like a citizen of that Jerusalem of which
                that Man of Peace says,
        who *was peaceable with those who hated peace:*
            *Pray for the peace of Jerusalem.*

For he knew that the throne of Solomon would not stand
                except in peace,
                since it is written:
        *In peace is his place and his abode in Sion.*

2. Following the example of our most blessed Father Francis, I was seeking this peace with panting spirit—I a sinner and utterly unworthy who after our blessed father's death had become the seventh Minister General of the Friars. It happened that about the time of the thirty-third anniversary of the Saint's death, under divine impulse, I withdrew to Mount La Verna, seeking a place of quiet and desiring to find there peace of spirit. While I was there reflecting on various ways by which the soul ascends into God, there came to mind, among other things, the miracle which had occurred to blessed Francis in this very place: the vision of a winged Seraph in the form of the Crucified. While reflecting on this, I saw at once that this vision represented our father's rapture in contemplation and the road by which this rapture is reached.

3. The six wings of the Seraph can rightly be taken to symbolize the six levels of illumination by which, as if by steps or stages, the soul can pass over to peace through ecstatic elevations of Christian wisdom. There is no other path but through the burning love of the Crucified.[8]

The impression of sufficiency created by the six stages is strong. But the first and third sections of the Prologue make clear that they are themselves bounded by the Father's emanation in his Word and by the return of the sacrificed Word. That return is the "way" to peace. As the reenactor of Francis's vision of the crucifixion, Bonaventure journeys toward the peace that is the goal of the entire treatise. Everything else is subordinate to this intercession and recession. The extent of this subordination in the quotation is greater than may at first appear. All our intellectual steps up the difficult grade are only preparation for the way of that peace which surpasses all understanding and which is identified with the prime mover of all intermediate apprehension.

The art of the exordium consists of a series of equations that locate the space of the peace that exists beyond life and death, without attempting to explain it. Thirty-three years after the passing (*transitum*) of Francis, whose life was peace and who succeeded in finding ultimate peace, the seventh Minister General, whose vision is in seven parts, ascended the Mount of the quiet place in search of the peace that is the Mount of Jerusalem, the peace of Zion. The top of that Tuscan Mount, which is now the place in which we hear of the ascent, is also the place of transfiguration where Francis received the stigmata, as *"after six days* . . . Christ *led his disciples up a mountain and was transfigured before them"*[9]—in his thirty-third year. When we have passed into "peace through ecstatic elevations," or when we are capable of discerning within the six gradations of the Seraph the road by which we come to the rapture in contemplation, we will have already, as it were, crossed unawares the Alps of meditation. We will then have journeyed, Bonaventure tells us in the first chapter, to the quiet of contemplation ("ad quietem contemplationis") through the six levels of meditation that bring us to perfecting wisdom: "ad *scientiam illuminantem,* et hoc in meditatione; ad *sapientiam perficientem,* et hoc in contemplatione."[10]

Bonaventure's procedure in the *Itinerarium* is to raise meditation toward the condition of contemplation, and toward contemplation's ultimate goal— repose. He explains that "no one comes to contemplation except by penetrating meditation,"[11] and that in the course of the *Itinerarium* we must make our approach through the six stages of meditation described in chapters one to six. It is clear that even at the start we must already be standing with him on the summit of the Mount. Without that prevenient repose no other commencement would be possible.

Thus contemplation is more than the goal of meditation. It is also the gracious or mediatory activity that makes possible the dialectical procedures of meditation itself. From this point of view, the goal of the *Itinerarium* is to raise to a level of human self-consciousness the concept of Christian peace that is the condition of Christian contemplation. Bonaventure creates this theological self-awareness by marshaling his concepts of *reductio, abstractio,* and *contuitio;* and, correlatively, by elaborating the philosophical metaphor *speculatio.* From the scaffolding of imagined symmetries, Bonaventure erects the framework of his philosophical concepts. This framework is conceived in the nature of a wedge whose two sides meet not in a material convergence but in a dimensionless line of division. The activity pursued in this framework, in other words, is to locate, in chapter seven, a meaningful abstraction that is integrally related to its satellite conceptions yet is in no way contingent upon them.

The philosophical method of the first six chapters is differentiated from that of the seventh even in the titles that Bonaventure devised "so that," he tells us, "their contents may be the more easily understood." After the Prologue the treatise is headed by the subtitle "Incipit Speculatio Pauperis in Deserto," and then all but the seventh chapter are introduced by a descriptive formula including the phrase "de speculatione." More than that, the words speculatio and speculum recur throughout the treatise in multiform ways. Bonaventure "seems haunted," as George Boas puts it, "by the basic metaphor of the universe's being a sort of mirror . . . in which God is to be seen."[12] We earlier suggested that Bonaventure's apparent repetitiveness in the Prologue anticipates the final goals of the treatise. When in the close of the same Prologue, the language of speculatio echoes all around us, we know that something of great interest to our journey is afoot: "speculationes subiectas propono, insinuans, quod parum aut nihil est speculum exterius propositum, nisi speculum mentis nostrae tersum fuerit et politum."[13] The language of the mirror is used throughout the first six chapters of the treatise, until finally, in the first section of the seventh chapter, we learn that the contemplation of the mirror (*speculetur; speculando*) must now be abandoned:

> when finally in the sixth stage
> our mind reaches that point
> where it contemplates
> in the First and Supreme Principle
> and in the *mediator of God and men,*
> Jesus Christ, those things whose likenesses can in no way be found
> in creatures
> and which surpass all penetration
> by the human intellect,
> it now remains for our mind,
> by contemplating these things,
> to transcend and pass over not only this sense world
> but even itself.[14]

What is the nature, and what are the limits, of this kind of speculative vision? Bonaventure hints at an answer in chapter four when he asks how it is that "when it has been shown / that God is so close to our souls / that so few should be aware / of the First Principle within themselves?"—"tam paucorum est in se ipsis primum principium *speculari.*"[15] His answer is that the mind, "lying totally in these things of sense / . . . cannot reenter into itself / as into the image of God"; not until, that is, by "the reformation of the image, through the theological virtues, through the delights of the spiritual senses and through mystical ecstasies" our "spirit has been made hierarchical."[16] The apex of this hierarchy is an image beyond creaturely imagination: "the *mediator of God and men.*" The activity of speculatio, of the first six chapters, seeks to effect this reformation of the image as a precondition of the mediation or passover to be achieved in the seventh chapter.

How speculatio can effect this reformation is understood when we grasp that the mirror language of the treatise is itself constituted by the essential principles of Bonaventure's epistemology. These are duly recorded in the first six stages of the ascent. To begin with, Bonaventure's conception of sensation is itself formulated as part of a denial of the possibility of restrictively objective knowledge. As such it participates in the similar denial that characterizes the philosophical tradition stretching from Plato to Kant. "The external sensibles," Bonaventure asserts, enter the senses only by a reduction: "not through their substance, but through their likenesses, which are first produced in the medium; and from the medium they enter into the organ and from the exterior organ into the interior organ and from this into the apprehensive faculty."[17] It is our power of judgment, Bonaventure explains, that subsequently

> causes the sensible species, received in a sensible way through the senses, to enter the intellective faculty by a process of purification and abstraction. . . . . [In this] is power flowing not from images of the imagination but from the truth of apprehension. . . . Judgment takes place through our reason abstracting from place, time and mutability, and thus from dimension, succession and change.[18]

For Bonaventure, all forms of human knowledge, both internal (psychological) and external, are spiritualized by these processes of reduction and abstraction, so that the objective data we collect concerning an object in its medium, under one kind of glass as it were, is also partly a reflection of a subjective disposition stored up or implanted under a different glass. As a consequence, all our best earthly knowledge is speculative. It consists of an oscillation between external and internal mirrors.

Bonaventure's conception of ideas, as Etienne Gilson has emphasized, is always a matter of *ut regulans et motiva.* In other words, where Bonaventure tends toward Aristotle's empiricism in maintaining that all our knowledge begins with the senses, he cleaves closer to a version of Plato's Idealism and innatism in stressing the active role of intellect in assimilating the data first generated by sensibles. Gilson has shown that in Bonaventure's development of his conception of the apprehending intellect he adopted what he considered to be Augustine's view that there is "a direct action of the divine ideas upon our thought which yet does not imply the perception of these ideas." For Bonaventure the result is that "in our acquisition of principles there is something innate, but the principles themselves are not such."[19] This is what lies behind Bonaventure's insistence in the *Itinerarium* that "those laws by which we judge with certainty . . . sensible things . . . are infallible and cannot be doubted by the intellect of the one who apprehends them, since they are as if ever present and cannot be erased from the memory of the one who recalls them."[20]

Gilson has further explained that for Bonaventure "a superior faculty must interpose to give the soul the reflective consciousness of its faculty of sensation" and to produce, thereby, a "genuine stream of thought." Gilson points out that in Bonaventure's view the principles within the mind must "organize the multiplicity of our sensible experiences, directing them towards fixed centres, the simple or universal first principles of knowledge or ethics" and that, accordingly, for Bonaventure the process of abstraction necessarily implies "the intervention of the eternal principles and of God." This intervention of the transcendent is of particular interest in the *Initiarium*, though it is at first extremely difficult to pinpoint. Gilson remarks, for example, that "the careful reader will find express confirmation of this in the *Itinerarium*," but he does not himself locate such confirmation. He does the next best thing, however, when he notes that, in the epistemology exemplified by the *Itinerarium*, abstraction must itself give way to contuition—to the "indirect apprehension by thought of an object which itself eludes us, the presence of which is in some way implied in that of the effects which follow from it."[21] In various ways, Bonaventure's use of contuition is at the heart of the seventh and final stage of the *Itinerarium*, where it is clearly identified with peace itself.

The achievement of peace or recession in contuition is embodied, I suggest, in the larger symbolic form into which the local symbols of the *Itinerarium* are fitted. This embracing form is outlined in the following passages from the beginning and end of the seventh chapter (a small part of which we cited earlier):

> 1. We have, therefore, passed through
> these six considerations.
> They are like
> the six steps of the true Solomon's throne,
> by which we arrive
> at peace,
> where the true man of peace
> rests in a peaceful mind
> as in the interior Jerusalem.
>
> They are also like
> the six wings of the Seraph
> by which the mind of the true contemplative
> can be borne aloft,
> filled with the illumination of heavenly wisdom.

They are also like the first six days,
in which the mind has been trained so that it may reach
the sabbath of rest.

After our mind has beheld God
outside itself
through his vestiges and in his vestiges,
within itself
through his image and in his image,
and above itself
through the similitude of the divine Light shining above us
and in the Light itself,
insofar as this is possible in our state as wayfarers
and through the exercise of our mind,
when finally in the sixth stage
our mind reaches that point
where it contemplates
in the First and Supreme Principle
and in the *mediator of God and men,*
Jesus Christ,
those things whose likenesses can in no way be found
in creatures
and which surpass all penetration
by the human intellect,
it now remains for our mind,
by contemplating these things,
to transcend and pass over not only this sense world
but even itself.
In this passing over,
Christ is the *way and the door;*
Christ is the ladder and the vehicle,
like the Mercy Seat placed above the ark of God
and the *mystery hidden from eternity.*

2. Whoever turns his face fully to the Mercy Seat
and with faith, hope and love,
devotion, admiration, exultation,
appreciation, praise and joy
beholds him hanging upon the cross,
such a one makes the Pasch, that is, the passover,
with Christ.

6. . . . if you wish to know how these things come about,
ask grace not instruction

.   .   .   .   .   .   .   .   .   .   .   .   .   .   .   .   .   .   .   .   .

> not light but the fire
> that totally inflames and carries us into God
> by ecstatic unctions and burning affections.
> This fire is God,
> and *his furnace is in Jerusalem*

. . . . . . . . . . . . . . . . . . . . . .

> Let us, then, die
> and enter into the darkness;
> let us impose silence
> upon our cares, our desires and our imaginings.
> With Christ crucified
> let us pass *out of this world to the Father*

. . . . . . . . . . . . . . . . . . . . . .

> Let us rejoice with David saying:
> *My flesh and my heart have grown faint;*
> *You are the God of my heart,*
> *and the God that is my portion forever.*[22]

Bonaventure suggests that we have reached the present moment by juxtaposing the data gleaned from ascending through three symmetrical sets of investigations. Those investigations are presented as pairs of facing mirrors, each of which in itself constitutes a mode of image reformation achieved by reduction and abstraction. The mind beheld God outside itself—"mens nostra contuita est Deum *extra se*"—

> through his vestiges and in his vestiges,
> within itself
> through his image and in his image,
> and above itself
> through the similitude of the divine Light shining above us
> and in the Light itself.[23]

The structure of the ascending symmetry symbolized by the wings of the Seraph is replaced in the fifth and sixth chapters by a parallel juxtaposition in the paired cherubim over the propitiatory. In the sixth chapter Bonaventure directs that "the eye of our intelligence . . . be raised" or prepared to contuit— "ad contuitionem"—"the most blessed Trinity, / so that the second Cherub [Good] / may be placed alongside the first [Being]."[24]

In the seventh chapter, finally, the separate acts of imperfect knowing aggregate around a recognition of the intervention or repose that in itself has no likeness, no mirror image, and yet gives being to all creation. The space of exception all along implicit between the enclosing wings of the Seraph now opens into the *"mystery hidden from eternity,"* the unseen space at the center of the propitiatory. The six mirrors of the stairway ascent ("scala") have now become the dialectical sides of the vehicle that locates God's intervention in earthly being.

In the final stages of the *Itinerarium* human rationality achieves more than rational knowledge by acknowledging its incomplete status. In the seventh chapter the contemplating mind enters into the phase of repose toward which the processes of speculation and contuition, and with them the structure of the *Itinerarium*, have been promoting it. All along, implicitly, that mind has been learning to acknowledge the speculative nature of its knowledge; and it has been growing accustomed to a shuttle existence in the gulf or passage between imperfect apprehensions. In the *Hexaemeron*, Bonaventure would later write that "when the center of a circle has been lost, it can be found only by two lines intersecting at right angles."[25] In the *Itinerarium*, the center is less palpable than such intersection may imply. Here the relocated centerpoint is without dimension. Its transcendent nature is suggested by the unfilled propitiatory mid-space. Here the final preparation for transcendent illumination is completed in the ascent to the sixth mirror vision in the sixth section of the sixth chapter. This is the vision of the framing cherubs that look to transcendence itself:

> look at the Mercy Seat and wonder
> that in Christ
> personal union exists
> with a trinity of substances and a duality of natures;
> that complete agreement exists
> with a plurality of wills;
> that mutual predication of God and man exists
> with a plurality of properties;
> that coadoration exists
> with a plurality of excellence,
> that coexaltation above all things exists
> with a plurality of dignity;
> that codomination exists
> with a plurality of powers.[26]

Thereafter, in the next—last—section of the sixth chapter, the contemplator already begins his passage through the center of conceptualized symmetries. The mind exceeds its own ideas or forms in a grace that is indeed snatched from beyond the reach of conventional art. The dynamic symbol thus created is one of paschal sacrifice, intervention, passage, and repose. It includes both our awareness of the data that are known and our recognition of the data that are known to be unknown:

> it [the mind] now reaches something perfect.
> It reaches the perfection of its illuminations
> on the sixth stage,

> as if with God on the sixth day of creation;
> nor does anything more remain
> except the day of rest on which
> through mystical ecstasy
> the mind's discernment comes to rest
> *from all the work which* it *has done.*[27]

In the last lap of the journey, "the mind's discernment comes to rest" and rest becomes the mind's discernment. As foretold in the Prologue, now "the way" is only through "burning love of the Crucified": Whoever

> turns his face fully to the Mercy Seat
> and with faith, hope and love,
> devotion, admiration, exultation,
> appreciation, praise and joy
> beholds him hanging upon the cross,
> such a one makes the Pasch, that is, the passover,
> with Christ.[28]

In this passover, the vision of Christ is presented as "the way and the door" ("via et ostium")[29] because the previously intuited intersection of the scale or scales of being is now opened by transcendent intervention. This intervention is rendered in the *Itinerarium* by the propitiatory space between and above the cherubim. Through this midpoint between all symmetries, says Bonaventure, the divine furnace leads to the peace of Jerusalem. Flesh and spirit, matter and angelic energy, melt away from the center of repose. But this recession is not a mystical obliteration. Rather, it is an integral function of the logos that reflects the Father's transcendence by separating the opposites of being. In Bonaventure's christology this separation is effected in paschal sacrifice and repose. The intercession of the Word, which is located yet remains unimaginable and incomprehensible, makes all other imagination and knowledge possible.[30]

## APPENDIX C

# Coleridge, Baxter, and the Poetics of Trichotomy

Coleridge's search for an imagination that could transcend its own images was not restricted to Milton's poems, although Milton was for him the great exemplar of such imagination. In the writings of Milton's Puritan contemporary, Richard Baxter, for example, Coleridge carried out an investigation that is closely analogous to his scrutiny of Milton. In the following pages I would like to reconstruct the terms and results of that investigation, since they seem to me strongly suggestive of the meanings Coleridge believed he had found in Milton.[1] I will then proceed to Baxter's texts themselves. I propose to show that Coleridge was more right about Baxter than he knew. Particularly in *The Saints Everlasting Rest*, we find a segregative imagination that is highly compatible with Milton's dividing muse.

### THE QUEST FOR PROTHESIS

Coleridge was certain that Baxter had found a way to escape the delusive effects of a dialectic of contraries. Coleridge describes these effects in his *Logic* as follows:

> Dichotomy, or the primary Division of the Ground into Contraries, is the necessary form of reasoning, as long as and wherever the intelligential faculty of Man weens [sic] to possess within itself the center of it's [sic] own system; and vice versa. . . . The adoption of Dichotomy under the supposition of it's being the legitimate and only form of distributive Logic, naturally excites, and seems to sanction the delusive conceit of Self-sufficiency.[2]

The philosophical means for escaping such dichotomy, Coleridge announces, was first proposed by Baxter. Coleridge argues that Baxter not only anticipated Kant's triadic distribution of the categories of thought, but that Baxter saw clearly, as Kant did not, the separateness and anteriority of the source term:

> I cannot doubt, but that the merit of substituting Trichotomy for the then, and alas! the still prevailing Method of Dichotomy, which forms the prominent excellence in Kant's Critique of the pure reason, belongs to R. Baxter, a century before the publication of Kant's Work. Nay, it appears that the claim of our Countryman rests on a stronger as well

as older plea. For Baxter *grounds* the necessity of Trichotomy, as the
Principle of Real Logic, on an absolute Idea presupposed in all intelli-
gential Acts: whereas Kant adopts it merely as a fact of Reflection.[3]

Coleridge emphasizes the absolute Idea that forms the logical and theological
keystone of Baxter's trichotomy, just as it does, he suggests, in "the Pythagorean
*Tetractys,* i.e. the eternal Foundation or Source of Nature." The absolute Idea
of transcendent unity is indivisible. Yet it is at the heart of all division, both
in our conceptualization of reality and in the emanation of reality itself:[4]

> this being sacred to contemplation of Identity, and prior in order of
> Thought to *all* division, is so far from interfering with Trichotomy as the
> universal form of Division (more correctly of distinctive Distribution in
> Logic) that it implies it. Prothesis being by the very term anterior to
> thesis can be no part of it—thus in

Prothesis

Thesis           Antithesis

Synthesis

> we have the Tetrad indeed in the intellectual and intuitive Contempla-
> tion; but a Triad in discursive Arrangement and a Tri-unity in Result.[5]

It may be tempting to suppose that this schematization is equivalent to the
model of reconciled contraries in the fourteenth chapter of the *Biographia.*
But there is something else here. In this account the Prothesis of logic and the
transcendent monad to which it corresponds do not merge with ("can be no
part of") the dialectics that they generate.

To understand Coleridge's conception of trichotomy and to be able to apply
it to Baxter's Puritan imagination, we should note that Coleridge identified two
distinct Neoplatonic conceptions of the One. In his view these conceptions
correspond to two different stages in human consciousness. Coleridge here
anticipates the account of the two kinds of Neopythagorean One that E. R.
Dodds presented in 1928. Dodds showed that, for the Neopythagorean schools
of the first centuries of the common era, there was both an absolutely transcendent One and a One that is the principle of everything and contains everything in itself.[6] Coleridge's manuscript note on the same point, first printed by
Brinkley in 1955, describes both the Neopythagorean sources and the philosophical filaments that stretch from them to the Anti-Nicene Fathers and to
the seventeenth century. As part of his planned exposition of Baxter's contribution, Coleridge tells us, he hopes to expound

> the equality asserted by the Pythagorean School of the Tetractys and
> the Triad—namely, that the former contemplates the Deity as unman-

ifested, or if we may hazard the expression or indeed any expression of the Inexpressible, as the Monad or Absolute One, not yet unfolded and still containing in itself the Triad—while the Deity, as self-manifested, was contemplated by them as the Triad, in which the Monad was revealed as the first name or position of the three, Source and principle of all. . . . The same Idea is expressed in the Schools of Theology and the philosophizing Greek Fathers of the Church as an eternal generation. It is here introduced, however, as the ground and reality, and so far therefore (as Baxter has implied) the proper explanation of the universal, tho' long neglected, Form of Logic—the logical Tetractys—in which the Monad has it's correspondent in the Prothesis, and the Triad in the Thesis, Antithesis, and Synthesis . . . while in the logical Triad, or Trichotomy, which is the form of all manifestation, the Prothesis takes the name and place of the thesis.[7]

What particularly interests Coleridge here is the transcendent aspect of the emanating One. We may not grasp this immediately, since most of us are more familiar with Coleridge's descriptions of the One in its unfolded immanence, as for example, in this passage from *The Friend*:

EVERY POWER IN NATURE AND IN SPIRIT *must evolve an opposite, as the sole means and condition of its manifestation*: AND ALL OPPOSITION IS A TENDENCY TO RE-UNION. This is the universal law of Polarity or essential Dualism, first promulgated by Heraclitus, 2000 years afterwars republished, and made the foundation both of Logic, of Physics, and of Metaphysics by Giordano Bruno. The Principle may be thus expressed. The *Identity* of Thesis and Anti-thesis is the substance of all *Being*; their *Opposition* the condition of all *Existence*, or being manifested; and every *Thing* or Phaenomenon is the Exponent of a Synthesis as long as the opposite energies are retained in that Synthesis.[8]

Yet this account and Coleridge's explanation of the power of the poet as that which "reveals itself in the balance or reconciliation of opposite or discordant qualities" are for Coleridge far less than exhaustive descriptions of creative being. In *The Statesman's Manual* we come closer to a full complement of Coleridge's conceptions. On one page we have the immanentist "translucence of the eternal through and in the temporal."[9] On the next, Coleridge seeks the transcendent Prothesis that is outside the thesis and can be no part of it. "Suffer me to inform or remind you," he adds,

that there is a threefold necessity. There is a logical, and there is a mathematical necessity; but the latter is always hypothetical, and both formally only, not in any real object. Only by the intuition and immediate spiritual consciousness of *the idea of God, as the One and Absolute,* at once the ground and the cause, who also containeth in himself the ground of his own nature, and therein of all natures, do we arrive at the third, which alone is a real objective, necessity. Here the immediate consciousness decides: the idea is its own evidence, and is insusceptible of all other. It is necessarily groundless and indemonstrable; because it is itself the ground of all possible demonstration. . . . All the necessity of causal relations (which the mere understanding reduces, and must reduce to co-existence and regular succession in the objects of which they are predicated, and to habit and association in the mind predicating) depends on, or rather, inheres in, *the idea* of the omnipresent and absolute. [10]

Coleridge seized on Baxter's trichotomy because he saw in it a program for marking off the transcendent One that is in the midst of, or prior to, phenomenal and conceptual reconciliations. As is the case with so many of Coleridge's large projects, his systematic account of Baxter's trichotomy was never written. He collected his materials, formed his insight, then lost heart. [11] Turning directly to Baxter's works, however, it is not difficult to find a practical use for Coleridge's rich insight.

### TRICHOTOMY AND *THE SAINTS EVERLASTING REST*

Baxter presents a theosophical account of trichotomy in his *Methodus theologiae christianae* (London, 1681). [12] There he argues that a dialectic of trichotomy must shape our account of reality because, in various ways, reality has already been shaped and determined by the Maker's projection of a similar dialectic. Representative of his elaborate christology in the *Methodus* is his analysis of the Covenant between the Halves in Genesis 15. The dichotomous halves, he says, are in fact groups of three organized by Christ's transcendent mediation. [13] The stamp of this exegesis is familiar.

The *Methodus,* in fact, is an immense Ramist catalogue in the spirit of Gouge's dividing Word. But the work of Baxter in which a dialectic of trichotomy is functionally most significant and in which, moreover, it suggests a Puritan poetics analogous to Milton's, is the *Fourth Part* of *The Saints Everlasting Rest* (1650). [14] Here in his most influential work the structures of trichotomy emerge in the process of meditating and imagining. It is significant that this emergence occurs in the period of Baxter's life when, according to later autobiographical remarks, he was first becoming aware of the need to replace logical dichotomy with a kind of trichotomy. [15]

Modern critics have usually turned to *The Saints Everlasting Rest* to deny Eliot's charges against the poetic barrenness of the Puritan mind by arguing against Eliot on his own terms. They have tried to find in Baxter the theological principles that Eliot regarded as the reflection of an integrated sensibility, that is, the union of spirit and body in the mystery of incarnation and the incorporation of the abstract Word in sensory image—the principles, in other words,

that are dramatized in Counter-Reformation devotion. Louis Martz, for example, has asserted that the second part of the following passage (from "Why
sure it will be . . .") is evidence of English Puritan acceptance of the Counter-
Reformation reunion of the powers of the soul:[16]

> Here therefore you must understand, That the meer pure work of
> *Faith* hath many disadvantages with us, in comparison of the work of
> *Sense*. Faith is imperfect, for we are renewed but in part; but *Sense*
> hath its strength, according to the strength of the flesh: *Faith* goes
> against a world of resistance, but *Sense* doth not. *Faith* is supernatural,
> and therefore prone to declining, and to languish both in the habit and
> exercise, further than it is still renewed and excited; but sense is natural,
> and therefore continueth while nature continueth. The object of Faith
> is far off; we must go as far as Heaven for our Joyes; But the object of
> sense is close at hand. It is no easie matter to rejoyce at that which we
> never saw, nor ever knew the man that did see it: and this upon a meer
> promise which is written in the Bible; and that when we have nothing
> else to rejoyce in, but all our sensible comforts do fail us: But to rejoyce
> in that which we see and feel, in that which we have hold of, and
> possession already; this is not difficult. Well then, what should be done
> in this case? Why sure it will be a point of our Spiritual Prudence, and
> a singular help to the furthering of the work of Faith, to call in our
> Sense to its assistance: If we can make us friends of these usual enemies,
> and make them instruments of raising us to God, which are the usual
> means of drawing us from God, I think we shall perform a very excellent
> work. Sure it is both possible and lawfull, yea, and necessary too, to do
> something in this kinde; for God would not have given us either our
> Senses themselves, or their usual objects, if they might not have been
> serviceable to his own Praise, and helps to raise us up to the appre-
> hension of higher things. [17]

Martz has usefully identified Baxter's application to Counter-Reformation attitudes, but the larger purpose of that application is, I believe, very much in
the spirit of the Reformation itself. Baxter's full proposal only feigns capitulation
to his usual enemies while it harbors the relish of a man who is preparing to
dynamite the devil. In his hour of siege he will turn Satan's resources against
Satan, fire aganst fire. He will use the engines of sense—that tragically draw
us away from God—against sense, "to raise us up to the apprehension of higher
things." Baxter does not surrender his awareness of the corruption inherent in
the sensory world. At this stage of the argument, he does not say how, in
practice, he will go about raising us to an apprehension of higher things. But
he has not forgotten the keystones of his theology: the pure work of Faith, and
the promise written in the Bible. "Look not," he will more freely admonish

later, "that Sense should apprehend thy blessed object."[18] He has a strategy. He will "do something in this kinde."

Baxter's doing follows the dialectical procedures that he would later call trichotomy, which can be traced by reconstructing the configuration of his emphases, keeping always in mind the significance of his never-forgotten object, Rest. For the Everlasting Rest of the saints forms, after all, the object both of his meditative program and of his culminating exemplary meditation. In *The Saints Everlasting Rest* we witness a passionate search: both the discourse and the meditative exemplum are modulated with high drama. Together they tell a scared love story, and they are both moved by a discontent that brings about large shifts in the point of view. These shifts at first appear to be no more than undercurrent motions. But upon closer examination we find that they are sustained and directed with such power that they join what for Baxter is the great gulf stream of Puritan crisis and conversion. To speak of dramatic changes, therefore, is not to say that Baxter's underlying principles are contradictory. A large part of the power and interest of *The Saints Everlasting Rest* has to do with the split that Baxter dramatizes between his two selves. One self is for the time being overwhelmed and helpless. The other moves steadily to salvation. Baxter's meditative self—his exercitant—is propelled into a spiritual trauma in which, at the final stage, he is to abandon all efforts of self-direction, even while Baxter's control over the ultimate outcome of that trauma pursues a providential fait accompli.

The drama as a whole, after all, is foreseen by the psalm-like prologue to the meditative discourse and anticipated from the beginning of the meditation itself. In chapter one, subtitled "Reproving our Expectations of Rest on Earth," Baxter asserts that the object desired by spiritual meditation, like the object of all quests for heavenly perfection, cannot be reached in this life. He tells us that we cannot preview Rest in any moment of earthly existence:

> Doth this Rest remain? How great then is our sin and folly, to seek and expect it here? . . .

> It is gross Idolatry to make any Creature or means, our Rest. To settle the Soul upon it, and say, Now I am well, upon the bare enjoyment of the Creature; what is this, but to make it our god? . . .

> I am persuaded, our discontents, and murmurings with unpleasing condition, and our covetous desires after more, are not so provoking to God, nor so destructive to the sinner, as our too sweet enjoying, and Rest of Spirit in a pleasing State. . . . Wheresoever your desires stop, and you say, Now I am well; that condition you make your God. [19]

Settling the soul upon any creature or means and making it our Rest is for Baxter gross idolatry. His exercitant must not stop to adore, too sweetly enjoying, any earthly moment. He must not say, "Now I am well." In the language of Goethe's Faust, this would be to declare, "Verweile doch. Du bist so schön."[20] This would be the moment of Satan's triumph. Indeed, for Baxter, meditation is a Faustian wager that he is determined his exercitant must not lose. To avert this disaster Baxter harnesses a kind of Faustian desperation (this time more reminiscent of Marlowe than of Goethe) in which the exercitant, speaking harsh words to his objectified self,[21] is plunged into the imagining of failure and damnation:

> Methinks I even hear the voice of his foregoers! Methinks I see him coming in the clouds, with the *attendants* of his *Angels* in Majesty and in Glory! O poor secure sinners, what will you now do? where will you hide your selves? or what will cover you? mountains are gone, the *Earth* and *Heavens* that were are passed away; the devouring fire hath consumed all, except your selves, who must be the fuel for ever: O that you could consume as soon as the *Earth*! and melt away as did the *Heavens*! Ah, these wishes are now but vain; the Lamb himself would have been your friend, he would have loved you, and ruled you, and now have saved you; but you would not then, and now too late: Never cry, *Lord Lord*; too late, too late man; why dost thou look about? can any save thee? whither dost thou run? can any hide thee? O wretch! that has brought thy self to this![22]

The tentativeness of the exercitant's perceptions is reinforced by another facet of Baxter's remote control. He commits the exercitant to a mode of tenseless being by forcing him to float between an imagined Plotinian there-and-then, which he knows he cannot possibly reach, and an earthly here and literal now, which he has discovered he cannot abide. Throughout the meditative progress, forces of temporal duality threaten to pull the meditation apart and to leave the exercitant in a no-time, no-place world of fantasy. This kind of apparent Rest is empty wish-fulfillment. Already in the opening paragraph he has begun to slip into a crevasse between earth and heaven, an illusion in which desire stops and he adopts his projected condition as a machine-made god:

> Rest! Not as the stone that rests on the *earth*, nor as these clods of flesh shall rest in the grave; so our beast must rest as well as we; nor is it the satisfying of our fleshly lusts, nor such a rest as the carnal world desireth: no, no, we have another kind of Rest than these: Rest we shall from all our labours, which were but the way and means to Rest.[23]

The ambiguous syntax reflects a confusion in the exercitant's mind: We have another kind of Rest—*or*, we shall have?

To ask such questions may seem, at first, to aim at a distinction without a difference. But soon the exercitant relaxes into fantasies of heavenly being. He is perfectly at home recounting the daily round of after-life realities:

> Before a *Saint* was weak and despised, so full of pride and peevishness and other sins, that we could scarce oft-times discern their graces: But now how glorious a thing is a *Saint!* . . . Now we are all of one *judgement*, of one *name*, of one *heart*, of one *house*, and of one *glory. O sweet reconcilement!* Oh Happy Union! . . . O what a mighty change is this! From the Dunghill to the Throne![24]

The exercitant leaps ahead to possess as immediate knowledge that which is the gift of salvation alone. He has begun to count himself as one with the very saints whose everlasting Rest is, after all, the distant goal of his prayerful meditation. He is heading for a fall that his own heady descriptions are preparing for him. Even the first paragraph ends with suspect exhilaration. Although he is engaged in confessing total ignorance, he begins to anticipate the emotion he hopes to experience: "O the frame that my soul will then be in! O how love and joy will stir!" Yet, he says stirringly, "I cannot express it! I cannot conceive it."[25] He admits to present failure but he is entranced by the joy of illusion.

His missteps lead to the larger trauma that the exercitant is storing up for himself. At first sight his procedure seems safe enough. Since the goal of any meditative effort is to effect a change in the will or affections, the exercitant proceeds to refine the grounds of his affections by successive considerations of devotional Love, Joy, and Desire. Thus, under the heading of Love we find such commonplaces as these:

> Canst thou love a little shining *Earth?* Canst thou love a walking piece of clay? and canst thou not love *that God, that Christ, that Glory,* which is so truly and unmeasurably lovely? . . . Dost thou love for excellency? why thou seest nothing below but baseness, except as they relate to thy enjoyments above. Yonder is the *Goshen,* the region of light, this is a Land of palpable darkness.[26]

And under the heading of Joy he offers himself the following reasonable inducements:

> If *Lipsius* thought when he did but read *Seneca,* that he was even upon *Olympus* top, above mortality and human things: What a case shall I be in when I am beholding Christ? If *Julius Scaliger* thought twelve Verses in *Lucan* better than the whole German Empire; What shall I think mine Inheritance worth? . . . If the heaven of glass which the *Persian* Emperour framed, were so glorious a piece; and the heaven of silver which the Emperor *Ferdinand* sent to the great Turk, because of their rare artificial Representations and Motions; what will the Heaven of Heavens then be?[27]

All this sounds too easy, almost glib, yet how can such harmless prodding get anyone into the deep trouble I propose to show? For Baxter, I believe, the answer is that the mode of argumentation that the exercitant employs, conventional as it surely is, represents a mere logic of contraries that misconstrues reality (both natural and divine) and betrays the individual into the illusion of Rest already achieved.

Baxter's critique of a logic of illusion is first expressed in the difficulties to which he commits his exercitant in 1650. In fact, as I suggested earlier, it is possible that in these climactic sections of *The Saints Everlasting Rest* lies one of the principal referents for the entry in the *Reliquiae* that so excited Coleridge a century later. Initially commenting on the *Methodus* (1681), Baxter wrote:

> Having long . . . been purposing to draw up a Method of Theology, I now began it: I never yet saw a Scheme, or Method of Physics or Theology, which gave any Satisfaction to my Reason: tho' many have attempted to exercise more accurateness in Distribution, than all others that went before them . . . yet I could never yet see any whose Confusion, or great Defects, I could not easily discover, but not so easily amend. *I had been Twenty Six Years convinced that Dichotomizing will not do it;* but that the Divine Trinity in Unity, hath exprest it self in the whole Frame of Nature and Morality.[28]

Baxter goes on to amplify "I now began it" by saying, "I set upon, and finished all the Schemes, and half the Elucidations in the end of the Year 1669, and the beginning of 1670." Computed by "Twenty Six Years," the time during which Baxter gestated his ideas of trichotomy falls squarely in the crisis period preceding the composition of *The Saints Everlasting Rest.* Baxter recalls, in addition, that he had "long been thinking of a true Method, and making some small Attempts, but I found my self insufficient for it; and so continued only thinking of it, and studying it all these Years."[29] Baxter's concern in these retrospective passages is with the emergence of his theosophical system. Our interest, however, is only in the discovery embodied in his dramatic meditation. What did it mean for Baxter to be (as he remembers it) only thinking of trichotomy and to have actually made some small attempts in that vein?

Of course, by 1696—at a distance of nearly fifty years—it is unlikely that Baxter himself could have reconstructed answers to such explicit questions. But Coleridge's faith in Baxter was, I believe, not misplaced. In the meditation of *The Saints Everlasting Rest* Baxter worked toward a three-part recognition and a three-part method of the kind that he was later to call trichotomy. To the exercitant's own great but by no means everlasting discomfort, he is made to discover that, indeed, dichotomizing will not do it.

The exercitant's dichotomous analysis of Love, for example, in which he ranges a walking piece of clay against that Glory so truly and unmeasurably lovely, finally leaves him in the lurch: "O that I were able! O that I could feelingly say, *I love thee!* even as I feel I love my friend, and my self! Lord, that I could do it! but alas, I cannot; fain I would, but alas, I cannot. Would I not love thee, if I were but able?"[30] By the time he passes on to the discourse concerning Joy, he is beginning to be more aware of the colossal lifelessness of his symmetries. We begin to hear self-accusations that are directed not at the failings of the sinner in general but at his present employment in particular:

> Ah wretched, fleshly, unbelieving heart! that can think of such a day, and work, and life as this, with so low and dull and feeble joys!
>
> Is it possible that there should be any defect of joy? or my heart not raised, when I am so raised? If one drop of lively faith were mixed with these considerations, O what work they would make in my breast! and what a Heaven-ravished heart should I carry within me![31]

What is increasingly called into question is not only the credibility of his dialectical perceptions, but the integrity of the self or heart that has been accepted, until now, as an instrument of differentiation. The exercitant is headed for a many-sided crisis.

THE FINDING OF CHRISTIAN LOSS

At the very end of the dialectical evocation of Joy, the wave of doubt finally breaks against the exercitant's consciousness. It happens immediately after he applies to the method of dichotomy for a preview of the heavenly Temple itself: "It is said in *Ezra* 3:12 that when the foundations of the second Temple were laid, many of the ancient men, who had seen the first house did weep, *i.e.* because the second did come so far short of it: what cause then shall we have to shout for joy, when we shall see how glorious the heavenly Temple is, and remember the meanness of the Church on earth?"[32] Without external prompting and without apparent warning, the convenient exchange of recollected weeping for prospective joy is blocked totally. All at once the exercitant's lot is loss, defeat, sterility:

> But alas, *what a loss am I at in the midst of my contemplations!* I thought my heart had all this while followed after, but I see it doth not; And shall I let my Understandings go on alone? or my tongue run on without Affections? what life is in empty thoughts and words? . . .
>
> Rather let me run back again, and look, and find, and chide this lazy loitering heart, that turneth off from such a pleasant work as this. . . .
>
> Lord, what's the matter that this work doth go on so heavily? Did I think my heart had been so backward to rejoyce? If it had been to mourn, and fear, and despair, it were no wonder: I have been lifting at this stone, and it will not stir. . . .
>
> But besides my darkness, deadness, and unbelief, I perceive there is something else that forbids my full desired Joy: this is not the time

and place where so much is given: the time is our Winter, and not our Harvest: the place is called the Valley of Tears.[33]

As a result of this afflicting realization, the exercitant's exploration of theological Desire is qualitatively different from his previous analyses. If until now he has imagined that his theological affection and knowledge—his heart and understanding—were merging inevitably by dint of his dialectical talents, now he begins to acknowledge that he must "run back" to an anterior and interior focus of attention. He must find the loss that persists in the dead center of his contemplations. Now his effort is to penetrate to the antecedent of the grammar of contraries that until this instant constituted his entire spiritual activity. He must somehow change his dialectical stock in trade: "nor shall Flesh and Spirit be combating within me, nor my soul be still as a pitched Field, or a stage of contention, where Faith and Unbelief . . . do maintain a continual distracting conflict."[34] Instead of continuing to marshal a dialectic that can yield—or seem to yield—distinct objects, the exercitant increasingly adequates his conception of Rest (and of Truth and divine Reality) to the longing of the mind itself. For Baxter the emergence of this longing is correlated with retreat from an alleged sensory grasp of higher things:

> Up then, O my soul, in thy most raised and fervent desires! Stay not till this Flesh can desire with thee; its Appetite hath a lower and baser object. Thy Appetite is not sensitive, but rational; distinct from its; and therefore look not that Sense should apprehend thy blessed object, and tell thee what and when to desire.[35]

How far Baxter has brought his exercitant from the use of the sensory, and how distant his ultimate position will be from one classic mode of Roman Catholic meditation, may be gathered from the passage below, which both encapsulates the method of Bernard of Clairvaux and fixes it in a lower order of meditation. Even in the salad days of his dialectic on Joy the exercitant has already turned away from the union of earthly sign and heavenly signified that he identifies with Cistercian spirituality. Instead he makes a vain attempt to salvage that dialectic by redistributing it in a dichotomy of inverse proportions:

> If *Bernard* were so ravished with the delights of his Monastery (where he lived in poverty, without the common pleasures of the world) because of its green banks, and shady bowers, and herbs, and trees, and various objects to feed the eyes, and fragrant smels [sic] and sweet and various tunes of Birds, together with the opportunity of devout Contemplations, that he cries out in admiration, Lord, what abundance of delights dost thou provide, even for the poor? How then should I be ravished with the Description of the Court of Heaven? where in stead of herbs, and trees, and birds, and bowers, I shall enjoy God and my Redeemer, Angels, Saints, and unexpressible pleasures? and therefore should with

more admiration cry out, Lord, what delights hast thou provided for us
miserable and unworthy wretches that wait for thee![36]

By the time Baxter's exercitant draws near to the end of his journey, he has
learned that for him even such reaching as this represents only a logic of
fantasizing, a conjuring that is of no lasting consequence for his earthbound
rational being. His dialectic has turned out to be merely the pursuit of doubleness in his own nature:

> The twins are yet a striving in my bowels: the spirit is willing, the flesh
> is weak: the spirit longs, the flesh is loth. The flesh is unwilling to lie
> rotting in the earth: the soul desires to be with thee. My spirit cryeth,
> Let thy Kingdom come, or else let me come unto thy Kingdom; but the
> flesh is afraid lest thou shouldest hear my prayer, and take me at my
> word. What frequent contradictions dost thou find in my requests? be-
> cause there is such contradiction in my self.[37]

He has discovered that there is a disparity in his being that is to be filled only
by longing. And he has realized that there is no describable object to be found
which can image that longing. He therefore leaves the dialectical twins striving
in a kind of animated suspension from which no synthesis can be expected.
Yet his abandonment of dialectical synthesis does not leave him without an
imaginative home. His failed dichotomizing of the three grounds of heavenly
affection (Love, Joy, Desire) has expanded into a procedure in which the absence of merging is understood as a divine thing unto itself. This is the Rest
he has sought all along.

The species of knowledge thus gained is for Baxter not a coincidence of
opposites. It cannot be described by the terminology of paradox or of mystical
self-obliteration. The consciousness of being that maintains the structures of
oppositions abides as the closest possible approximation to selfhood and to a
Christlike receptor of knowledge and affliction:

> Ah my dear Lord, I feel thy meaning; its written in my flesh; its
> engraven in my bones: My heart thou aimest at. . . . Though I cannot
> so freely say "My heart is with thee, my soul longeth after thee" yet
> can I say, I long for such a longing heart. . . . O blessed be thy grace
> that makes advantage of my corruptions, even to contradict and kill
> themselves. For I fear my fears, and sorrow for my sorrows, and groan
> under my fleshly groans: I loath my lothness, and I long for greater
> longings; and while my soul is thus tormented with fears and cares, and
> with the tedious means for attaining my desires, it addeth so much to
> the burden of my troubles, that my wearinesss thereby is much in-
> creased, which makes me groan to be at Rest.[38]

The awareness thus created is of unmerged contraries and of sacrificial Rest at
their core. The exercitant learns that God's meaning for man is not a sum of

dialectical parts. No object is produced at the heart of his cognitive yearnings: he fears his fears and sorrows for his sorrows. If anything, his cognition is in interminable delay. He has learned that the "heart," the fullest expression of God's intentions for human kind, is continuously re-created as the boundaries of a cognitive chasm, the place of Rest and of God.

In the last moments of the meditation, when sabbatic Rest sits inaccessible on the horizon of contemplation, the exercitant quietly carries forward the *impedimenta* of his journey. The final brief section contains at least ten reiterations (perhaps more, depending on how we count) of the three pairs of antinomies set out earlier.[39] Nothing of the boundary-making process is abandoned, that is, even after the exercitant has realized that his methodology has proven to be seriously inadequate. Here it is useful to recall the *Reliquiae* statements singled out by Coleridge: " I never yet saw a Scheme, or Method of Physicks or Theology, which gave any Satisfaction to my Reason. . . . I had been Twenty-Six Years convinced that Dichotomizing will not do it." The Baxter who composed *The Saints Everlasting Rest* was possessed of a similar conviction and a similar desire for a dialectic that would include an independent anterior term, a prothesis, as Coleridge calls it. Baxter's exercitant makes his way toward the equivalent of this kind of dialectical achievement when he recognizes that all his dichotomizing has been inadequate and that something else is needful: "Lord, my soul it self also is in a straight," he says "and what to chuse I know not well; but yet thou knowest what to give."[40]

The required gift, we may say, is located in the "straight" of his earlier dialectic:

> Reading and Hearing will not serve: my Meat is not so sweet to my Ear or to my Eye: it must be a taste or feeling that must entice away my soul: though arguing is the means to bind my will, yet if thou bring not the matter to my hand, and by the influence of thy Spirit make it not effectual, I shall never reason my soul to be willing to depart. . . . It is not thy ordinary discoveries that will here suffice.[41]

In Baxter's meditation the discovery of the Prothesis is made—tasted and felt—in the separation, or enticing to departure, that gives life to Love and Joy and Desire. Dialectical arguing of the conventional sort is a necessary part of the divine process, but it cannot suffice of itself. The entire process must be made effectual by the intervention of the divine Spirit in the heart of loss. At this moment the plight of the exercitant becomes emblematic of Christian reality.

Barbara Lewalski has said recently that Protestant meditation strove to develop an "all-encompassing 'incarnational' symbolism whose focus is the individual."[42] In Baxter's case Lewalski's formula works well if we substitute "crucifixional" for "incarnational." Baxter's embracing symbolism is very much of the Christian individual, but it suggests loss and absence rather than fulfillment. The exercitant's biblical metaphors, heavy with spousal longing, describe this unfulfilled reality:

> Thy desolate Bride saith, *Come*, for thy Spirit within her saith, *Come* who teacheth her thus to pray with groanings after thee, which cannot be expressed; The whole Creation saith, *Come*, waiting to be delivered from the bondage of corruption into the glorious liberty of the Sons of God: Thy self hath said, *surely I come; Amen, Even so come* LORD JESUS.[43]

This dialectic of unresolved antinomies is not the possession of mere reasoning. The whole Creation waits suspended in the "bondage of corruption," from which only the intercession of the Son can deliver it. The exercitant's quest ceases, therefore, in the recognition of Christ as longed-for Rest within the welter of dichotomies. Coleridge was justified in believing that he saw in Baxter's trichotomy an attempt to reach a knowledge of the anterior One. In Baxter's terms and in Coleridge's, this is knowledge of the intervening Prothesis from which all being emanates.

# NOTES

CHAPTER 1

1 T. S. Eliot, *Milton: Two Studies* (1936 and 1947; reprint, London: Faber and Faber, 1968), pp. 10ff., 20–21, 31ff.
2 Eliot, *Selected Essays, 1917–32* (New York: Harcourt, Brace, 1936), pp. 15ff.
3 Edmund Burke, *The Sublime* (London, 1757), p. 44.
4 Gotthold Ephraim Lessing, *Laocoön: An Essay on the Limits of Painting and Poetry*, trans. Edward Allen McCormick (New York: Bobbs-Merrill, 1962), p. 74. For Lessing's debt to du Bos and Mendelssohn, see McCormick, p. xx. It has been noticed that Lessing's assertion concerning Milton contains an allusion to the poetics of compensation described in *Paradise Lost* III.26–55: see *Lessing's Laocoön*, ed. A. Hamann and L. E. Upcott (Oxford, 1895), p. 262.
5 McCormick, p. 88.
6 Ibid., p. 85; emphasis added.
7 Don Cameron Allen, "Milton's Amarant," *Modern Language Notes*, 72 (1957): 257; *The Harmonious Vision: Studies in Milton's Poetry* (Baltimore: Johns Hopkins University Press, 1970), p. 99.
8 Douglas Bush, *"Paradise Lost" in Our Time: Some Comments* (Ithaca: Cornell University Press, 1945), pp. 95–97.
9 Leland Ryken, *The Apocalyptic Vision in "Paradise Lost"* (Ithaca: Cornell University Press, 1970), pp. 91, 193–94. Roland Mushat Frye offers valuable comments on the views represented by Allen, Bush, and Ryken: see n. 10 and n. 13 below.
10 Roland Mushat Frye, *Milton's Imagery and the Visual Arts: Iconographic Tradition in the Epic Poems* (Princeton: Princeton University Press, 1978).
11 Ibid., pp. 347–48.
12 Ibid., pp. 140, 194.
13 Milton, Frye writes, relies upon "words and phrases to elicit visual counterparts with which his readers would be familiar, but he transforms even that which he elicits"; Milton, he exclaims, goes "beyond ordinary experience . . . to suggest the transcendent." The commodiousness of Frye's frame of iconographic reference has made it possible for him to clarify how the principle objects and locations in Milton's poetic world have been made to form markedly nonvisual entities. A number of his comments make this point quite unforgettably:

"The Chaos which separates Hell from the Universe in *Paradise Lost* is essentially unpaintable. . . . Its defining terms prohibit even the possibility of finding an equivalent in art. . . . Milton explicitly cancels every dimension, every limit, every measure. . . . In his insistence upon the invisibility of the Father, Milton is closer to the first millennium of Christian art than to the centuries which immediately preceded him. . . . The eye of God, like the hand, was at once a Biblical and an artistic symbol of deity. Milton's use of such symbols does provide some visual references for his God the Father, but the visualization remains minimal and the synecdoche becomes very nearly an abstraction. . . . Milton's descriptions of God the Father represent a visual *via negativa*. . . . . Milton sought to evoke in the reader's mind the familiar image of the dove of the Holy Spirit, but at the same time it was necessary for him to go beyond that simple image to convey a massiveness and pervasiveness of power which could not be suggested by any simple picture of a dove. At most, then, his description must be 'dove-like' without actually representing a dove. In conveying that conception, Milton could rely on greater support from the magnificent poetry of Genesis than from anything in the visual tradition, though artists had frequently used the dove to represent the Spirit of God moving upon the water. . . . As for facial and physical characteristics, the Son in Milton's epics is described in no more visual terms than the Father. . . . The Son of God is never given a physical description in *Paradise Regained"* (*Milton's Imagery and the Visual Arts*, pp. 145, 250, 142, 149–55, 341).

14  "St. Augustine's Rhetoric of Silence: Truth vs. Eloquence and Things vs. Signs," in *Renaissance and Seventeenth-Century Studies*, ed. Joseph A. Mazzeo (New York: Columbia University Press, 1964), p. 19.

15  See Frye, *Milton's Imagery and the Visual Arts*, pp. 186–87, 201–05, 251–53, 265–66.

16  My interest in Milton's methods of image depletion, and the qualities of his imagination more generally, is in some ways analogous to theoretical concerns of such contemporary Revisionist and Deconstructive critics as Harold Bloom, Jacques Derrida, and Geoffrey Hartman. I have learned much from their brilliant work, but in this book I have drawn my critical vocabulary largely from Milton's writings and what I take to be Milton's intellectual inheritance. For an interesting discussion of Milton's poetry using the language of contemporary literary theory (Structuralist and Post-Structuralist), see Donald F. Bouchard, *Milton: A Structural Reading* (Montreal: McGill-Queens University Press, 1974).

17  See Eliot, *Milton,* pp. 40ff.

18  Ibid., pp. 11–18. Eliot's second, more moderate essay of 1947 recants little if anything of this central stricture. On the score discussed here he merely allows that *Paradise Lost* is indeed a remarkable feat of a defective imagination.

19  See "Hamlet and His Problems" (1919) in Eliot, *Selected Essays*, pp. 124–25, "The Metaphysical Poets" (1921), ibid., p. 247, and *The Sacred Wood: Essays on Poetry and Criticism* (London: Methuen, 1920; reprint, 1964), p. 10. In *Romantic Image* (New York: Random House, 1964), pp. 138–61,

Frank Kermode does much to correct the false impressions of Milton's verse created by Eliot's "dissociation" theory. In his "Conclusion," p. 165, Kermode issues the modern clarion call for a just and ample appreciation of Milton's imagery.

20 Eliot, *Milton*, pp. 33–34.

21 For useful discussion of these matters see Geoffrey H. Hartman, *The Unmediated Vision: An Interpretation of Wordsworth, Hopkins, Rilke and Valery* (New Haven: Yale University Press, 1954), pp. 128, 164–65, in particular.

22 New Critical views of Eliot's theories have been discussed by William K. Wimsatt, Jr., and Cleanth Brooks in *Literary Criticism: A Short History* (New York: Random House, 1957), pp. 667ff. Brooks has since written about the need to pay more attention to the processes of exclusion that contribute to determining the nature of many poetic objects: see "I. A. Richards and the Concept of Tension," in *I. A. Richards: Essays in His Honor*, ed. Reuben Brower et al. (New York: Oxford University Press, 1973), pp. 135–56.

23 Wimsatt, *The Verbal Icon: Studies in the Meaning of Poetry* (New York: Farrar, Straus, 1964), p. 270. And Maritain, we might add, with his "stress," as Wimsatt puts it, on "the radiance of a concrete form" (p. 270), returns us by a back door to Eliot's incarnationist theory.

24 See "The Metaphysical Poets," Eliot, *Selected Essays*, p. 24.

25 Samuel Taylor Coleridge, *Biographia Literaria*, ed. J. Shawcross, 2 vols. (Oxford: Oxford University Press, 1907), vol. 2, p. 12 and vol. 1, p. 202.

26 *Table Talk* (7 August 1837), in *The Complete Works of Samuel Taylor Coleridge*, ed. W. G. T. Shedd, 7 vols. (New York, 1854), vol. 6, 409–10. Besides Frye's monumental work, three interesting studies of the painting, sculpture, and architecture that could have influenced Milton are those of Roy Daniells, *Milton, Mannerism and Baroque* (Toronto: University of Toronto Press, 1963), J. B. Trapp, "The Iconography of the Fall," in *Approaches to "Paradise Lost": The York Tercentenary Lectures*, ed. C. A. Patrides (London: Edward Arnold, 1968), pp. 223–65, and Murray Roston, *Milton and the Baroque* (London: Macmillan, 1980).

27 *Biographia Literaria*, ed. Shawcross, vol. 2, pp. 102–03.

28 *Seven Lectures on Shakespeare and Milton by the Late S. T. Coleridge*, ed. John Payne Collier (London, 1856), pp. 64–66; emphases added.

29 See *The Literary Remains*, ed. Henry Nelson Coleridge (London, 1835), vol. 2, p. 348.

30 *The Friend*, in *Complete Works*, ed. Shedd, vol. 2, p. 163.

CHAPTER 2

1 Allen, *The Harmonious Vision: Studies in Milton's Poetry* (Baltimore: Johns Hopkins University Press, 1954), p. 25. Allen believes that the poem

implies three kinds of higher unity: timelessness, immutable Nature, and the harmony of God (p. 29). The challenging nature of Milton's presentation of harmony was in effect first recognized by Arthur E. Barker, "The Pattern of Milton's Nativity Ode," *University of Toronto Quarterly*, 10 (1940): 167–81, when he showed that the Hymn divides into three large movements, the *last* of which introduces dissonance and discord. But Barker did not feel that this sequence poses any particular aesthetic problems. Following hard on Barker's conclusions, however, A. S. P. Woodhouse, "Notes on Milton's Early Development," *University of Toronto Quarterly*, 13 (1943): 66–101, tried to distinguish the harmony of the spheres (of the second movement) as the Ode's aesthetic center and the banishment of the pagan gods (of the third movement) as its intellectual core.

Among others who have been struck, in different ways, by the apparent lack of harmony in the Ode are Malcolm Mackenzie Ross, *Poetry and Dogma: Transfiguration of Eucharistic Symbols in Seventeenth-Century English Poetry* (New Brunswick, N.J.: Rutgers University Press, 1954), who finds "no poetic continuity . . . in the representation of Christ" (p. 191); Wylie Sypher, *Four Stages of Renaissance Style: Transformations in Art and Literature, 1400–1700* (Garden City, N.Y.: Doubleday, 1955), who calls the poem Mannerist because its conflict of opposing forces is left unresolved (p. 106); and Donald Friedman, "Harmony and the Poet's Voice in Some of Milton's Early Poems," *Modern Language Quarterly*, 30 (1969): 523–34, who describes Milton's early, wavering engagement of the metaphor of harmony. A recent study of the incompleteness of the Ode's structures of harmony is that of I. S. Maclaren, "Milton's Nativity Ode: The Function of Poetry and Structures of Response in 1629 (with a Bibliography of Twentieth-Century Criticism)," in *Milton Studies*, 15 (1981): 181–200, which argues for the necessary supplement of reader response. "The harmony to be sung," he writes, "cannot be sung alone" (p. 194).

2 Rosemond Tuve, *Images and Themes in Five Poems of Milton* (Cambridge: Harvard University Press, 1957), p. 62. Three inheritors of Tuve's views are Lawrence W. Hyman, "Christ's Nativity and the Pagan Deities," *Milton Studies*, 2 (1970): 103–12, Joan Webber, "The Son of God and Power of Life in Three Poems by Milton," *ELH*, 37 (1970): 175–94, and Lawrence W. Kingsley, "Mythic Dialectic in the Nativity Ode," *Milton Studies*, 4 (1972): 163–76. In a kindred spirit is Maren-Sofie Røstvig's comparison of Milton's Ode and Francesco Giorgio's *De Harmonia Mundi* in which numerical harmony is represented by "a complete reconciliation of opposites, as in the Platonic *lambda*" (p. 49): "The Hidden Sense: Milton and the Neoplatonic Method of Numerical Composition," in *The Hidden Sense and Other Essays: Norwegian Studies in English*, 9 (1963): 44–58. See also Røstvig's "Elaborate Song: Conceptual Structure in Milton's 'On the Morning of Christ's Nativity,'" in *Fair Forms*, ed. Maren-Sofie Røstvig

(Cambridge: Brewer, 1975), pp. 54–84, where further numerical analysis leads to the suggestions that "the concepts of the circle, the centre, and the 'well-balanced world' hung on hinges . . . have been worked into the structure of the poem to permit Milton's gift to the child to contribute an image of his acts as Creator and Redeemer" (p. 55).

3 Tuve, *Images and Themes*, p. 45.

4 Ibid., p. 57.

5 Unless otherwise noted, all quotations from Milton's poetry are taken from *John Milton: Complete Poems and Major Prose*, ed. Merritt Y. Hughes (New York: Odyssey Press, 1957). References are by book and line numbers.

6 E. M. W. Tillyard, *Milton* (London: Chatto and Windus, 1930), p. 36.

7 See *Paradise Lost*, VII.165–73. Louis L. Martz, *Poet of Exile: A Study of Milton's Poetry* (New Haven: Yale University Press, 1980), pp. 50–59, observes that as part of Milton's "technique of the naive" the pagan deities are presented as "the supernatural beings of antique folklore, who exist in their own right as a part of nature, are part of man's primitive consciousness of forces that lie beyond his control" (pp. 57–58). This valuable suggestion is compatible with a variety of interpretations of the Ode's other levels of meaning.

8 Jon S. Lawry, *The Shadow of Heaven: Matter and Stance in Milton's Poetry* (Ithaca, N.Y.: Cornell University Press, 1968), offers useful comments on Milton's use of "a consecrative musical rest" and "a stillness that awaits theophany" (pp. 33–34).

9 Laurence Stapleton, "Milton and the New Music," *University of Toronto Quarterly*, 23 (1953): 217–26; reprinted in *Milton: Modern Essays in Criticism*, ed. Arthur E. Barker (New York: Oxford University Press, 1965), p. 36.

   Milton's interest in, and indebtedness to, Ante-Nicene theology has been studied in illuminating detail by Harry F. Robins, *If This Be Heresy: A Study of Milton and Origen* (Urbana: University of Illinois Press, 1963). In a related vein, Balachandra Rajan, *The Lofty Rhyme: A Study of Milton's Major Poetry* (London: Routledge & Kegan Paul, 1970), has tried to justify "the structural asymmetry of the poem" by directing our attention to "its imaginative centre of gravity" (p. 15). Rajan speaks in interesting (even if shorthand) terms of Milton's representation of the intervention of the logos into history (pp. 13, 21). With respect to Barker's account of the Ode's structure, Rajan believes that there is "something further in the shape of the poem which defines the points at which it turns and the manner of its turning" (p. 14).

10 *Clement of Alexandria*, trans. G. W. Butterworth, in the Loeb Classical Library (Cambridge: Harvard University Press, 1968), p. 23. On Milton's conceptions of Christ's self-emptying see Barbara Kiefer Lewalski, *Milton's Brief Epic: The Genre, Meaning, and Art of* Paradise Regained (Provi-

dence, R.I.: Brown University Press, 1966), pp. 149ff., 156ff., and Michael Lieb, "Milton and the Kenotic Christology: Its Literary Bearing," *ELH*, 37 (1970): 342–62. The exchange of visual for musical notations is, of course, an ancient reflex of Western thought. See Leo Spitzer, *Classical and Christian Ideas of World Harmony: Prolegomena to an Interpretation of the Word "Stimmung,"* ed. Anna Granville Hatcher (Baltimore: Johns Hopkins University Press, 1963), p. 143n., for comments on the Greek "reapplication of the visual" in acoustical or musical similes.

11 *Clement of Alexandria*, p. 25.

12 *The Writings of Clement of Alexandria*, trans. William Wilson, in the *Ante-Nicene Christian Library* (Edinburgh, 1869), vol. 2, pp. 242–43.

13 Ibid., vol. 2, p. 244.

14 R. C. Lilla, *Clement of Alexandria: A Study in Christian Platonism and Gnosticism* (Oxford: Oxford University Press, 1971), p. 5n.

15 Philo, *Quis Rerum Divinarum Heres*, xxvi.130–32 and xliv.215. Here and below I have quoted from *Philo*, trans. F. H. Colson, G. H. Whitaker, and Ralph Marcus, 12 vols., in the Loeb Classical Library (London: W. Heinemann, 1929–53). For the sake of easy reference I have used the standard Latin titles of individual works followed by section and subsection numbers.

16 Philo, *De Plantatione*, ii.10; *De Fuga et Inventione*, xx.112.

17 Philo, *De Vita Mosis*, xx.97; cf. Colson's footnote.

18 See Paul Heinisch, *Der Einfluss Philos auf die älteste christliche Exegese (Barnabas, Justin und Clemens von Alexandria)* (Münster: Eichendorff, 1908), p. 142. See also Appendix A below for a more detailed description of Philo's views.

19 Woodhouse's note on "strikes" is illuminating: "produces instantaneously, at a stroke, rather than produces with sudden force, as L. E. Lockwood assumes. . . . This meaning is not recorded in *OED*, which treats the verb under 88 headings, but it is confirmed, e.g. by 'Descend with all the gods . . . / To strike a calm' (Beaumont and Fletcher, *Maids Tragedy* I.2.263–4, and 'Dark Night, / Strike a full silence' (ibid., 212–13)": *A Variorum Commentary on the Poems of John Milton, the Minor English Poems*, ed. A. S. P. Woodhouse and Douglas Bush, 2 vols. (New York: Columbia University Press, 1972), vol. 2, part 1, p. 73. But Woodhouse perhaps presses his point too far (and perhaps chooses inappropriate analogues) by neglecting Milton's cumulative rhythmic emphasis on strikes and by ignoring the close relation of "dividing," two lines earlier, to the meaning created.

20 This is the text of lines 143–44 in the 1673 edition. The 1645 version is given below.

21 A fuller account of this tradition is presented in chapter 4.

22 Milton's 1648 translation of Psalm 85 highlights the propitiatory location as

well as the spatial relation of the logos voice to God's symmetrical Daughters
or angelic blessings:

> *And now* what God the Lord will speak
>   I will *go straight and* hear,
> For to his people he speaks peace
>   And to his Saints *full dear,*
> To his dear Saints he will speak peace,
>   But let them never more
> Return to folly, *but surcease*
>   *To trespass as before.*
> Surely to such as do him fear
>   Salvation is at hand
> And glory shall *ere long appear*
>   *To* dwell within our Land.
> Mercy and Truth *that long were miss'd*
>   Now *joyfully* are met;
> *Sweet* Peace and Righteousness have kiss'd
>   *And hand in hand are set.*          [29–44]

Milton or the printer explained that words in "a different character" indicated additions to the literal rendering. Line 34, "To his dear Saints he will
speak peace," should also have been italicized.

On the tradition of the four Daughters of God (Justice, Truth, Mercy,
and Peace) see Woodhouse's rich footnote. We should note, however, that
in the Ode the stationing of Mercy in the middle or center is in any case
closer to the pattern of Exodus 25. In his study of Blake's implicit reading
of the Nativity Ode in *Europe,* Leslie Tannenbaum has recently emphasized the possible Wisdom-literature affiliations of the divine muse represented in Milton's poem: *Biblical Tradition in Blake's Early Prophecies:
The Great Code of Art* (Princeton: Princeton University Press, 1982),
pp. 152–84.

23  See Philo, *Quis Rerum Divinarum Heres,* xxvi.
24  For other views of Milton's early handling of a divine time scheme see
    Lowry Nelson, Jr., *The Baroque Lyric* (New Haven: Yale Univeristy Press,
    1961), pp. 32–52; Ralph Waterbury Condee, *Structure in Milton's Poetry:
    From the Foundation to the Pinnacles* (University Park: Pennsylvania State
    University Press, 1979), pp. 34–44; M. Christopher Pecheux, "Milton and
    *Kairos,*" *Milton Studies,* 12 (1979): 119–211; and Edward W. Tayler, *Mil-
    ton's Poetry: Its Development in Time* (Pittsburgh: Duquesne University
    Press, 1979), pp. 35–44.
25  G. Wilson Knight, *The Burning Oracle: Studies in the Poetry of Action*
    (Oxford: Oxford University Press, 1939), p. 64.

CHAPTER 3

1 All quotations from Milton's prose are taken from *Complete Prose Works of John Milton*, ed. Don M. Wolfe et al., 8 vols. (New Haven: Yale University Press, 1953—).

2 On this point see M. Y. Hughes's introduction to *John Milton: Prose Selections* (New York: Odyssey Press, 1947), pp. xxxv–xxxvii.

3 Stanley E. Fish, *Self-Consuming Artifacts: The Experience of Seventeenth-Century Literature* (Berkeley: University of California Press, 1972), pp. 272–90. Other critics who offer useful comments on *Church-Government* are Thomas Kranidas, *The Fierce Equation: A Study of Milton's Decorum* (The Hague: Mouton, 1965), pp. 55ff.; K. G. Hamilton, "Structure in Milton's Prose," in *Language and Style in Milton*, ed. Ronald David Emma and J. Shawcross (New York: Frederick Ungar, 1967), pp. 304–32; John F. Huntley, "The Images of Poet and Poetry in Milton's *The Reason of Church-Government*," in *Achievements of the Left Hand: Essays on the Prose of John Milton*, ed. Michael Lieb and J. Shawcross (Amherst: University of Massachusetts Press, 1974), pp. 83–120; and Keith W. Stavely, *The Politics of Milton's Prose Style* (New Haven: Yale University Press, 1975), pp. 34–46.

4 In *Complete Prose Works*, ed. Wolfe et al., vol. 1, p. 751n., Ralph Haug notes that Milton's use of the word *moments* in the passage is "the only citation in *NED* of this sense of the word of 'motion or movement.'" Further scrutiny of the passage shows that Milton's usage is more multiple than Haug suggests.

5 *Republic*, IV.436 in *The Republic and Other Works*, trans. B. Jowett (Garden City: Doubleday, 1973), p. 127.

6 Calvin, *Institutes of the Christian Religion*, ed. John T. McNeill, trans. Ford Lewis Battles (Philadelphia: Westminster Press, 1960), vol. 2, pp. 1229–54.

7 See Jacques Courvoisier, "La dialectique dans l'ecclesiologie de Calvin," *Revue d'histoire et de philosophie religieuses*, 44 (1964): 350ff.

8 Calvin, *Institutio Christianae Religionis* (Geneva, 1590), p. 253$^r$. For Calvin's and Augustine's vocabulary of severity, separation, and unity, see the texts quoted in the next note and note 13 below.

9 In Calvin's quotation of Augustine's Latin the last sentence reads as follows: "Haec (inquit) qui diligenter cogitat, nec in conseruatione vnitatis negligit disciplinæ seueritatem, nec intemperie correctionis disrumpit vinculum societatis" (*Institutio*, p. 253$^r$). According to the text in Migne, Calvin's quotation is fully accurate except that where he quotes "intemperie correctionis," Augustine—or a different manuscript of Augustine—has "im-

moderatione coercitionis": *Patrologiae cursus completus . . . Series [latina]*, ed. Jacques Paul Migne, 221 vols. (Paris, 1844–65), vol. 43, p. 94.

10  Augustine, *The City of God*, trans. John Healey, revised by R. V. G. Tasker (London: Dent, 1950), pp. 327, 338.

11  See also chapter four below.

12  See Hughes, *Complete Poems*, p. 41.

13  Augustine's Latin, *Patrologiae . . .[latina]*, vol. 43, p. 93 is "Et revera si contagio peccandi multitudinem invaserit, divinæ disciplinæ severa misericordia necessaria est." Calvin, *Institutio*, p. 253ᶜ, writes: "Vnum istud praecipuem commendat, si contagio peccandi multitudinem inuaserit, viuidæ disciplinæ severam misericordiam esse necessarium."

14  How thoroughly Milton acquiesced in this particularized form of a servant and to a great command to personal obscurity is attested twelve years later in a passage from the *Second Defense*. While justifying God and himself for his blindness, he writes:
"There is a certain road which leads through weakness, as the apostle teaches, to the greatest strength. May I be entirely helpless, provided that in my weakness there may arise all the more powerfully this immortal and more perfect strength; provided that in my shadows the light of the divine countenance may shine forth all the more clearly. For then I shall be at once the weakest and the strongest, at the same time blind and most keen in vision. By this infirmity may I be perfected, by this completed. So in this darkness, may I be clothed in light." (*Complete Prose*, vol. 4, part 1, pp. 589–90).
The poet's recompense of strength for weakness is here viewed as one instance of paradigmatic Christian service. An archetypical pattern of compensation may be particularly implied by the shaded, obscure place of God, who is himself all light. Indeed, the pattern of a wing-surrounded space and the self-emptied form of a servant seem to coalesce a few sentences later when Milton further describes his personal fate and discipline: "Nor do these shadows around us seem to have been created so much by the dullness of our eyes as by the shade of angels' wings. And divine favor not infrequently is wont to lighten these shadows again, once made, by an inner and far more enduring light."

CHAPTER 4

1  James Whaler's work shows a strong interest in logical usage: in "The Miltonic Simile," *PMLA*, 46 (1931): 1034–74, his findings in this area are exhaustively recorded. The second part of Tuve's *Elizabethan and Metaphysical Imagery: Renaissance Poetics and Twentieth-Century Critics* (Chicago: University of Chicago Press, 1947) is devoted to "The Logical Functions of Imagery" (pp. 251–410). Among later studies that touch on

aspects of the same subject are those of L. D. Lerner, "The Miltonic Simile," *Essays in Criticism*, 4 (1954): 297–308; Kingsley Widmer, "The Iconography of Renunciation: The Miltonic Simile," *ELH*, 25 (1958): 258–69; Christopher Ricks, *Milton's Grand Style* (Oxford: Oxford University Press, 1963); Christopher Grose, *Milton's Epic Process: Paradise Lost and Its Miltonic Background* (New Haven: Yale University Press, 1973), pp. 125–39; Walter J. Ong, "Logic and the Epic Muse: Reflections on Noetic Structures in Milton's Milieu," in *Achievements of the Left Hand: Essays on the Prose of John Milton*, ed. Michael Lieb and John T. Shawcross (Amherst: University of Massachusetts Press, 1974), pp. 239–68; R. D. Bedford, "Similes of Unlikeness in *Paradise Lost*," *Essays in Criticism*, 80 (1975): 179–96; Dennis H. Sigman, "The Negatives in *Paradise Lost*," *Studies in Philology*, 73 (1976): 320–41; and Lee A. Jacobus, *Sudden Apprehension: Aspects of Knowledge in* Paradise Lost (The Hague: Mouton, 1976), pp. 119–67. Conventional assumptions regarding the apparent synthesizing work of Milton's images are presented in philosophical categories by Don Parry Norford, "'My Other Half': The Coincidence of Opposites in *Paradise Lost*," *Modern Language Quarterly*, 36 (1975): 21–53.

2  Geoffrey Hartman, "Milton's Counterplot," in *Beyond Formalism: Literary Essays, 1958–1970* (New Haven: Yale University Press, 1970), pp. 121–22; reprinted from *ELH*, 25 (1958). The essays by Widmer, Ong, Bedford, and Sigman listed in the preceding note usefully reinforce or complement Hartman's emphasis on differentiation. A detailed and profound analysis of structures and images of division in *Samson Agonistes* is presented by Mary Ann Radzinowicz in *Toward* Samson Agonistes: *The Growth of Milton's Mind* (Princeton: Princeton University Press, 1978), pp. 15–50. But Radzinowicz argues that the ultimate aim of Milton's handling of dialectical divisions is the creation of a harmony of resolution. She also believes that that harmony, particularly for the Milton of the later poems, is more psychotherapeutic and humanistic than theological. The place of deific transcendence in this dialectical model is located in finite human interchange (see pp. 50–66, 273–84).

3  In "Voice of the Shuttle: Language from the Point of View of Literature," Hartman deepens his insights concerning the discriminating, dividing activity of Milton's images: see *Beyond Formalism*, pp. 339–44; reprinted from *The Review of Metaphysics*, 23 (1969). A programmatic attempt to include the reader in the logical activity of Milton's images and, at the same time, to decompose the independent unities of Milton's works is S. E. Fish's *Surprised by Sin: The Reader in* Paradise Lost (London: Macmillan, 1967), and the essay discussed in chapter three above, "Reason in *The Reason of Church Government*," in *Self-Consuming Artifacts: The Experience of Seventeenth-Century Literature* (Berkeley: University of California Press, 1972), pp. 265–302.

4 John Milton: *Complete Shorter Poems*, ed. John Carey (London: Longman, 1971), p. 119.

5 Other suggestive linkages of a divine division and an angelic new music occur in Milton's early poems. The antidote to Comus's "backward mutters of dissevering power" (817), for example, is associated with the Lady's musical power expressed as "an unusual stop of sudden silence" that interrupts "barbarous dissonance" (546–61). And in the "Ad Leonoram, Romae Canentem," Leonora's singing teaches us to hear a harmony of divine silence that intervenes not only between audible sounds but even between natural pauses. In the sonnet Milton associates this intercession with a Neoplatonic "third mind" (5) that inserts God's transcendent presence within our material world.

6 For a still current report on where the quest stands, see *A Variorum Commentary on the Poems of John Milton: The Minor English Poems*, ed. A. S. P. Woodhouse and Douglas Bush (London: Routledge & Kegan Paul, 1972), vol. 2, part 2, pp. 467–69.

7 See H. F. Robins, "Milton's First Sonnet on His Blindness," *Review of English Studies*, 7 (1965): 360–66.

8 *Commentaries on the Last Four Books of Moses*, trans. Charles William Bingham (Edinburgh, 1853), vol. 2, p. 157.

9 See the informative account by John S. Coolidge, "Christian Liberty and Edification," in *The Pauline Renaissance in England: Puritanism and the Bible* (Oxford: Oxford University Press, 1970), pp. 23–54.

10 All citations from the Bible are according to the Authorized Version.

11 Skepticism regarding this claim is expressed by Milton J. French, ed., *The Life Records of John Milton*, 5 vols. (New Brunswick: Rutgers University Press, 1954), vol. 3, p. 83 and William Riley Parker, *Milton: A Biography* (Oxford: Clarendon Press, 1968), vol. 2, p. 860.

12 John Diodati, *Pious and Learned Annotations upon the Holy Bible* (London, 1651; third edition).

13 Gervase Babington, *Works* (London, 1637).

14 *John Milton: Complete Shorter Poems*, ed. Carey, p. 479. Northrop Frye, "The Typology of *Paradise Regained*," in *Milton: Modern Essays in Criticism*, ed. Arthur E. Barker (New York: Oxford University Press, 1965), p. 443.

15 *N&Q*, 8 (1961): 178.

16 See, for example, C. A. Ward, *N&Q*, Ser. 6, 11 (1885): 516; Leon Howard, "'That Two-Handed Engine' Once More," *Huntington Library Quarterly*, 15 (1952): 173–84; John M. Steadman, *N&Q*, 3 (1956): 249–50; and Ernest Tuveson, "'The Pilot of the Galilean Lake'," *Journal of the History of Ideas*, 27 (1966): 453–56.

17 See Tuve, *Elizabethan and Metaphysical Imagery*, pp. 288ff. (especially p. 332 n.1) and Frances A. Yates, "Ramism as an Art of Memory," *The Art*

*of Memory* (Chicago: University of Chicago Press, 1966), pp. 231–42. For a list of studies of Milton's relations to Ramist logic see Jacobus, *Sudden Apprehension*, p. 121 n.2, to which should be added, most particularly, Grose, *Milton's Epic Process*, pp. 125–39. It is interesting to note that the topic of "disjunctive syllogism" occupies a central place in Milton's *Art of Logic* (see Jacobus, pp. 136ff.).

18 Walter J. Ong, *Ramus, Method, and the Decay of Dialogue: From the Art of Discourse to the Art of Reason* (Cambridge: Harvard University Press, 1958), p. 199.

19 Ibid., p. 202.

20 Yates, *The Art of Memory*, pp. 234–37.

21 Ibid., p. 278; William Perkins, *Works* (Cambridge, 1603), pp. 830, 841.

22 Ong, "Logic and the Epic Muse," p. 253.

23 For Gouge's place in the story of Ramist dialectic in England see Wilbur Samuel Howell, *Logic and Rhetoric in England, 1500–1700* (Princeton: Princeton University Press, 1956), pp. 199–200.

24 William Gouge, *A Learned and Very Useful Commentary on the Whole Epistle to the Hebrews* (London, 1655), pp. 443–44.

25 Ibid., pp. 443–49.

26 Gouge, *The Whole Armour of God*, reprinted in an impressive folio edition, London, 1627. My references are to this edition.

27 Ibid., pp. 166–67.

28 Thomas Jackson, *MAPAN AΘA: or Dominus Veniet. Commentaries Upon these Articles of the Creed. Never heretofore Printed* (London, 1657), p. 3786.

29 Gouge, *Commentary on Hebrews*, p. 450.

30 Ong, "Logic and the Epic Muse," p. 234.

31 Ibid., p. 247.

32 Ibid., pp. 264–65.

33 F. W. Farrar, *The Epistle of Paul the Apostle to the Hebrews* (Cambridge, 1888), pp. xliii, xlix. Biblical scholarship in our time has continued to investigate the extent of Philo's intellectual influence on Hebrews. C. Spicq, *L'Epitre aux Hebreux*, 2 vols. (Paris: Gabalda, 1952–53), argues for a heavy, multifaceted debt of this kind, while Ronald Williamson, *Philo and the Epistle to the Hebrews* (Leiden: E. J. Brill, 1970), denies the existence of important theological similarities, even though he does not doubt that much of Philo's language and imagery passed directly into Hebrews. Yet, the differences between Spicq's and Williamson's positions tend to disappear when the subject is the structure of the symbols, which Philo and the author of Hebrews have very much in common.

34 James Moffatt, *A Critical and Exegetical Commentary on the Epistle to the Hebrews, The International Critical Commentary* (1924; reprint, Stony Point, S.C.: Attic Press, 1979), p. xx.

35 Grotius's *Annotationes in Acta apostolorum; in Epistolas S. Pauli* appeared at Paris in 1646. It was reprinted with other distinguished commentaries in the *Annotata ad Actus Apostolicos, Epistolas et Apocalypsin: Sive Criticorum Sacrorum*, 19 vols. (London, 1660).

36 In the opening sentence of his dedicatory epistle to the *Christian Doctrine* Milton declares his commitment to the Reformation reinvestigation of the "original state" of Christianity: *Complete Prose Works of John Milton*, ed. Don M. Wolfe et al. (New Haven: Yale University Press, 1973), vol. 6, p. 117. For illuminating commentary on the Philonic strains of Ante-Nicene Christianity, see Harry F. Robins, *If This Be Heresy: A Study of Milton and Origen* (Urbana: University of Illinois Press, 1963).

37 Grotius, *Critici Sacri*, vol. 7, p. 4165. Grotius, of course, reproduces Philo's Greek. I have quoted the same sentences from the translation by F. H. Colson and G. H. Whitaker in *Philo*, in The Loeb Classical Library (London: W. Heinemann, 1932), vol. 4, pp. 347–49. Andrew Willet, fellow of Milton's college and close friend of George Downham (Milton's immediate model in the *Art of Logic*) comments in detail on various aspects of Philo's exposition of Genesis 15 in his *Hexapla in Genesin* (London, 1608), pp. 171–75. Willet, however, does not discuss Philo's exposition of the logos severer. For the varieties of debt that Grotius records, see especially *Critici Sacri*, vol. 7, pp. 4267–75. On Philo's elaboration of the logos severer as a theistic alternative to Heraclitus's pantheistic logos of coincident opposites, see Appendix A below.

38 For a listing of Philo's numerous exegeses of this same pattern see Harry Austryn Wolfson, *Philo: Foundation of Religious Philosophy in Judaism, Christianity and Islam*, 2 vols. (Cambridge: Harvard University Press, 1947), vol. 1, pp. 334ff.

CHAPTER 5

1 Frank Kermode, "Adam Unparadised," in *The Living Milton*, ed. Kermode (London: Routledge & Kegan Paul, 1960), p. 100; and Louis L. Martz, *Poet of Exile: A Study of Milton's Poetry* (New Haven: Yale University Press, 1980), pp. 96, 88ff., 93.

2 By worshipping mere images, Michael informs Adam, men disfigure "not God's likeness, but thir own, / Or if his likeness, by themselves defac't" (XI.521–22).

3 *Complete Prose Works of John Milton*, ed. Don M. Wolfe et al., 8 vols. (New Haven: Yale University Press, 1973), vol. 6, p. 388. Cf. Martz, *Poet of Exile*, pp. 203–44.

4 Water (*mayim*) and sky (*shamayim*—'water there'?) are near cognates in the Hebrew of Genesis 1.

5 Ernst Cassirer, *The Philosophy of Symbolic Forms*, trans. Ralph Manheim,

3 vols. (New Haven: Yale University Press, 1953–57), vol. 2, pp. 193–94.
A strong argument could no doubt be made for viewing Eve's mirror self-
discovery under the aspect of a Lacanian mirror-phase of identity formation:
cf. Jacques Lacan, *Ecrits: A Selection,* trans. Alan Sheridan (New York:
W. W. Norton, 1977); and Geoffrey H. Hartman, *Saving the Text: Literature / Derrida / Philosophy* (Baltimore: Johns Hopkins University Press,
1981), pp. 26–28. I present Cassirer's model both because it is indigenous
to the same Platonic tradition that includes Milton and Coleridge and because it efficiently represents the view that Milton dismantles and transcends.

Milton's symbol usages may also be said to bear striking resemblances
to the Kant-descended, Cassirer-engendered assault on symbolism offered
in such a work as *Symbol and Metaphor in Human Experience* (Princeton:
Princeton University Press, 1949) by Martin Foss. These resemblances were
in fact noted thirty years ago—and summarily dismissed with only partial
justification. Foss's strictures on "the symbolic endeavor to reduction and
fixation" and his advocacy of a "metaphorical process" that stems from a
continuous "critique" and "negation" of symbol formation (pp. 22–46) provide close theoretical analogues to what Milton performs in his poem.
Malcolm M. Ross, *Poetry and Dogma: The Transfiguration of Eucharistic
Symbols in Seventeenth-Century English Poetry* (New Brunswick, N.J.:
Rutgers University Press, 1954), threw Milton's interpreters off a relevant
scent when, soon after the publication of Foss's book, he dismissed such
"holocaust" symbolic methods as unthinkable in *Paradise Lost.* But Ross
was right to insist that the conclusions or final stages of Foss's theory are
not relevant to the meanings of a poem like Milton's—at least not the
meanings Milton would have understood or intended. Ross writes, "[the]
sphere of knowledge which seems to be inhabited by Foss's semantic [has]
no claim whatsoever to ontological root. . . . Metaphor is preferred to symbol because it is a wholly noncommittal process of the imagination, whereas
symbol is involved in statement and even belief. . . . Such metaphysics of
process, in which symbolic belief and practice exist only to be annihilated
in a metaphorical holocaust or vision, must in the end deny the ontological
claim of the poetic as well as the religious symbol" (p. 23). In *The Verbal
Icon: Studies in the Meaning of Poetry* (New York: Farrar, Straus, 1964)
the obverse of the same objection is succinctly formulated by William K.
Wimsatt when he labels Foss's larger theory "a monism of the expressive
process" (p. 121). However, the early stages of consciousness described in
Foss's symbolic theory—those concerned with critique and negation—are
strongly relevant to Milton's methods. For yet another view of the negating
potentialities of symbols, see Wilbur Marshall Urban, *Language and Reality: The Philosophy of Language and the Principles of Symbolism* (New
York: Macmillan, 1939), pp. 426–29.

6 Cassirer, *Philosophy of Symbolic Forms*, vol. 2, p. 194.

7 Ibid., vol. 2, p. 112.

8 Ibid., vol. 2, pp. 114–15.

9 Ibid., vol. 2, p. 202.

10 Interestingly enough Cassirer's formulation, with its emphasis on individual spiritual determination, is an attempt to elude the pantheism that he and Coleridge both identified in Schelling: see *Philosophy of Symbolic Forms*, vol. 2, p. 38 and J. A. Appleyard, *Coleridge's Philosophy of Literature: The Development of a Concept of Poetry, 1791–1819* (Cambridge: Harvard University Press, 1965), p. 206. See also, Appendix C below.

11 *Philosophy of Symbolic Forms*, vol. 3, p. 448.

12 Ibid., vol. 2, pp. 241–45.

13 Ibid., vol. 2, p. 245.

14 *Seven Lectures on Shakespeare and Milton by the Late S. T. Coleridge*, ed. John Payne Collier (London, 1856), pp. 64–66; emphases added.

15 D. G. James, *Scepticism and Poetry: An Essay on the Poetic Imagination* (London: Allen and Unwin, 1937), p. 17.

16 Stanley Fish shows the logic of such an approach in *Surprised by Sin: The Reader in* Paradise Lost (London: Macmillan, 1967) and *Self-Consuming Artifacts: The Experience of Seventeenth-Century Literature* (Berkeley: University of California Press, 1972).

17 *Complete Prose Works*, vol. 6, pp. 211–12.

18 James Holly Hanford and James G. Taaffe, *A Milton Handbook* (New York: Appleton-Century-Crofts, 1970), pp. 256–57.

19 B. Rajan, Paradise Lost *and the Seventeenth Century Reader* (Ann Arbor: University of Michigan Press, 1967), pp. 127–28.

20 See chapter one above.

21 Hughes cites Isaiah 16:8–9 and Jeremiah 48:32.

22 F. R. Leavis, *Revaluation* (New York: W. W. Norton, 1963), pp. 47ff. J. B. Broadbent, "Milton's Paradise," *Modern Philology*, 51 (1954): 170, offers a partial refutation of Leavis's appraisal.

23 See Martz, *Poet of Exile*, pp. 221–26, for a discussion of the Ovidian character of Eve's love song.

24 Howard Schultz, *Milton and Forbidden Knowledge* (New York: Columbia University Press, 1955), pp. 182–83.

25 Lee A. Jacobus, *Sudden Apprehension: Aspects of Knowledge in "Paradise Lost"* (The Hague: Mouton, 1976), p. 206.


CHAPTER 6

1 Prolusion VII. Cited from the translation provided by Merritt Y. Hughes in *John Milton: Complete Poems and Major Prose* (New York: Odyssey Press, 1957), p. 623.

2 Cf. the word "mantling" in V.277ff. Milton's use of bird imagery has been discussed by Anne Davidson Ferry in *Milton's Epic Voice: The Narrator in* Paradise Lost (Cambridge: Harvard University Press, 1963), pp. 20–43.

3 For the relationship between iconoclasm and covenantal renewal in these and related lines, see my *Poetry of Civilization: Mythopoeic Displacement in the Verse of Milton, Dryden, Pope, and Johnson* (New Haven: Yale University Press, 1974), pp. 41–80.

4 For eloquent accounts of the feeling created by this pattern, see Geoffrey H. Hartman, "Milton's Counterplot," in *Beyond Formalism: Literary Essays 1958–1970* (New Haven: Yale University Press, 1970), pp. 113–15, and Louis L. Martz, *Poet of Exile: A Study of Milton's Poetry* (New Haven: Yale University Press, 1980), pp. 231ff.

5 By verse count, the language of this description furnishes the churning, still center of the entire poem. A useful summary of various views on the centrality (numerical and other) of this image is available in *Paradise Lost*, ed. Alastair Fowler (London: Longman, 1971), pp. 345–46n. See also p. 583 for Fowler's interesting comments on Solomon "the just divider" and Sofala-Ophir.

 For possible relations of number symbolism to structure in Milton's poetry, see Maren-Sofie Røstvig, *The Hidden Sense and Other Essays: Norwegian Studies in English*, IX (1963): 44–58, G. Qvarnström, *Poetry and Numbers: On the Structural Use of Symbolic Numbers, Scripta minora Regiae Societatis Humaniorum Litterarum Lundensis* (Lund: C. W. K. Gleerup, 1966), and *The Enchanted Palace: Some Structural Aspects of* Paradise Lost (Stockholm: Almquist, 1967), and Galbraith Miller Crump, *The Mystical Design of* Paradise Lost (Lewisburg, Pa.: Bucknell University Press, 1975).

6 See Ernst Cassirer, *The Philosophy of Symbolic Forms*, trans. Ralph Manheim (New Haven: Yale University Press, 1966), vol. 2, p. 107 and Martin Foss, *Symbol and Metaphor in Human Experience* (Princeton: Princeton University Press, 1949), p. 93.

7 Harry F. Robins, *If This Be Heresy: A Study of Milton and Origen* (Urbana: University of Illinois Press, 1963), p. 92. Of parallel interest are the essays by Michael Lieb, "Milton and the Kenotic Christology: Its Literary Bearing," *ELH*, 37 (1970): 342–60, and "'Holy Rest': A Reading of *Paradise Lost*," *Studies in English Literature*, 17 (1977): 129–47. Lieb's longer study, *The Dialectics of Creation: Patterns of Birth & Regeneration in* Paradise Lost (Amherst: University of Massachusetts Press, 1970), deals with patterns of divine creation and Satanic uncreation.

8 See Denis Saurat, *Milton: Man and Thinker* (London: Jonathan Cape, 1946), pp. 113–25; Robins, *If This Be Heresy*, pp. 82–95; and R. J. Zwi Werblowsky, "Milton and the *Conjectura Cabbalistica*," *Journal of the Warburg and Courtauld Institutes*, 18 (1955): 90–113.

9 Robins, *If This Be Heresy*, p. 91.

10 Saurat, *Milton: Man and Thinker*, p. 125.

11 Robins, *If This Be Heresy*, p. 94.

12 *The Writings of Clement of Alexandria*, trans. William Wilson, in the *Ante-Nicene Christian Library* (Edinburgh, 1869), vol. 4, p. 244.

13 For Milton's comments on uncontingent, logical disjunction, see *A Fuller Institution of the Art of Logic*, trans. Allan H. Gilbert, in *The Works of John Milton*, ed. Frank Allen Patterson, et al., 18 vols. (New York: Columbia University Press, 1935), vol. 11, p. 363. See also Leon Howard, "'The Invention' of Milton's 'Great Argument': A Study of the Logic of 'God's Ways to Men,'" *Huntington Library Quarterly*, 9 (1945): 149–73. Howard performs a very useful service by explaining the pervasive relevance to *Paradise Lost* of the Ramist system that Milton explicated in the *Art of Logic*: it was, he notes, "a distinctive method of thinking in 'dichotomies,' moving from the general to the particular by a consistent division of ideas into pairs of mutually exclusive classes until all thought was reduced to its fundamental 'arguments'" (p. 151). Howard, however, too quickly extends to *Paradise Lost* the implications of his general observation that "the Ramean system, as Milton developed it . . . failed" when it came to treating the efficient cause, "for there was, he admitted, no apparent possibility of dividing the efficient cause into mutually exclusive species according to the proper method of dichotomy" (p. 155). Milton, Howard wrongly assumes, therefore ignored both the first cause and its "chain of causation . . . as an unfathomable mystery"; Howard believes that the cause and causation have "no part in the invention of *Paradise Lost*" (p. 158) and that, indeed, theology per se is "somewhat incidental" in the poem (p. 168). Therefore, he does not allow that in *Paradise Lost* Milton may have tried, in fact, to transcend the dichotomous limits of the Ramist system by resorting, in the final logical stage, to a kind of *reductio* in which all thought could, after all, be reduced to its fundamental theological argument, its first cause. For some recent discussions of other kinds of Ramist influences on Milton, see Lee A. Jacobus, *Sudden Apprehension: Aspects of Knowledge in* Paradise Lost (The Hague: Mouton, 1976).

14 Susan Sontag, *Against Interpretation and Other Essays* (New York: Dell, 1966), pp. 13–23. The Miltonic view of one kind of interpretation as self-aggrandizement was no doubt understood and adopted by more than one great writer following in Milton's footsteps. Meville's Ahab, as Tony Tanner points out, is a false interpreter of just this kind: see *City of Words: American Fiction 1950–1970* (London: Jonathan Cape, 1976), p. 22.

15 W. K. Wimsatt, Jr., and Monroe C. Beardsley in *The Verbal Icon: Studies in the Meaning of Poetry* (New York: Farrar, Straus, 1964), p. 12.

CHAPTER 7

1 "Inaction and Silence in Paradise Regained," in *Calm of Mind: Tercentenary Essays on* Paradise Regained *and* Samson Agonistes *in Honor of*

*John S. Diekhoff,* ed. Joseph Anthony Wittreich, Jr. (Cleveland: Case Western Reserve University Press, 1971), pp. 27ff.

2 On Milton's "interpretative freedom" in the poem see Frank Kermode's valuable comments in *The Art of Telling: Essays on Fiction* (Cambridge: Harvard University Press, 1983), pp. 191–93. John Carey, ed., *John Milton, Complete Shorter Poems* (London: Longman, 1971), p. 432, would restrict the meaning of "unrecorded" to a musical usage.

3 See Northrop Frye, "The Typology of *Paradise Regained*," in *Milton: Modern Essays in Criticism,* ed. Arthur E. Barker (New York: Oxford University Press, 1965), p. 445. Barbara Kiefer Lewalski, *Milton's Brief Epic: The Genre, Meaning, and Art of* Paradise Regained (Providence: Brown University Press, 1966), p. 163, argues that the poem's action "advances" to a "grand climax of full understanding and total victory" in the fourth book. This view has been questioned by Burton Weber, *Wedges and Wings: The Patterning of* Paradise Regained (Carbondale: Southern Illinois University Press, 1975), pp. 72ff. See also Jon S. Lawry, *The Shadow of Heaven: Matter and Stance in Milton's Poetry* (Ithaca: Cornell University Press, 1968), pp. 342ff.

4 Here and throughout this chapter I am indebted to Frank Kermode's suggestive essay, "Milton's Hero," *Review of English Studies,* 4 (1953): 317–30.

5 See *A Variorum Commentary on the Poems of John Milton,* vol. 4, *Paradise Regained,* ed. Walter MacKellar, with a review of Studies of Style and Verse Form by Edward R. Weismiller (London: Routledge & Kegan Paul, 1975), p. 141.

6 For a Derridean analysis of Milton's management of the "interplay of presence and absence" see Donald F. Bouchard, *Milton: A Structural Reading* (Montreal: McGill-Queens University Press, 1974), pp. 165ff. Geoffrey H. Hartman, *Saving the Text: Literature / Derrida / Philosophy* (Baltimore: Johns Hopkins University Press, 1981), p. 106, speaks in a related vein of the word as wound in II.90–92 and Luke 2:34–35.

7 *Complete Prose Works of John Milton,* ed. Don W. Wolfe et al. (New Haven: Yale University Press, 1973), vol. 6, p. 265.

8 For a different view of Milton's handling of these matters see Laurie B. Zwicky, "Kairos in *Paradise Regained*: The Divine Plan," *ELH,* 31 (1964): 271–77. On the distinction between *kairos* and *chronos* see James T. Barr, *Biblical Words for Time* (London: SCM Press, 1962) and Frank Kermode, *The Sense of an Ending: Studies in the Theory of Fiction* (London: Oxford University Press, 1966), pp. 47ff.

9 Erich Auerbach, *Mimesis: The Representation of Reality in Western Literature,* trans. Willard R. Trask (Princeton: Princeton University Press, 1953), p. 10.

10 Ibid., pp. 14–15.

11  Cassirer, *Philosophy of Symbolic Forms*, trans. Ralph Manheim (New Haven: Yale University Press, 1966), vol. 2, p. 244.

12  In more familiar typological formulations, both type and antitype are endowed with solid historical presence: see Erich Auerbach, *Scenes from the Drama of European Literature*, trans. Ralph Manheim (New York: Meridian Books, 1959), p. 53, and Theodore Ziolkowski, "Some Features of Religious Figuralism in Twentieth-Century Literature," in *Literary Uses of Typology*, ed. Earl Miner (Princeton: Princeton University Press, 1977), pp. 346–47. Thomas M. Davis points out that in Protestant exegesis "prophecy implies future fulfillment; typology asserts that the consummation has occurred": see "The Traditions of Puritan Typology" in *Typology and Early American Literature*, ed. Sacvan Bercovitch (Amherst: University of Massachusetts Press, 1972), p. 43. From this point of view Milton's emphasis on the prevenient and displaced status of present fulfillment represents a deepening of existing Protestant tendencies. See also my essay "Milton and the Scene of Interpretation: From Typology toward Midrash," in *Midrash and Literature*, ed. Geoffrey H. Hartman and Sanford Budick, forthcoming, Yale University Press.

13  For this Heraclitean model see Appendix A.

14  Lewalski, *Milton's Brief Epic*, pp. 148ff.

15  See Davis, "Traditions of Puritan Typology," p. 17. Cf. also Lewalski, *Milton's Brief Epic*, p. 167.

16  Perhaps the greatest of the medieval elaborations of the mercy-seat image and the "way into the holiest of all" of Hebrews is Bonaventure's *Itinerarium Mentis in Deum*. Louis Martz has indicated the place of the *Itinerarium* in Milton's theological heritage: *The Paradise Within: Studies in Vaughan, Traherne, and Milton* (New Haven: Yale University Press, 1964), pp. 17ff. and 103ff. See Appendix B below for a discussion of Bonaventure's propitiatory symbolism.

17  Northrop Frye, "The Typology of *Paradise Regained*," p. 444, focuses on only one part of Milton's pattern when he argues that in the tower scene "the center of religion passes from the temple Christ is standing on into the Christian temple, the body of Christ above it."

APPENDIX A

1  For a detailed accounting of such searches see Erwin R. Goodenough, "A Neo-Pythagorean Source in Philo Judaeus," *Yale Classical Studies*, 3 (1932): 117–64.

2  See chapters two and three above.

3  John Burnet, *Early Greek Philosophy* (4th ed., London: Black, 1930), p. 143. Two recent revisionist views of Heraclitus's thought are offered in W. K. C. Guthrie's *A History of Greek Philosophy* (Cambridge: Cam-

bridge University Press, 1967), especially vol. 1, pp. 469–73, and Charles H. Kahn's *The Art and Thought of Heraclitus: An Edition of the Fragments with Translation and Commentary* (Cambridge: Cambridge University Press, 1980). See also Ed. L. Miller, "The Logos of Heraclitus: Updating the Report," *Harvard Theological Review*, 14 (1981): 161–76.

4  Philo, *Quis Rerum Divinarum Heres*, xliii.213–14. Here and throughout I have quoted from the Loeb Classical Library translation of Philo's works by F. H. Colson, G. H. Whitaker, and Ralph Marcus, 12 vols. (London: W. Heinemann, 1929–1953).

5  *Legum Allegoriae*, iii.7–8. On the "man with an issue" and Philo's contemptuous allusion to Heraclitus's famous dictum, "everything flows," see Colson's and Whitaker's appendix, vol. 1, p. 482.

6  *Quis Rerum Divinarum Heres*, xxvi.130–l.248 is the most methodical of Philo's expositions in this vein. For a listing of numerous other discussions of the same kind, consult Harry Austryn Wolfson, *Philo: Foundations of Religious Philosophy in Judaism, Christianity and Islam* (Cambridge: Harvard University Press, 1947), vol. 1, pp. 334ff.

7  Cf. *Quis Rerum Divinarum Heres*, xliii.212.

8  Ibid., xxvi.130.

9  This may be part of what Philo wishes to imply in an obscure passage of the *Quaestiones in Exodum* when he asserts that Scripture expects us to comprehend "the multisymbolism of intelligible things . . . through the clear vision of the eyes": "one who learns," he explains, "by seeing rather figuratively can, by attributing certain forms to certain symbols, achieve a correct apprehension of them." True symbolizing, in this account, is in effect re-symbolizing in a particular divine mode: *Quaestiones et Solutiones in Exodum*, II.Q.52.

10  For a penetrating discussion of this meaning of logos see Guthrie, *A History of Greek Philosophy*, vol. 1, p. 422.

11  There is potential for grim confusion in the fact that by Philo and the Greek Fathers the terms matter and material were often used—in this context—in sharp opposition to corporeality and corporeal: matter and material might here designate a substance of such absolute refinement that it could be identified with God himself. See, for example, Origen's response to Celsus on this point: *The Ante-Nicene Christian Library*, ed. Alexander Roberts and James Donaldson (Edinburgh, 1872), vol. 23, pp. 406–07.

   The special qualities of Philo's design may better be appreciated by comparison with apparent close kin such as the following passage from the fifth book of Plotinus's *Enneads*: "Bring a vision actually before your sight, so that there shall be in your mind the gleaming representation of a sphere, a picture holding all things of the universe moving or in repose or (as in reality) some at rest, some in motion. Keep this sphere before you, and from it imagine another, a sphere stripped of magnitude and of spatial

differences; cast out your inborn sense of Matter, taking care not merely to
attenuate it: call on God, maker of the sphere whose image you now hold,
and pray Him to enter. And may He come bringing His own universe with
all the gods that dwell in it. . . . ." [*Enneads,* trans. Stephen Mackenna,
revised by B. S. Page (London: Faber and Faber, 1962), p. 429] Where
Philo can envision intervention and abruption within a sustained representation of the material universe, Plotinus images wholesale negation, substitution, or annihilation. In Plotinus's view the mind must necessarily
choose between incompatible orders of being.

12  *De Plantatione,* ii.10; *De Fuga et Inventione,* xx.112.

13  *Quis Rerum Divinarum Heres,* xxxviii.187.

14  Ibid., xxxv.170.

15  See *De Opificio Mundi,* ix.32–34, and *Quis Rerum Divinarum Heres,*
    xxxi.156.

16  Cf. *Quis Rerum Divinarum Heres,* xxvi.130–32 and xliv.215. Wolfson,
    *Philo,* vol. 1, pp. 335–36, thinks it likely that Philo derived the term "sev-
    erer" or "cutter" for the immanent logos from the above passage from
    Genesis and from a hint in Exodus 39:3, quoted by Philo as "the plates of
    gold he cuts into hairs," where Philo similarly understands the "he" as
    referring to the logos. Wolfson makes clear Philo's emphasis on the sub-
    ordinate, agent status of the immanent logos (vol. 1, pp. 340–42).

17  *Quaestiones et Solutiones in Exodum,* II.Q.68.

18  *Quis Rerum Divinarum Heres,* xxxiv.166.

19  Philo's commentary on the Isaiah passage appears in *De Deo,* 6–9;
    cf. Wolfson, *Philo,* vol. 1, pp. 220–21 and 340–41.

20  Erwin R. Goodenough, *Jewish Symbols in the Greco-Roman Period,*
    13 vols. (New York: Bollingen, 1953–68), vol. 10, pp. 93–94.

21  *De Vita Mosis,* xx.97.

22  Goodenough, "A Neo-Pythagorean Source," p. 132.

23  *De Vita Mosis,* xx.97.

24  For a related reason, perhaps, Philo suggests that in the account of Paradise
    in Genesis the location of the Tree of Knowledge is carefully omitted: "to
    prevent the man unversed in natural philosophy from regarding with won-
    der the spot where that knowledge dwells"—*Legum Allegoriae,* I.xviii.60.

APPENDIX B

1  See Martz, *The Paradise Within: Studies in Vaughan, Traherne and Milton* (New Haven: Yale University Press, 1964), pp. 17ff., 103ff.

2  Ewert H. Cousins, *Bonaventure and the Coincidence of Opposites* (Chicago: Franciscan Herald Press, 1978), pp. 272–73. In the introduction to
   his translation of the *Itinerarium, The Mind's Road to God* (New York:

Bobbs-Merrill, 1965), pp. x, xiv–xv, George Boas notes similarities between Philo's and Bonaventure's exegetical methods.

3 Cousins, *Bonaventure and the Coincidence of Opposites*, pp. 224, 18–20.

4 Ibid., pp. 224–25.

5 Cousins sums it up nicely: "In the *Itinerarium* Christ can be considered as the center of the universe as well as the center of the soul, since two of the wings of the Seraph symbolize the material world. However, when we analyze the *Itinerarium*, it becomes clear that the emphasis is on Christ the center of the soul and not as center of the universe. . . . In the middle period, Bonaventure developed the theme of Christ the center of the soul. In the final period the emphasis shifted to Christ the center of the universe and history" (pp. 62–63).

6 See Boyd M. Berry, *Process of Speech: Puritan Religious Writing and Paradise Lost* (Baltimore: Johns Hopkins University Press, 1976), pp. 104ff.

7 Bonaventure, *The Soul's Journey into God, The Tree of Life, The Life of St. Francis*, trans. Ewert H. Cousins (New York: Paulist Press, 1978), p. 56. It should be noted that Cousins's translation is somewhat innovative in that where the Latin original is distinguished by particular rhetorical intensity, he breaks the text into "sense lines" (cf. Cousins's explanation, p. 46). All quotations in English are cited from this edition and are hereafter designated *SJG*. All quotations and references in Latin are given according to the standard text of the *Itinerarium* in Bonaventure's *Opera Omnia*, 10 vols. (Claras Aquas [Quaracchi], 1891), vol. 5, pp. 295–313, and are designated *IMD*.

8 *SJG*, pp. 53–54.

9 *SJG*, p. 62.

10 *SJG*, p. 62; *IMD*, I.5; *SJG*, p. 63; *IMD*, I.8.

11 *SJG*, p. 63.

12 *The Mind's Road to God*, p. 7n. See also Patricia J. Eberle, "The Lover's Glass: Nature's Discourse on Optics and the Optical Design of the *Romance of the Rose*" and James L. Miller, "Three Mirrors in Dante's *Paradiso*," *University of Toronto Quarterly*, 46 (1977): 241–62, 263–79, respectively.

13 *IMD*, Prol.4.

14 *SJG*, p. 111 (*IMD*, VII.1).

15 Ibid., p. 87; *IMD*, IV.1—my emphases.

16 *SJG*, pp. 87, 90.

17 Ibid., p. 71.

18 Ibid., pp. 72–73.

19 Gilson, *The Philosophy of St. Bonaventure*, trans. Dom Illtyd Trethowan and F. J. Sheed (Paterson, N.J.: St. Anthony Guild Press, 1965), pp. 395–96, 374.

20 *SJG*, pp. 73–74.

21 Gilson, *The Philosophy of St. Bonaventure*, pp. 358–59, 396, 398–400. See also George H. Tavard, *Transiency and Permanence: The Nature of Theology According to St. Bonaventure* (St. Bonaventure, N.Y.: Franciscan Institute, 1954), pp. 237–47 and J. Guy Bougerol, *Introduction to the Works of Bonaventure*, trans. José de Vinck (Paterson, N.J.: St. Anthony Guild Press, 1964), pp. 75–82.

22 *SJG*, pp. 110–16.

23 *IMD*, VII.1; *SJG*, p. 111.

24 *SJG*, p. 102; *IMD*, VI.1.

25 *Collationes in Hexaemeron*, coll.I.n.24.

26 *SJG*, p. 108.

27 Ibid., p. 109.

28 Ibid., pp. 111–12.

29 Ibid., p. 111; *IMD*, VII.1.

30 Raniero Sciamannini, *La contuizione bonaventuriana* (Florence: Citta di vita, 1957), p. 97, emphasizes the affirmative and exemplarist aspects of Bonaventure's contuition.

APPENDIX C

1 See chapter one above.

2 MS Logic, II.37–38, reprinted in *Coleridge on the Seventeenth Century*, ed. Roberta Florence Brinkley (Durham, N.C.: Duke University Press, 1955), pp. 118ff.

3 Ibid., pp. 118–19.

4 The correspondence between Prothesis and monad is only implicit here. It is explicit in the next passage cited below.

5 Ibid., pp. 119–20. Coleridge wrote these comments in connection with Part III, p. 69 of the *Reliquiae Baxterianae* (London, 1696). The comments appear on the backboard of Coleridge's copy, now in the Harvard University Library.

6 E. R. Dodds, "The *Parmenides* of Plato and the Origin of the Neoplatonic One," *Classical Quarterly*, 22 (1928): 129–42.

7 Brinkley, ed., *Coleridge on the Seventeenth Century*, pp. 120–21.

8 *The Friend*, ed. Barbara Rooke, in *The Collected Works of Samuel Taylor Coleridge* (London: Routledge & Kegan Paul, 1969), vol. 1, p. 94. For other statements to the same effect see *Biographia Literaria*, ed. J. Shawcross (Oxford: Oxford University Press, 1907), vol. 2, p. 12 and *The Statesman's Manual* in *The Complete Works of Samuel Taylor Coleridge*, ed. W. G. T. Shedd (New York, 1884), vol. 1, pp. 436–37.

9 Coleridge, *The Statesman's Manual*, pp. 437–38.

10 Ibid., pp. 438–39; emphases added.

11 Working without all the evidence now available, René Wellek believed that Coleridge's claims for Baxter were of no significance—for Coleridge's thought or Baxter's: see *Immanuel Kant in England* (Princeton: Princeton University Press, 1931), pp. 85–87, 279–80n. For a more appreciative view of Coleridge's comments on Baxter's trichotomy vis-à-vis Kant, see John H. Muirhead, "Parting with Kant: The Principle of Trichotomy," *Coleridge as Philosopher* (1930; reprint, London: Allen and Unwin, 1954), pp. 82–88. Although Muirhead seems somewhat embarrassed by Coleridge's Neopythagorean emphasis (see p. 86n.), he offers the following illuminating view of Coleridge's interest in trichotomy by referring to Coleridge's marginal notes on Kant's *Allgemeine Naturgeschichte*: "For the use which he was prepared to make of the principle [of trichotomy] we have to go beyond the limits not only of the ordinary but of the critical logic, seeing that the method which trichotomy prescribes is the opposite of that which underlies both. Instead of starting with opposing concepts, in one or other of which, taken separately, we are to find the truth, we have to 'seek first for the Unity as the only source of Reality, and then for the two opposite yet correspondent forms by which it manifests itself. . . .'" (p. 86). Muirhead veers closer to Wellek's position, however, when he asserts that "the doctrine of trichotomy is only the logical statement of the metaphysical doctrine of 'the law of polarity or essential dualism' which Coleridge conceived of as running through all nature, and in *The Friend* . . . speaks of as 'first promulgated by Heraclitus, 2,000 years afterwards republished and made the foundation both of Logic, of Physics, and of Metaphysics by Giordano-Bruno'" (p.85n.). Thus Muirhead too misses Coleridge's swerve from the pantheistic inevitablities of the Heraclitean dialectic: that swerve is effected by his application to an absolutely segregated third term, the Unity of the Neopythagorean monad that is somehow discontinuous with the opposites by which it is manifested. Muirhead's own citation of the following passage from Coleridge's critique (again in the margins of the *Allgemeine Naturgeschichte*) of the principle of dichotomy should help fix in our minds Coleridge's yearning for "a higher or deeper ground" than a logic of contraries could provide: "the inevitable result of all *consequent* reasoning, in which the speculative intellect refuses to acknowledge a higher or deeper ground than it can itself supply, is—and from Zeno the Eleatic to Spinoza ever has been—Pantheism, under one or another of its modes" (p. 84).

12 Wellek omits the *Methodus* from his survey of Baxter's works related to trichotomy, yet the *Methodus* is extremely useful for grasping the context of Baxter's ideas. Wellek's charge, for example, that Baxter's dialectical speculations "are not original with him, but go back . . . to Thomas Campanella's Podromus Philosophiae" is better than answered in the *Methodus*, where Baxter explains his debt to Campanella as well as to many other strands of influence: "Diu credidi omnem legitimam divisionem esse bi-

membrem; & ad Dichotomiam maxime propendebam: Et adhuc de mere
Logicis, (*e.g.* affirmationibus aut negationibus, *&c.*) ita judico, & in talibus
per hunc librum Dichotomiam eligo: Cum Dieterico enim Dialect. li.I.c.28
p. 188. dico [*Distributio, si subjectae rei natura patiatur debet esse bi-
membris; ut quicquid est, aut est Creator, aut Creatura: Animal aut est
rationale, aut irrationale.* ] Quando vero a re sujecta sumenda est methodus plerumque Trichotomiam praeferendam sentio. *Trinitas* enim in *Unitate,* & *Unitias* in *Trinitate* a Deo ipso in omnia sua opera *nobiliora* activa
clare impressa sunt. A rebus autem Methodus est. Hoc sicut Campanella,
D. Glissonus & Scholasticorum plurimi observarunt, ita per totum hunc
librum patefacere ego conatus sum. In Deo ipso Trinitatem in Unitate non
tantum *Personarum,* sed & primorum conceptuum, & Attributorum, Pri-
malitatum, seu conceptuum formalium, & Relationum, operationum, &c.
quantum datur explicavi" (sig $N^5v$). Dietericus is the Semi-Ramist Conrad
Dietrich (1595–1673). Coleridge, we note, suggests that his own knowledge
of the *Methodus* is only second hand: see Brinkley, ed., *Coleridge on the
Seventeenth Century,* pp. 118–19.
13 Baxter, *Methodus,* vol. 1, pp. 410–19.
14 First published: London, 1650. In *Coleridge's Meditative Art* (Ithaca: Cornell University Press, 1975), pp. 26–47, Reeve Parker has considered the
   analogical premises of "This Lime-Tree Bower My Prison" in relation to
   Baxter's methods in *The Saints Everlasting Rest.*
15 In the passage from the *Reliquiae* (1696; Part III, p. 69) cited by Coleridge
   (see n. 5 above), Baxter indicates that in the *Methodus* he attempted to
   deal with philosophical dissatisfactions first formulated twenty-six years earlier. On page 70, Baxter goes on to write that he was hard at work on the
   *Methodus* as early as 1669.
16 See Martz, *The Poetry of Meditation: A Study in English Religious Literature of the Seventeenth Century* (New Haven: Yale University Press,
   1965), pp. 171–75.
17 Baxter, *The Saints Everlasting Rest,* 7th ed., rev. by author (London:
   1658), pp. 749–50.
18 Ibid., p. 800. Here we should note U. Milo Kaufman's assertion in *The
   Pilgrim's Progress and Traditions in Puritan Meditation* (New Haven: Yale
   University Press, 1966), p. 145, that Baxter "opens the door to a sacramen-
   talism" when he says, "There is yet another way by which we may make
   our senses here serviceable to us; and that is, by comparing the objects of
   Sense with the objects of Faith; and so forcing Sense to afford us that
   *Medium,* from whence we may conclude the transcendent worth of Glory,
   by arguing from sensitive delights as from the less to the greater" (p. 753).
   But if we attempt to calculate Baxter's ratio of sensory object to transcendent
   Glory we discover the infinite disproportion and mental impossibility that
   he soon applies as weapons against the mind's tendencies to a sacramen-
   talism.

19  Baxter, *The Saints Everlasting Rest*, pp. 587, 588, 590–91.

20  *II Faust*, V.11582, in the line numbering of *Goethes Faust*, ed. Robert Petsch (Leipzig: Bibliographisches Institut, 1925).

21  See Baxter, *The Saints Everlasting Rest*, pp. 777–79 and 801 for numerous examples of the exercitant's self-dramatizing oscillations between "my" and "thy."

22  Ibid., p. 778.

23  Ibid., p. 777.

24  Ibid., p. 779.

25  Ibid., p. 778.

26  Ibid., pp. 782–83.

27  Ibid., pp. 790–91.

28  *Reliquiae Baxterianae*, Part III, p. 69. The emphases are mine—and Coleridge's.

29  Ibid., p. 70 and 69.

30  Baxter, *The Saints Everlasting Rest*, p. 786.

31  Ibid., pp. 792 and 794.

32  Ibid., p. 797.

33  Ibid., p. 797; emphases added.

34  Ibid., p. 798.

35  Ibid., p. 800.

36  Ibid., p. 791.

37  Ibid., p. 804.

38  Ibid., pp. 804–05. I have substituted quotation marks for Baxter's brackets.

39  In the following representative passages we note particularly how Baxter manages the dialectics of Love, Joy, and Desire so that they yield to, or recede from, a state of resignation to the unknowability of God, which is the halfway house to Peace or Rest: (a) "I am contented therefore, O my Lord, to stay thy time, and go thy way, so thou wilt exalt me also in thy season, and take me into thy barn when thou seest me ripe. In the meantime, I may desire, though I am not to repine; I may look over the hedge, though I may not break over; I may believe and wish, though not make any sinful hast; I am content to wait but not to lose thee; and when thou seest me too contented with thine absence, and satisfying and pleasing my self here below; I quicken up then my dull desires, and blow up the dying spark of love" (ibid., p. 806); (b) "O let not my soul be ejected by violence, and dispossessed of its Habitation against its will, but draw it forth to thy self by the secret power of thy love, as the Sun-shine in the Spring draws forth the creatures from their Winter Cels; meet it half way, and entice it to thee, as the Loadstone doth the Iron, and as the greater flame doth attract the less; Dispel therefore the Clouds that hide from me thy love, or remove the Scales that hinder mine eyes from beholding thee: for only the Beams that stream from thy Face, and the fore-sight or taste of thy

great Salvation can make a soul unfeignedly to say, *Now let thy servant depart in peace"* (ibid., pp. 806–07).

40 Ibid., p. 805.
41 Ibid., p. 807.
42 B. Lewalski, *Donne's Anniversaries and the Poetry of Praise: The Creation of a Symbolic Mode* (Princeton: Princeton University Press, 1973), pp. 106, 161.
43 Baxter, *The Saints Everlasting Rest*, p. 808.

# INDEX